MIDDLE AGES, RENAISSANCE AND REFORMATION

TEACHERS GUIDE

With tremendous gratitude
we wish to acknowledge
and express our appreciation
to those who assisted in the
making of this manual:

Ned Bustard
Christi McCullars
Shea Foster
Emily Fischer
and Aaron Larsen

Veritas Press

Veritas Press

Dear Friends,

We hope this guide will be helpful as you study the New Testament, Greece, and Rome this year. You are about to take a journey through the past where you can see God's providence, judgement, and provision for His people on a daily basis. This study should help build an understanding of the world into which Christ was born, the tremendous suffering our Lord bore for our sins and the persecution our Christian forefathers experienced. And then we finally see a victory of sorts for Christianity with the Edict of Milan. God was faithful to His people through the years just as He is today. What a joy it is for young children to come to realize God's faithfulness as they learn from the past.

There are 32 events/people featured in the cards in this series. That is approximately one per week. A few of the cards have extra projects which may spread into the following week. The projects are only suggestions, so use your imagination and have fun with your group. You will note that the projects vary to appeal to different ages. You may choose the ones you think are appropriate for your student(s). We recommend singing the song daily for the first several weeks, after that three times a week is usually enough. Remember, the reason for the song is to help memorize the chronology of the events. It is also good to have the children recite events, in proper order, rather that singing it after the song has been memorized. A sample school week might be planned as follows:

MONDAY: Sing the song (you may want to have a student come to the front of the room and hold up the flashcards in order as the class sings). Present the new card. Read what it says on the back and discuss it. Allow different students to read it out loud if you can. Then allow the students to answer questions on the worksheet. The questions are based on information on the cards.

TUESDAY: Sing the song. Orally review questions from this card's worksheet and from previous events. Obviously you cannot review every questions every day, so do a sampling. Assign different children different sources from the resource list on the card and allow them to look up the information and share it with the class.

WEDNESDAY: Sing the song. Orally review questions from the worksheet. Do one of the projects.

THURSDAY: Sing the song. Orally review from this week and previous weeks. Discuss how this card relates to those before it. Do another project, if there is one.

FRIDAY: Give test. Use remaining time for class instruction and drill. If you have already studied the Old Testament/Ancient Egypt series we strongly encourage review and testing of that series. Appendix 1 is provided for testing the student(s) on four different cards each week.

Having fun makes it easy to learn. Using the cards for games is one way. Ask the children to shuffle them and then see who can get their cards in order the fastest. Or have four to six students mix up their cards and then play Go Fish. This allows them to get familiar with the titles. Or you can get in a large room and see who can make their own timeline the fastest. A good way to drill questions in a classroom is to divide the children into two teams and ask questions in order. Teams receive a point for each right answer.

We have found one of the best ways to file the cards is to laminate them, punch a hole in the top right corner, and keep them on a large ring. The children can add the newest card and also have the previous cards handy. Another idea is to laminate them, put a Velcro strip on the card and on the wall, and start a timeline that children can put up and take down over and over again. An extra set of cards mounted at the end of the room for a reference timeline is a good idea too.

In order to encourage children to read historical fiction related to classroom work, we suggest a book chart to show points earned for each book read by each student. After receiving a certain number of points we allow the child to have a special lunch with their teacher. You could have a mom bring in a special lunch or allow the winners to go out.

Each worksheet, test, or writing assignment should receive three grades, one each for Content, Grammar and Linguistics (Spelling).

GRADING: A grading scale you may find helpful is to count ten points for essay questions, five points for one sentence answers and two points for fill in the blank answers. The percentile grade will then be the total number of points achieved divided by the total number of points possible.

GRAMMAR: The child should answer the questions in a complete sentence in which they first restate the question. For example: What is the Scripture reference for Creation? The Scripture reference for Creation is Genesis 1-2. This grade should be applied to an application grade in grammar, but should not affect history content grades. We suggest application at twenty percent of the overall grade.

LINGUISTICS: The children should spell all words correctly. You should deduct for misspelled words once the rule for spelling a particular word has been mastered. For example: i before e except after c. Once this has been covered a child's grade would be reduced if they spelled receive as receive. If they are using a history card to do their worksheet they should be taught that those words to be transcribed directly from the card should be spelled correctly. This grade would be applied towards a linguistics application grade. Again we suggest twenty percent, but not to affect their history grade.

When you look at the tests you will see that there are not the same number of questions on each test or worksheet. We assign five points per question, with the listings of the chronology receiving two points per item listed. Partial credit may be counted because the questions are essay and they may have portions correct. Some students may ask why they are receiving three grades on each paper. We believe that it is important for a student to realize that grammar and linguistics matter in history class as well as in grammar class. All three contribute to help make students understood by others, and are thus intertwined.

Finally we welcome your feedback and comments. We hope that his resource will enrich the education of those children entrusted to you, and will help them understand the comprehensive responsibility that God requires of them.

Sincerely,

Marlin and Laurie Detweiler
Veritas Press
September 15, 1998

MIDDLE AGES, RENAISSANCE, AND REFORMATION
Teachers Guide

TABLE OF CONTENTS

St. Augustine Converts to Christianity
Worksheet

1. Who was Augustine's mother? What impact did she have upon him?

2. What was Augustine's religious background before his conversion?

3. In what year did Augustine convert to Christianity?

4. Who baptized Augustine? When?

5. What official roles/titles did Augustine have within the Church?

St. Augustine Converts to Christianity

Worksheet, Page 2

6. What is the book by Augustine entitled *"Confessions"* about?

7. What is the book by Augustine entitled *"City of God"* about?

8. Who were the Donatists?

9. Describe the differences between Augustine and Pelagius regarding their belief in the nature of man.

10. How important are Augustine's writings today? Why?

St. Augustine Converts to Christianity
Project

Reading and Discussion

On the following page is an excerpt from Augustine's *"Confessions."* The reading of the excerpt is obviously difficult for young children. The intent of this project is to introduce students to Augustine's writings and to some of the theological underpinnings about which he wrote.

The following discussion questions are intended to raise the student's awareness of the depths of the riches found in Scripture and communicated by men like Augustine. This type of exercise will lay the foundation for later probing of the deep truths of the Bible. This will enable the student to willingly and more comfortably go beyond "milk to meatier matters."

Define: *invoke, infinite* and *mortality*
1. What is meant by "restless is our heart until it rests in Thee?"
2. Augustine talks about praising God and calling upon Him. He says, "In my faith which Thou hast given me, which Thou hast inspired in me through the humanity of Thy Son." From where does our faith come? Would we have faith if God hadn't given it to us?
3. What is meant by the quote of God saying "I fill heaven and earth"? What terms are used to describe this attribute of God? (Omnipresence which has the Latin root "omni", sovereignty)

15th century minature
of St. Agustine's
City of God

St. Augustine Converts to Christianity
Project, Page 2

The Confessions of Saint Augustine

Book One, Chapters One and Two

In God's searching presence, Augustine undertakes to plumb the depths of his memory to trace the mysterious pilgrimage of grace which his life has been—and to praise God for his constant and omnipotent grace.

Chapters One

"Great art thou, O Lord, and greatly to be praised; great is thy power, and infinite is thy wisdom." And man desires to praise thee, for he is a part of thy creation; he bears his mortality about with him and carries the evidence of his sin and the proof that thou dost resist the proud. Still he desires to praise thee, this man who is only a small part of thy creation. Thou hast prompted him, that he should delight to praise thee, for thou hast made us for thyself and restless is our heart until it comes to rest in thee. Grant me, O Lord, to know and understand whether first to invoke thee or to praise thee; whether first to know thee or call upon thee. But who can invoke thee, knowing thee not? For he who knows thee not may invoke thee as another than thou art. It may be that we should invoke thee in order that we may come to know thee. But "how shall they call on him in whom they have not believed? Or how shall they believe without a preacher?" Now, "they shall praise the Lord who seek him," for "those who seek shall find him," and, finding him, shall praise him. I will seek thee, O Lord, and call upon thee. I call upon thee, O Lord, in my faith which thou hast given me, which thou hast inspired in me through the humanity of thy Son, and through the ministry of thy preacher.

Chapters Two

And how shall I call upon my God—my God and my Lord? For when I call on him I ask him to come into me. And what place is there in me into which my God can come? How could God, the God who made both heaven and earth, come into me? Is there anything in me, O Lord my God, that can contain thee? Do even the heaven and the earth, which thou hast made, and in which thou didst make me, contain thee? Is it possible that, since without thee nothing would be which does exist, thou didst make it so that whatever exists has some capacity to receive thee? Why, then, do I ask thee to come into me, since I also am and could not be if thou wert not in me? For I am not, after all, in hell—and yet thou art there too, for "if I go down into hell, thou art there."

Therefore I would not exist—I would simply not be at all—unless I exist in thee, from whom and by whom and in whom all things are. Even so, Lord; even so. Where do I call thee to, when I am already in thee? Or from whence wouldst thou come into me? Where, beyond heaven and earth, could I go that there my God might come to me—he who hath said, "I fill heaven and earth"?

MIDDLE AGES, REFORMATION AND RENAISSANCE
Project 2

The instructions for this project can be found on Appendix 2-1.

The Fall of Rome and the City of God

I

If Rome wasn't built in a day, it didn't fall in a day either. Many people think of the Fall of Rome as having been sudden and dramatic. In reality it was a long, gradual decline. In the period from Constantine on, the "barbarians" had been becoming more "roman" and the Romans more "barbaric". In many cases, the barbarians didn't really want to destroy the Roman empire. They wanted to become a part of it, settle on its fertile land and enjoy its many luxuries. The Romans often let them settle on the empire's borders and grew to depend on them more and more as soldiers to defend it from other barbarians. The problem was that while the barbarians often appreciated Roman wealth and luxury, they rarely appreciated Roman learning and culture just as much. Often, great civilizations are destroyed, not by people who hate them, but by people who don't understand them.

II

For the common people, the fall of Rome wasn't all bad. Ordinary people often found that once the trouble and hardship of war and conquest were over, the new rulers lowered taxes and interfered less in their everyday business. On the other hand, They found out that they had less protection from the ruler's anger if they offended him. That is what an educated Roman named Boethius found. He was unjustly imprisoned, and eventually killed, by a German king he had served. While in prison, he wrote The Consolation of Philosophy, in which he combined his Christian faith and his classical learning to explain why such injustice occurs.

III

The decline of Rome was especially hard for educated, upper class Romans to understand. They had seen "Eternal Rome" as a symbol of strength and stability for 500 years and it seemed to them that their world was falling apart. St. Augustine was one of these educated Romans and his work The City of God was his attempt to understand the situation. He wrote that although the "City of Man", the human kingdom, was only destined to be temporary, there was a "City of God" which is eternal and should be the Christian's real hope.

Project 2, Page 3

Vocabulary

1. *dramatic:*
2. *decline:*
3. *barbaric:*
4. *luxuries:*
5. *culture:*
6. *interfered:*
7. *unjustly:*
8. *stability:*
9. *eternal:*

Key Word Outline

I ______________________________

1 ______________________________

2 ______________________________

3 ______________________________

4 ______________________________

5 ______________________________

6 ______________________________

7 ______________________________

8 ______________________________

II ______________________________

1 ______________________________

2 ______________________________

3 ______________________________

4 ______________________________

5 ______________________________

6 ______________________________

III

1 ______________________________

2 ______________________________

3 ______________________________

4 ______________________________

Project 2, Page 5

Answers

Vocabulary

1. *dramatic:* involving great conflicting forces
2. *decline:* a gradual wasting away
3. *barbaric:* primitive or unsophisticated
4. *luxuries:* comforts and pleasures
5. *culture:* refinement of intellectual or artistic development
6. *interfered:* to put oneself in the midst of something
7. *unjustly:* unfairly
8. *stability:* firmness of establishment
9. *eternal:* lasting forever

Key Word Outline

I The Fall of Rome
1. Rome, fall, day
2. Fall, sudden, dramatic
3. barbarians, more, roman
4. didn't, want, destroy
5. become, part, settle
6. Romans, let, depend
7. rarely, appreciated, culture
8. civilizations, destroyed, understand

II The Romans' Consolation in Philosophy
1. people, fall, bad
2. lower, taxes, business
3. less, protection, anger
4. educated, Boethius, found
5. unjustly, imprisoned, killed
6. prison, wrote, combined

III The City of Man and the City of God
1. decline, hard, educated
2. symbol, falling, apart
3. Augustine, attempt, understand

St. Augustine Converts to Christianity
Test

1. In which year did Augustine become a Christian?

2. Name two books written by Augustine. Describe the subject of each of them.

3. Who was Augustine's mother? What impact did she have on him?

4. When was Augustine baptized? By whom?

5. What roles/titles did Augustine hold in the Church?

6. What was the subject of his debate with Pelagius? What did Augustine believe about it? On what did he base his thinking?

St. Augustine Converts to Christianity
Test, Page 2

7. What did the Donatists believe? How did Augustine differ from them?

8. How important is what Augustine wrote to us today? Why?

Barbarian Invasion and Vikings

Worksheet

1. What is the approximate date of the Barbarians Invasion and Vikings?

____

____

____

2. What was the name of the historic period when barbarians and Vikings lived?

____

____

____

3. Who conquered the Roman Empire during the time period?

____

____

____

4. Describe what the barbarians were like.

____

____

____

____

____

Emporer Theodosius, last to rule the Empire before it split into an Eastern and Western Roman Empire

Barbarian Invasion and Vikings

Worksheet, Page 2

5. Fill in the following:

Tribe	Country Conquered	Date
Germanic	______________________	__________
Barbarians	______________________	__________
Vandals	______________________	__________
Visigoths	______________________	__________
Saxons	______________________	__________
Huns	______________________	__________

6. The Vikings ravaged the ________ coast from _____ to _____ and reached __________ around 1000 AD.

7. Who were the Vikings?

____

____

8. What occurred in 1453 that caused the end of the Middle Ages and the influence of the barbarians and Vikings?

____

____

____

____

____

BARBARIAN INVASION AND VIKINGS
Project

Map Skills

Using this map discuss the invasions of barbarian tribes in Europe. You may want to color each area the tribes invaded in a different color. For example: Vandals- orange, Franks- green, etc.

Barbarian Invasion and Vikings

Project 2

The Barbarian Invasions

Background

If an Italian country boy had been taken to visit Rome fifteen hundred years ago, he would have found much to see. There were temples and theaters and baths. There were aqueducts, sometimes with arches one hundred feet high, stretching far out into the country to bring pure water to the city. There was an open space known as the Forum, where the people came together for public meetings, and in this space were beautiful pillars and arches and statues of famous Romans. Around the Forum were palaces and temples and the Senate House, and directly in front of the Senate House was a platform on which speakers stood when they wished to address the people. The platform was called the rostrum, from the Latin word *rostrum*, meaning the beak of a warship, because it was adorned with the beaks of ships which the Romans had captured. Another open space was the great race-course, the "Circus Maximus," where 250,000 people could sit and watch leaping, wrestling, boxing, foot-races, and especially the famous four-horse chariot races. There was the Coliseum, too, where gladiators, generally captives or slaves, fought with one another or with wild beasts.

The Roman streets were narrow, and they seemed still narrower because many houses were built with their upper stories projecting over the lower, but in those narrow streets there was always something of interest. Sometimes it was a wedding procession with torches and songs and the music of the flute. Sometimes it was a funeral train with not only the friends of the dead man, but also trumpeters and pipers. In the long line walked hired actors wearing waxen masks made to imitate the faces of the dead person's ancestors. Early in the morning, one could see crowds of clients, each one hastening to the home of his patron, some wealthy man who was expected to give him either food or money.

Rome was built upon seven hills, and most of these men of wealth lived on either the Palatine or the Esquiline Hill. After a patron had received his clients, he ate a light meal and then attended to his business, if he had any. About noon he ate breakfast and had a nap. When he awoke, he played ball or took some other exercise. Then came his bath; and this was quite a lengthy affair, for there was not only hot and cold bathing, but there was rubbing and scraping and anointing. At the public baths were hot rooms and cold rooms and rooms where friends might sit and talk together, or lie on couches and rest. Dinner, the principal meal of the day, came at two or three o'clock. Oysters were often served first, together with radishes, lettuce, sorrel, and pickled cabbage. These were to increase the keenness of the appetite. Then came fish, flesh, and fowl, course after course. Next came cakes and fruits, and last, wine followed, mixed with water and spices. The formal banquets were much more elaborate than this, for a good host must load his table with as many kinds of expensive food as possible, and a guest who wished to show his appreciation must eat as much as he could.

The whole business of a feast was eating, and there was seldom any witty conversation. No one sang any songs or told any merry stories.

Such was the life of the wealthy Romans. Moreover, they kept hosts of slaves to save

Barbarian Invasion and Vikings

Project 2, Page 2

themselves from every exertion. Their ancestors had been brave, patriotic folk who loved their country and thought it was an honor to fight for it, but these idle, luxurious people had no idea of giving up their comfort and leisure to join the army and help defend their fatherland. Hired soldiers could do that, they thought. The time had come when Rome needed to be defended. In the early days, it had been only a tiny settlement, but it had grown in power until the Romans ruled all Europe south of the Rhine and the Danube, also Asia Minor, northern Africa, and Britain. Nearly all the people of Europe are thought to have come from Central Asia. One tribe after another moved to the westward from their early home in Europe, and when the hunting and fishing became poor in their new settlements, they went on still farther west. The Celts came first, pushing their way through Central Europe, and finally into France, Spain, and the British Isles. Later, the Latins and Greeks took possession of southern Europe. Meanwhile the Celts had to move faster than they wished into France, Spain, and Britain, because another race, the Teutons, had followed close behind them, and taken possession of Central Europe. These Teutons, who lived a wild, restless, half-savage life, roamed back and forth between the Danube and the shores of the Baltic Sea. They consisted of many different tribes, but the Romans called them all Germans. For many years the Germans had tried to cross the Danube and break into the Roman Empire, but the Roman armies had driven them back beyond the Danube, and had destroyed their rude villages again and again. Sometimes, however, the Germans were so stubborn in their efforts to get into the Empire that the Roman emperors found it convenient to admit certain tribes as allies.

Background Reading Activities

(These are activities you may want to do, before or after these readings)

1. Draw a map of Rome from the 1st paragraph's description.
2. Plan a daytimer calendar for a Roman businessman. Consilium per diem.
3. Write a menu for a Roman feast.
4. Compare the way of life for a Roman with the Barbarian life.

Barbarian Invasion and Vikings

Project 2, Page 3

ALARIC THE VISGOTH

As time went on, a tribe of Teutons called Goths became the most troublesome of all to the Romans. Part of them lived on the shores of the Black Sea, and were called Ostrogoths, or Eastern Goths, while those who lived near the shores of the Danube were called Visigoths, or Western Goths. Toward the end of the fourth century, the Visigoths found themselves between two fires, for another people, the Huns, were driving them into the Roman Empire, and the Romans were driving them back. The Visigoths could not fight both nations, and in despair they sent ambassadors to the Romans. "Let us live on your side of the river," they pleaded. "Give us food, and we will defend the frontier for you." The bargain was made, but it was broken by both parties. It had been agreed that the Goths should give up their arms, but they bribed the Roman officers and kept them. The Romans had promised to furnish food, but they did not keep their word. Hungry warriors with weapons in their hands make fierce enemies. The Goths revolted, and the Roman Emperor was slain. As the years passed, the Goths grew stronger and the Romans weaker. By and by, a man named Alaric became leader of the Visigoths. He and his followers had fought under Roman commanders. He had been in Italy twice, and he began to wonder whether it would not be possible for him and his brave warriors to fight their way into the heart of the Roman Empire. One night, he dreamed that he was driving a golden chariot through the streets of Rome and that the Roman citizens were thronging about him and shouting, "Hail, O Emperor, hail!" Another time when he was passing by a sacred grove, he heard, or thought he heard, a voice cry, "You will make your way to the city." "The city" meant Rome, of course; and now Alaric called his chief men together and laid his plans before them. First, they would go to Greece, he said. The warlike Goths shouted for joy, for in the cities of Greece were treasures of gold and silver, and these would fall into the hands of the victors. They went on boldly, and before long Alaric and his followers were feasting in Athens, while great masses of treasure were waiting to be distributed among the soldiers. The Greeks had forgotten how brave their ancestors had been, and Alaric had no trouble in sweeping over the country. At last, however, the general Stilicho was sent with troops from Rome, and would have been captured or slain if he had not succeeded in slipping away. Before this, the Roman Empire had been divided into two parts, the western and the eastern. The capital of the western part was Rome, that of the eastern was Constantinople.

A young man of eighteen who was emperor in the eastern part of the empire became jealous of Stilicho. "If he wins more victories, he will surely try to make himself emperor," thought the foolish boy; and he concluded that it would be an exceedingly wise move to make Alaric master-general of Eastern Illyricum. This was like setting a hungry cat to watch a particularly tempting little mouse; for Illyricum stretched along the Adriatic Sea, and just across the narrow water lay Italy. Of course, after a few years, Alaric set out for Italy. The boy emperor in the western part of the empire ran away as fast as he could go. He would have been captured had not Stilicho appeared. Then Alaric and his warriors held a council. "Shall we withdraw and make sure of the treasure that we have taken, or shall we push on to Rome?" questioned the warriors. "I will find, in Italy either a kingdom or a grave," declared the chief, but Stilicho was upon them, and they were obliged to retreat. Then the boy emperor returned to Rome to celebrate the victory and declare that he had never thought of such a thing as being afraid. Nevertheless, he hurried away to a safe fortress again, and left Rome to take care of itself. Alaric waited for six years, but meanwhile he watched everything that went on in Italy. The boy emperor had become a man of twenty-five, but he was as foolish as ever. Now he, as well as the Emperor in the East, concluded that Stilicho meant to become ruler of the empire, and he murdered the only man who could have protected it.

Then was Alaric's time, and he marched straight up to the walls of Rome, shut off food from the city, and commanded it to surrender. The luxurious Romans were indignant that a mere barbarian should think of conquering their city. Even after they were weakened by famine and pestilence, they told Alaric that if he would give them generous terms of surrender, they might yield; "but if not," they said, "sound your trumpets and make ready to meet a countless multitude." Alaric laughed and retorted, "The thicker the hay, the easier it is mowed." He would leave Rome, he declared, if they would bring him all the gold and silver of the city. Finally, however, he agreed to accept 5,000 pounds of gold, 30,000 pounds of silver, 4,000 robes of silk, 3,000 pieces of scarlet cloth, and 3,000 pounds of pepper.

Only two years later, Alaric came again, and this time the proud Romans were ready to obey whatever he commanded. He put the prefect of the city upon the throne, but a little later he came a third time and encamped before the walls of Rome. The trumpets blew blast after blast, and the invaders poured into the city. Alaric bade his men spare both churches and people, but the Goths killed all who opposed them, or whom they suspected of concealing their wealth. Then they went away, loaded down with gold and silver and silk and jewels. They were in no haste to leave Italy with its wine and oil and cattle and corn. Moreover, Alaric was not satisfied with sacking Rome; he meant to get possession of Sicily and then make an expedition to Africa. Suddenly all these plans came to an end, for he was taken ill and died. His followers turned aside a little river from its channel, wrapped the body of their dead leader in the richest of the Roman robes, and made his grave in the river bed. They heaped around it the most splendid of their treasures, and then turned back the waters of the stream to flow over it forever. Finally, lest the grave should become known and be robbed or treated with dishonor, they put to death the multitudes of captives whom they had obliged to do this work.

Barbarian Invasion and Vikings

Project 2, Page 5

Comprehension questions for Alaric the Visigoth

1. What was the Eastern Illyricum?

2. What was the agreement between the Romans and the Visigoths?

3. Who broke the bargain between the Romans and the Visigoths?

4. Describe Alaric's dream.

5. What did Alaric hear one day while passing a grove?

6. What position did the Eastern Roman Emperor give Alaric?

7. Which general saved Rome from Alaric? What was the general's fate at the hands of the Western Roman Emperor?

Barbarian Invasion and Vikings

Project 2, Page 6

8. How many times did Alaric attack Rome?

9. Describe Alaric's death and burial.

Barbarian Invasion and Vikings
Project 2, Page 7

Attila the Hun

While Alaric was winning his victories, the Huns had built on the banks of the Danube what they looked upon as their capital. The homes of the poorer folk were huts of mud or straw; but the king, Attila, and his chief men lived in houses of wood with columns finely carved and polished. There was plenty of some kinds of luxury in this strange capital, for the tables of the chiefs were loaded with golden dishes. Swords, shoes, and even the trappings of the horses gleamed with gold and sparkled with jewels. King Attila, however, would have no such elegance. "I live as did my ancestors," he declared and in his wooden palace he wore only the plainest of clothes. He ate nothing but flesh, and he was served from rough wooden bowls and plates. Nevertheless, he was proud of his wealth because it had been taken from enemies, and so was a proof of the bravery and daring of his people. This king of a barbarous tribe meant to become the greatest of conquerors. Even in the early years of his reign he had hoped to do this. It is said that one of his shepherds noticed one day that the foot of an ox was wet with blood. He searched for the cause, and discovered a sharp point of steel sticking up from the ground. He began to dig around it, and soon saw that it was a sword. "That must go to the king," he said to himself, and he set out for the palace. King Attila examined the weapon closely and declared, "This is the sword of Tiew. I will wear it as long as I live, for no one who wears the sword of the war-god can ever know defeat."

When Attila felt himself ready, he set out with his followers to conquer the world. Before long, Constantinople was in his power. The Emperor in the East called himself the Invincible Augustus, but he could not meet Attila, and to save his city and his life he had to give the barbarians 6000 pounds of gold and a large tract of land on the Roman side of the Danube.

Wherever Attila went, he was successful. His ferocious warriors rode like the wind. They would dash down upon some village, kill the inhabitants, snatch up whatever there was of booty, and level the homes of the people so completely that it was said a horse could gallop over the ruins without danger of stumbling. In the far East, he was thought to be a magician. "The Huns have a wonder-stone," declared the folk of that region, "and whenever they choose they can raise storms of wind or rain." It is no wonder that men trembled at the sound of Attila's name and shuddered at the thought of the Scourge of God, as he called

himself, when they heard any strange sound in the night. "Attila and his Huns are the children of demons," they whispered; and those who had seen them were ready to believe that this was true. They were of a different family from the Goths and Celts and Romans. They were short and thick-set, with big heads and dark, swarthy complexions. Their eyes were small and bright, and so deep-set that they seemed to be far back in their skulls. Their turned-up noses were so short and broad that it was commonly said they had no noses, but only two holes in their faces.

Although Attila had made peace with the Emperor in the East, before long he found an excuse for invading his empire. With the sword of Tiew in his hand, he swept across what is now Germany and France, killing and burning wherever he went. When he came to Orleans, he expected that city to yield as the others had done, but the people had just made their fortifications stronger, and they had no idea of surrendering to even the terrible Huns. But before long, Attila had got possession of the suburbs, he had weakened the walls with his battering-rams, and the people of Orleans began to tremble with fear. Those who could not bear arms were at the altars praying, and their bishop was trying to encourage them by declaring that God would never abandon those who put their trust in Him. "Go to the rampart," he bade a faithful attendant, "and tell me if aid is not at hand." "What did you see?" he asked when the messenger returned. "Nothing," was the reply. A little later the man was sent again, but he had nothing of comfort to report. A third time he climbed the rampart, and now he ran back to the bishop, crying, "A cloud! there is a cloud on the horizon as if made by an arms marching!" "It is the aid of God," the bishop exclaimed." It is the aid of God," repeated the people, and they fought with fresh courage. The cloud grew larger and larger. Now and then there was a flash of steel or the gleam of a war banner. The bishop was right; it was the brave Roman general Aetius with his army, and Orleans was saved.

Attila withdrew to the plain of Chalons. The Romans and their former foes, the Goths, had united against him, and on this plain was fought one of the most bloody battles ever known. It raged from the middle of the afternoon until night, and some of the people of the country believed that in the darkness the spirits of those who had fallen arose and kept up the fight in mid air. Attila retreated across the Rhine. If he had won the day the heathen Huns instead of the Christian Germans would have, become the most powerful people of Europe. That is why this conflict at Chalons is counted as one of the great battles of the world.

After a winter's rest, Attila started to invade Italy. He meant to go straight to Rome, but the strong city of Aquileia was in his way. After a long siege it yielded. Some of the inhabitants of that and other conquered cities fled to a group of marshy islands, where Venice now stands. City after city he captured and burned. But this wild Hun was not without a sense of humor. While he was strolling through the royal palace in Milan, he came across a picture showing Roman emperors on their thrones with Scythian chiefs kneeling before them and paying them tribute of bags of gold. Attila did not draw the sword of Tiew and cut the picture to fragments; he simply sent for a painter and said, "Put those kneeling men upon the thrones, and paint the emperors kneeling to pay tribute."

The Romans were thoroughly frightened, for now Attila was near their city. Aetius was calm and brave, but he was without troops. Then Leo, another brave bishop as courageous as the bishop of Orleans, put on his priestly robes, went forth to meet the Huns, and begged Attila to spare the city. Attila yielded, but no one knows why. A legend arose, that the apostles Peter and Paul appeared to him and declared that he should die at once if he did not grant the prayers of Leo. It is certain that before he started for Rome his friends had said to him, "Beware! Remember that Alaric conquered Rome and died." He had no fear of a sword, but he may have been afraid of such warnings as this. Whatever was the reason, he agreed to spare Rome if the Romans would pay him a large ransom.

The gold was paid, and Attila returned to his wooden palace on the Danube. Soon after this he suddenly died. His followers cut off their hair and gashed their faces, so that blood rather than tears might flow for him. His body was enclosed in three coffins, one of gold, one of silver, and one of iron. It was buried at night with a vast amount of treasure. Then, as in the case of Alaric, the captives who had dug the grave were put to death. His followers belonged to different races. Several chieftains tried to become king, but no one of them was strong enough to hold the tribes together, and they were soon scattered.

Comprehension questions for Attila the Hun

1. Which group of barbarians did Attila lead?

2. Describe how he came to wear the "sword of Tiew."

3. Who was Tiew?

4. Which Roman Empire did Attila invade first?

5. What was Attila's nickname?

Barbarian Invasion and Vikings

Project 2, Page 11

6. What happened when Attila seiged Orleans?

7. Who fought the battle of Chalons and what was the outcome?

8. What did Bishop Leo do for Rome?

9. Describe Attila's death and burial.

10. Who ruled the Huns after his death?

The following is an activity that you may want to do. It will help to bring the reading alive for your students.

Use the description of the Hun race to make masks. They can be simple paper plate or bag masks, or as elaborate as papier-mache over balloons.

GENSERIC THE VANDAL

Shortly after the death of Attila, Rome was once more in the hands of an invader, Genseric the Vandal. The Vandals were great wanderers. They slowly made their way from the shores of the Baltic Sea to the Danube, passed through what is now France, and went south into Spain. Only nine miles from Spain, just across what is now the Strait of Gibraltar, lay Africa.

Africa belonged to Rome. It was one of her most valued provinces because, while Italy could not raise enough grain to feed her people, Africa could supply all that was needed. Genseric longed to add Africa to his domain, and he was more fortunate than most men who wish to invade a country, for after a little while he received a cordial invitation to come to Africa and bring his soldiers with him. The invitation was given by no less a man than the brave general Boniface, the appointed governor of the province. This is the way it came about. Aetius was jealous of the success of Boniface, and he persuaded the mother of the child emperor to send the governor a letter recalling him. Then he himself wrote a letter to his "friend" Boniface with the warning that the empress was angry with him and he would lose his head if he risked it in Rome. Boniface was in a hard position. He concluded that the safest thing for him to do was to remain where he was, and ask Genseric to help him hold Africa.

Vandal bronze-gilt buckle with a man fighting a lion, showing the primitive workmanship of this destructive tribe.

Genseric did not wait to be urged. He hurried across the Strait of Gibraltar and began his victories. A Vandal conquest was more severe than that of any other tribe, for the Vandals seemed to delight in ruining everything that came into their power. They killed men, women, and children; they burned houses and churches and they destroyed whatever treasures they could not carry away with them. Some said that whenever they conquered a country, they cut down every fruit tree within its limits. This is why people who seem to enjoy spoiling things are sometimes called vandals.

After a while Boniface discovered how he had been tricked by Aetius, and he begged Genseric to leave the country, but the barbarian refused, and Boniface could not drive him away. Genseric and his followers settled in Africa, making the city of Carthage the capital of their kingdom. They became a nation of pirates. They built light, swift vessels and ran up on the shore of any country where they expected to find plunder.

All this time Genseric had his eyes fixed upon Italy, and again he was fortunate enough to be invited to a land which he was longing to invade. This time the widow of a murdered emperor begged him to come and avenge her wrongs. He wasted no time, but crossed the narrow sea and marched up to the walls of Rome. Behold, the gates were flung open, and once more Bishop Leo, now a hoary-headed man, came forth with his clergy, all in their priestly robes, to beg the Vandals to have mercy. Genseric made some promises, but they were soon broken. For fourteen days the Vandals did what they would. They were in no hurry; they had plenty of ships to carry away whatever they chose; and after they had chosen, there was little but the walls remaining. They snatched at gold and silver and jewels, of course, but they took also brass, copper, and bronze, silken robes, and even furniture. Works of art were nothing to them unless they were of precious metal and could be melted; and what they did not care to take with them, they broke or burned. The widowed empress had expected to be treated with the greatest honor, but the Vandals stripped off her jewels and threw her and her two daughters on board their ships to be carried to Africa as prisoners.

Genseric kept his nation together as long as he lived; and indeed, though the Romans made many expeditions against the Vandals, it was nearly eighty years before the pirates were conquered.

Comprehension questions for Genseric the Vandal

1. What country did Genseric desire to invade?

2. Who invited Genseric into the country and why?

3. What is a vandal? How did the term come to its current usage?

4. How did Genseric come to be invited to Italy?

5. What did Bishop Leo attempt to do for Rome once again? Was he successful?

6. What happened when Genseric invaded Italy?

Barbarian Invasion and Vikings

Project 2, Page 15

Clovis

Of all the Teutons who came to live on Roman territory, the most important were the Franks, or free men. They had no wish to wander over the world when they had once found a country that pleased them, and so, since they liked the land about the mouth of the Rhine, they settled there and held on to it, adding more and more wherever a little fighting would win it for them. Each tribe had its chief; but Clovis, one of these chiefs, came at last to rule them all. The country west of the Rhine, then called Gaul, was still partly held by the Romans, but Clovis meant to drive them away and keep the land for the Franks. When he was only twenty-one, he led his men against the Roman governor at Soissons and took the place. From here he sent out expeditions to conquer one bit of land after another and to bring back rich booty. The most valuable treasures were usually kept in the churches, and the heathen Franks took great delight in seizing these. Among the church treasures captured at Rheims was a marvelously beautiful vase. Now, the bishop of Rheims was on good terms with Clovis, and he sent a messenger to the young chief to beg that, even if the soldiers would not return all the holy vessels of the church, this one at least might be given back. Clovis bade the messenger follow on to Soissons, where the booty would be divided. At Soissons, when all the warriors were assembled, the king pointed to the vase and said, "I ask you, 0 most valiant warriors, not to refuse to me the vase in addition to my rightful part." Most of the soldiers were wise enough not to object to the wishes of so powerful a chief, but one foolish, envious man swung his battle-axe and crushed the vase, crying, "Thou shalt receive nothing of this unless a just lot gives it to thee." It is no wonder that the whole army was amazed at such audacity. Clovis said nothing, but quietly handed the crushed vase to the bishop's messenger. He did not forget the insult, however, and a year later, when he was reviewing his troops, he declared that this man's weapons were not in fit condition, and with one blow of his axe he struck the soldier dead, saying, " Thus thou didst to the vase at Soissons."

Clovis showed himself so much stronger than the other chiefs of the Franks that at length they all accepted him as their king. Soon after this, he began to think about taking a wife. The story of his wooing is almost like a fairy tale. In the land of Burgundy lived a fair young girl named Clotilda, whose wicked uncle had slain her father, mother, and brothers that he might get the kingdom. Clovis had heard how beautiful and good she was, and he sent an envoy to ask for her hand in marriage. The wicked uncle was afraid to have her marry so powerful a ruler, lest she should avenge the slaughter of her family; but he did not dare to refuse Clovis or to murder the girl after Clovis had asked that she might become his queen. There was nothing to do but to send her to the king of the Franks. Clovis was delighted with her, and they were married with all festivities.

Clotilda was a Christian, and she was much grieved that her husband should remain a heathen. She told him many times about her God, but nothing moved him. When their first child was born, Clotilda had the baby baptized. Not long afterwards, the little boy grew ill and died. "That is because he was baptized in the name of your God," declared Clovis bitterly. "If he had been consecrated in the name of my gods, he would be alive still." Nevertheless, when a second son was born, Clotilda had him baptized. He, too, fell ill, and the king said, "He was baptized in the name of Christ, and he will soon die." But the mother prayed to God, and by God's will the boy recovered. Still Clovis would not give up the gods of his fathers. It came to pass, however that he was engaged in a fierce battle near where Cologne now stands. His enemies were fast getting the better of him, and he was almost in despair, when suddenly he thought of the God of his queen, and he cried, "Jesus Christ, whom Clotilda declares to be the Son of the living God, if Thou wilt grant me victory over these enemies, I will believe in Thee and be baptized in Thy name." Soon the enemy fled, and Clovis did not doubt that his prayer had been answered. When he told Clotilda of this, she was delighted. She sent for the bishop and asked him to teach her husband the true religion. After a little, Clovis said to him, "I am glad to listen to you, but my people will not leave their gods." He thought a while and then he declared, " I will go forth and tell them what you have told me." He went out among his people, and, as the legend says, even before he had spoken a word, the people cried out all together, "We are ready to follow the immortal God." Then the bishop ordered the font to be prepared for the baptism of the king. The procession set out from the palace and passed through streets made gorgeous with embroidered hangings. First came the clergy, chanting hymns as they marched, and bearing the Gospels and a golden cross. After them walked the bishop, leading the king by the hand. Behind them came the queen, and after her the people. They passed through the door and into the church. The candles gleamed, the house was hung with tapestries of the purest white and was fragrant with incense, and there the king of the Franks, his sisters, and more than three thousand of his warriors, besides a throng of women and children, were baptized and marked with the sign of the cross. The times were harsh and rude, and even a king who was looked upon as a Christian ruler never dreamed of hesitating to do many cruel deeds. Clovis wished to enlarge his kingdom, and he could always find some excuse for attacking any tribe living on land next his own. He cared nothing for his word, and to get what he wanted, he was ready to lie or steal or murder. Clovis died in 511, but before that time all the lands between the lower Rhine and the Pyrenees Mountains had been obliged to acknowledge his rule. He took Paris as his capital, and went there to live. This was the beginning of France. The descendants of Clovis held the throne for nearly two centuries and a half. They were called Merovingians from Merovaeus, the grandfather of Clovis.

Barbarian Invasion and Vikings

Project 2, Page 17

Comprehension questions for Clovis

1. What group of people did Clovis lead?

2. What does Frank mean?

3. What country did Clovis invade and keep for the Franks?

4. Describe the vase incident at Soissons.

Barbarian Invasion and Vikings

Project 2, Page 18

Comprehension questions for Clovis

5. Describe Clovis' wife.

6. How was Clovis converted to Christianity?

7. Draw the scene of Clovis' baptism.

8. What country did Gaul become?

9. What line of kings were Clovis' descendants?

Barbarian Invasion and Vikings

Project 2, Page 19

The Coming of the Teutons to England

The Celts, as has been said before, left their old home in Asia in very early times and moved slowly across Europe. At length they came to the ocean. The tribes behind were pressing upon them, and the Celts were not stopped by so narrow a body of water as the English Channel. Many of them crossed to the British Isles. There they lived in small huts made of poles fastened together at the top. They knew how to make boats with planks and nails, but oftener they made them by covering wicker frameworks with skins. Their priests were called Druids, and it is thought that the great stones at Stonehenge, on Salisbury Plain, are the remains of rude temples in which sacrifices were offered. These Celts, or Britons, painted their bodies blue, for they thought this would make them seem more terrible to their enemies. Rough as they were, they were fond of pretty things, and they made themselves bracelets and necklaces. Those who lived inland were savage, but those who dwelt nearest to the Continent were somewhat civilized. They raised wheat and barley and kept many cattle. They had no towns, but gathered in little villages.

This is the way the Britons lived when the Romans came upon them. The Romans were always ready to conquer a new country, and they meant to subdue the British Isles. They obliged the Britons in the greater part of England to obey them, but they gave up trying to conquer the savage tribes of the northern part of the island, and finally, to keep them out they built two great walls with watchtowers and strongholds straight across the country. Some of the Teutons on the Continent were also troublesome, and therefore the Romans raised a line of forts around the southeastern shore of England. These Romans were famous road-makers, and they built excellent highways, several running across the island. They made settlements; they erected handsome town houses and country houses with statues and vases and pavements of many-colored marble, and they built many of their famous baths. The Romans were the rulers, and the Britons had to obey. It is probable that many of the Britons were obliged to enter the Roman army, and that many of those who did not become soldiers were treated as slaves.

The Romans could have conquered the troublesome northern tribes, but as we have seen, the Goths were pressing forward upon the boundaries of their empire, and Alaric had invaded Italy and plundered Rome itself. Every soldier in the Roman army was needed to help protect the empire, and none could be spared for the Britons, therefore officers and men sailed away from the British shores and left the people to take care of themselves.

The Britons could have done this better before they had anything to do with the Romans. At one time they were excellent fighters, but they had become so used to being led by Roman officers that when they were left alone they were helpless. The savages were coming down upon them from the north, and the three tribes of Teutons—the Saxons, Angles, and Jutes—were threatening them from the region between the Baltic and the North Sea. The Britons could not protect themselves, and they sent a pitiful appeal to the Roman commander Aetius to come and help them. "The barbarians," it said, "drive us to the sea, and the sea drives us back to the barbarians; and between them we are either slain or drowned." Aetius, however, was too busy trying to keep other barbarians from Rome to help people so far away as England, and he could do nothing for them. The Britons believed that of all their enemies the Teutons were the strongest, and they decided to ask them to come to Britain and help drive away the others. They might have the island of Thanet for their home, the Britons promised.

The Jutes came first, under the two brothers, Hengist and Horsa, it is said, and they were followed by the Angles and Saxons. These Teutons helped to drive away the other tribes, according to the bargain, but soon they found Thanet too small for them, and so, just as one tribe had been driving another to the westward for centuries, they drove the British westward. Some Britons were killed, some became slaves, and some hid away in the mountains of western England. The Teutons called these Wealh, or Welsh, that is, strangers or foreigners, and it is from this that the country of Wales takes its name.

The Britons were not conquered all at once by any means, for they fought most courageously, and probably it was many years before the Teutons became masters of the country. The Angles scattered so widely throughout the land that it took its name from them and became known as the land of the Angles, or Angle-land, and finally England. The Saxons, however, were strongest of the three peoples, and therefore their name is generally given to all the invaders. Their descendants take both names and are known as Anglo-Saxons.

The Britons had become Christians long before the coming of the Saxons, but the Saxons were heathen. After these savage invaders had been in England about a century, some young people of their race were sold in Rome as slaves. They had golden hair and blue eyes, and to a saintly monk named Gregory who was passing through the market-place they seemed exceedingly beautiful. "Who are they?" he asked. The answer was *Angles.* "Angli," that is, *angels.* Gregory never lost his interest in the Angles, and if he had been permitted, he would gladly have gone to England as a missionary. After some years he became Pope Gregory the Great, and then, although he himself could not go, he sent Saint Augustine (not of Hippo) to preach to them. The King of Kent had a Christian wife, and therefore Saint Augustine went first to him and asked if he might tell him about the religion of Christ. The King was willing to hear him, but not in a house, for if there was any magic about this new faith, he thought the evil spirits would have far less power in the open air. He listened closely, and then he went home to think over what he had heard. After a while he told Saint Augustine that he believed the Christian faith was true. This teaching spread over England, and soon it was no longer a heathen country.

Comprehension questions for the Teutons

1. Describe the life of the Celts, or Britons. What religion were they? How did they fight?

2. Who conquered most of the Britons first?

3. What happened to draw the Roman conquerors out of England?

4. What three barbarian tribes invaded the Britons?

5. Who were the Welsh?

6. What name was given to the inhabitants of England?

7. Describe the conversion of the Anglo-Saxons.

Barbarian Invasion and Vikings

Project 3

The War Room

In the Project 2 readings the battles and invasions occur very quickly. To help sort it all out, set up a "war room" with maps depicting the invasions. Use colored tacks to represent the battles. Color the sections on one large geographical wall map of Europe to represent the Teuton tribe that moved in. This is a good time to reflect on where the former inhabitants went. Did they stay in the area and learn to live with the invaders, or did they move on to other areas? The Norsemen were masters at adapting the cultures of the people they invaded. Through this living together, the Norsemen had great influence on European culture. Of course, the other Europeans had influence on the Norsemen also. You can also address geographical barriers such as mountains, rivers, and oceans and what motivates men to push beyond their boundaries.

Barbarian Invasion and Vikings
Project 4

Viking Library

Divide the students into groups. For a very small classroom or homeschool, have students choose a few topics. Use the following topics to make small books (you may want to use the images on the following page). Attach the books on a poster board, or to a pocket folder, for a nice presentation of the Vikings. Have students share their research with parents or another class of children. Use the resources on your cards to research the information.

Topics *(with some suggestions for information to include)*

Travel *(horses, snowy weather, bridges)*

Ships and sailing *(navigation, longships, merchant ships)*

Viking Explorations *(Iceland, Greenland, America)*

Food

Work *(Fisherman, Craftsmen, Merchants, Slaves, Warriors)*

Runes *(futhark, transcribe names with runes)*

Society *(royalty, thralls, family)*

Government *(things, althings, crime and punishment)*

Burial *(burial ships, grave goods, monuments)*

Norse Mythology

Norse religion vs. Christianity *(View of Universe, worship, afterlife, the conversion of the Vikings to Christianity)*

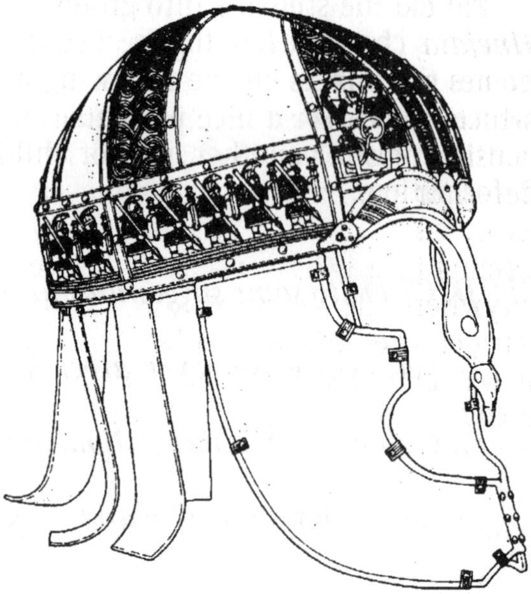

BARBARIAN INVASION AND VIKINGS

Project 5

Hnefatafl

Pre-dating chess by at least 1,000 years, *Hnefatafl* (nev-a-tah-full) was played in Viking homes as early as 400 A.D. A game of strategy which is translated as "King's Table", Hnefatafl consists of one piece called *Hnefi* ("King"), twelve defenders and twenty-four attackers all referred to as *Hunns* ("knobs") or *Taeflor* ("table-men"). Many gaming boards have been found Greenland to France—anywhere the Vikings had influence. Hnefatafl appears in various sizes and was called Ard-Ri ("High-King") in Scotland, Brandubh in Ireland (where it was played with dice), and Tablut in Finland just to name a few. The rules and gaming board changed over time but the basic idea of the game remained consistent. A mock battle between unequal forces—the weaker army in the center surrounded by a larger attacking force surrounding. The gaming pieces were made of antler, bone, clay, glass, horn, stone, wood, or even horse's teeth. The game was for two players, using twelve light pieces and a King for one and twenty-four dark pieces for his opponent.

History

There are many references to Hnefatafl in Old Norse literature, from sources ranging from the poems of the *Poetic Edda* to saga references such as *Orkeyinga Saga*, the Greenland *Lay of Astli, Hervarar Saga, Fridthjof's Saga* and more. Most often these references are to the playing pieces.

The earliest mention of the game reads:

> *Then in the grass the golden taeflor, the far-famed ones, will be found again, which they had owned in older days.*

Rigsthula speaks of the noble child Earl learning to swim and play Tafl. From *Hervarar Saga* come two riddles in the riddle-game between Odinn and King Heidrek:

> *Who are the maids that fight weaponless around their lord, the brown ever sheltering the fair ever attacking him?*

Answer: the pieces in Hnefatafl (in this case the brown pieces occupy the center attacked by the white pieces).

There have been numerous grave finds of game pieces. One runestone from Ockelbo, Sweden, shows two men balancing a boardgame on their knees, which reflects the saga references where arguments over the game frequently cause one or both players to leap to their feet, upsetting the Tafl-board and scattering the pieces. Fragments of actual game boards have been excavated as well.

Barbarian Invasion and Vikings

Project 5, Page 2

Set Up

The King goes in the center square, or Konakis ("the Throne") surrounded by his men while the attackers are set up around the board (see fig.1).

Objective

The goal is for the defenders to get the King to one of the corner squares so he can "escape" while the attackers win if they capture the King before he can escape. Because the game is uneven, it is good etiquette to play twice, switching sides. A score of pieces taken is recorded in order to establish the final winner.

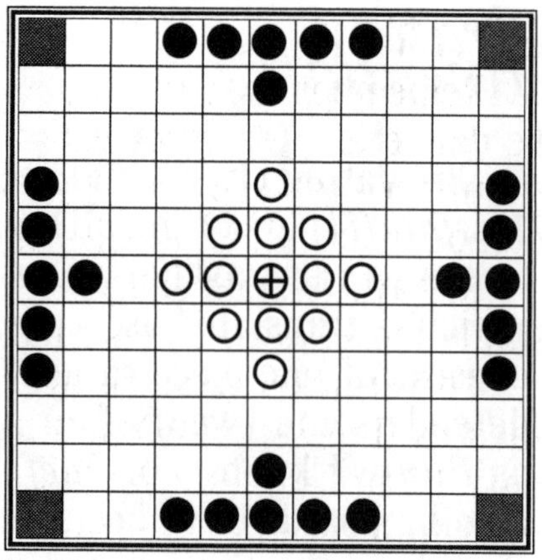

Figure 1: Set up for start of game

Rules

1. The Throne and the four corners are restricted and may only be occupied by the King. The King may re-enter the Throne and all pieces my pass through the Throne when it is empty. The four corners and the Throne can replace one of the two pieces required in capturing an opponents piece at any time, while the Throne is only hostile to the defenders while it is empty.

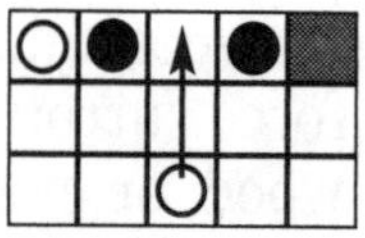

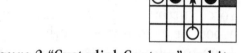

Figure 2: "Custodial Capture"—white captures both black pieces in one move

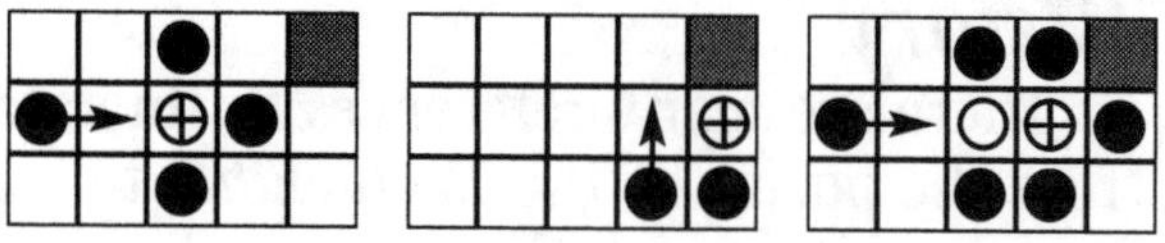

Figure 3: In each case black captures the King and wins

2. Turns alternate between players with the attackers getting to move first. All pieces slide orthogonally (up-down or left-right, no diagonal moves) as long as it doesn't jump over any pieces, like a rook in the game of Chess.

3. Defenders and attackers are captured if they are sandwiched between two enemy pieces, or between an enemy piece and a hostile square (the four corners and sometimes the Throne), along a column or row. The two enemy pieces should be either above and below or to the left and right of the attacked piece. A capture is only made if the trap is closed by the move of the opponent, and it is, therefore, allowed to move in between two enemy pieces (fig. 2). A captured piece is taken off the board for the rest of the game. The King may take part in a capture.

4. The King is captured like any other piece unless he is on the Throne or one of the four squares adjacent to the Throne. When on the Throne, the attackers must surround him in all four directions and when he is on a square next to the Throne, the attackers must surround him in the four points of the compass except the Throne. When the King is in danger of being captured on the attackers' next move, the attacker must announce, "Watch your King."

Barbarian Invasion and Vikings

Project 5, Page 3

Strategy

Remember that the King is a powerful piece! He can be placed into situations that would be dangerous for other defenders, and used as an anvil to kill attackers. The Attacker should try to keep the king pinned into the center part of the board. If he gets loose the defender has a big advantage.

Always remember that any piece can move from one side of the board to the other in a single move. Keep the big picture in mind at all times.

The attacker must be aggressive. It is tempting to place 8 pieces beside the corner squares thus stopping the King from escaping. This leaves your position much weaker with only 16 attackers to the 13 defenders one of which is the very powerful King. The time you need to block the corners will also give the defender time to get the king in motion.

The king has to make clever sacrifices to create paths into the open, but without weakening his own forces too much. It is important to rapidly establish a threat against at least one of the strategically important corners. The attackers should try to build walls at a larger distance. In the initial phase, it is advantageous for the attackers not to capture defenders unless absolutely necessary, as the defenders tend to block the way for their own king. When the attackers finally have managed to surround the defenders with their walls, they can start to capture defenders and tighten the trap.

Supplies

Clay or Glass beads
(to fashion playing pieces: twelve light defenders, a light King and twenty-four dark attackers)
Posterboard and Markers
(to illustrate playing board as shown in this manual)

or

Photocopy (at 200%) board and pieces in this manual

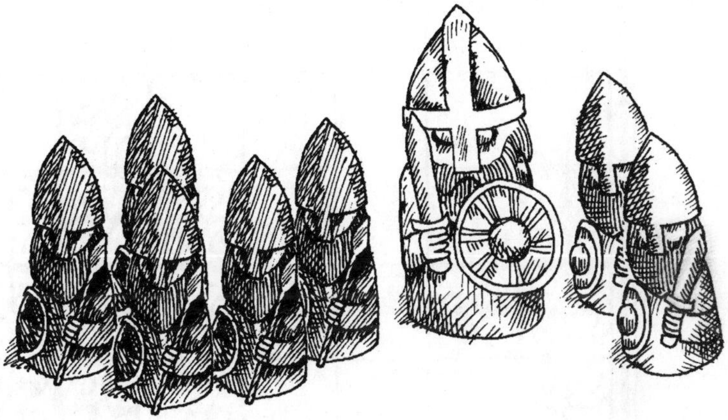

Barbarian Invasion and Vikings

Project 5, Page 4

Photocopy these on thick paper at 200% for a quick Hnefatafl game set.

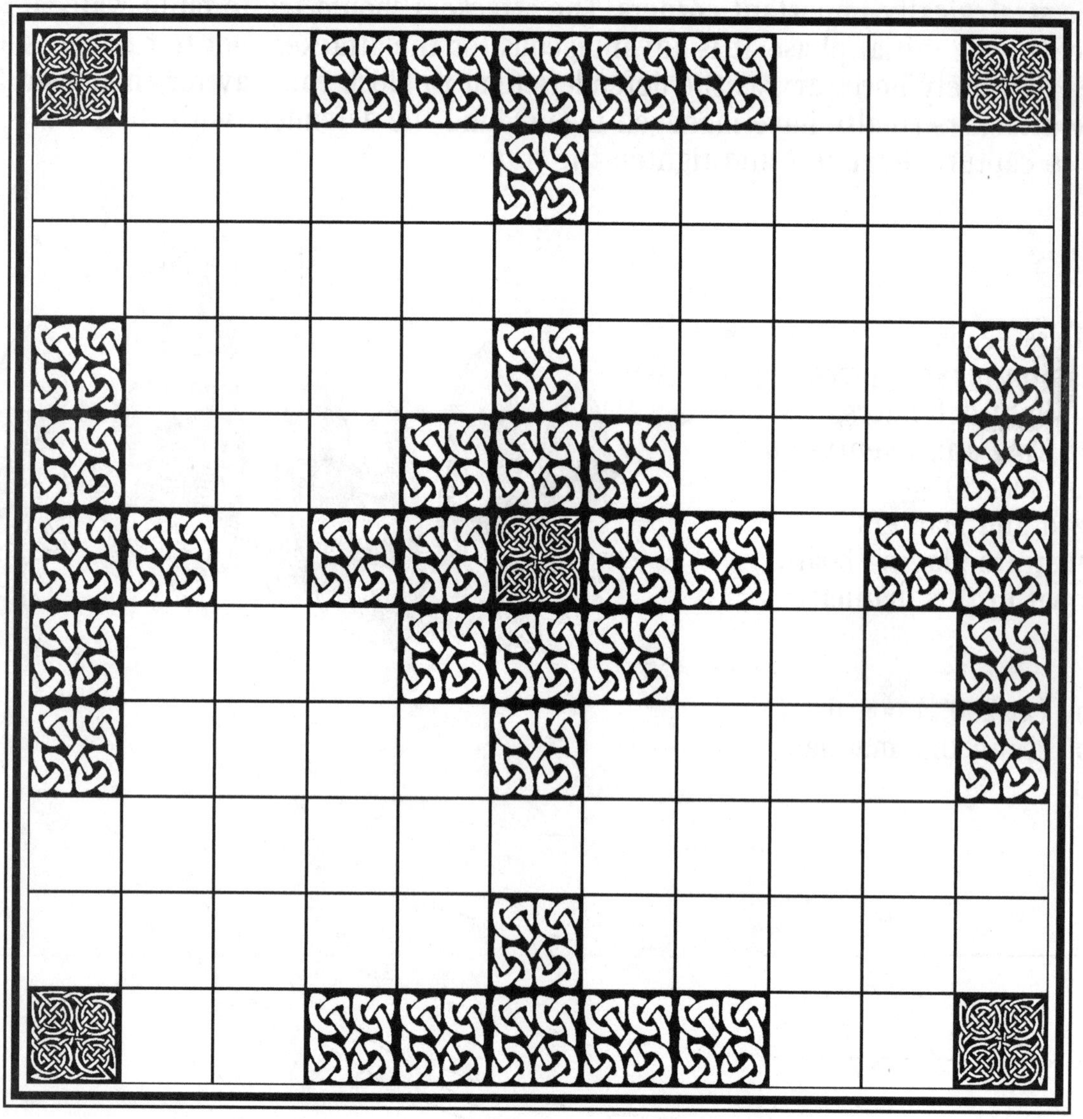

Barbarian Invasion and Vikings

Project 6

Viking Ship

Supplies (one per boat)

1 empty box of 100 3.5 floppy disks

4 pieces of brown construction paper

paint brush

brown paint

glue/hot glue gun

1/4 inch dowels, 12" long

1/4 inch dowels, 16" long

12" x 12" red cloth

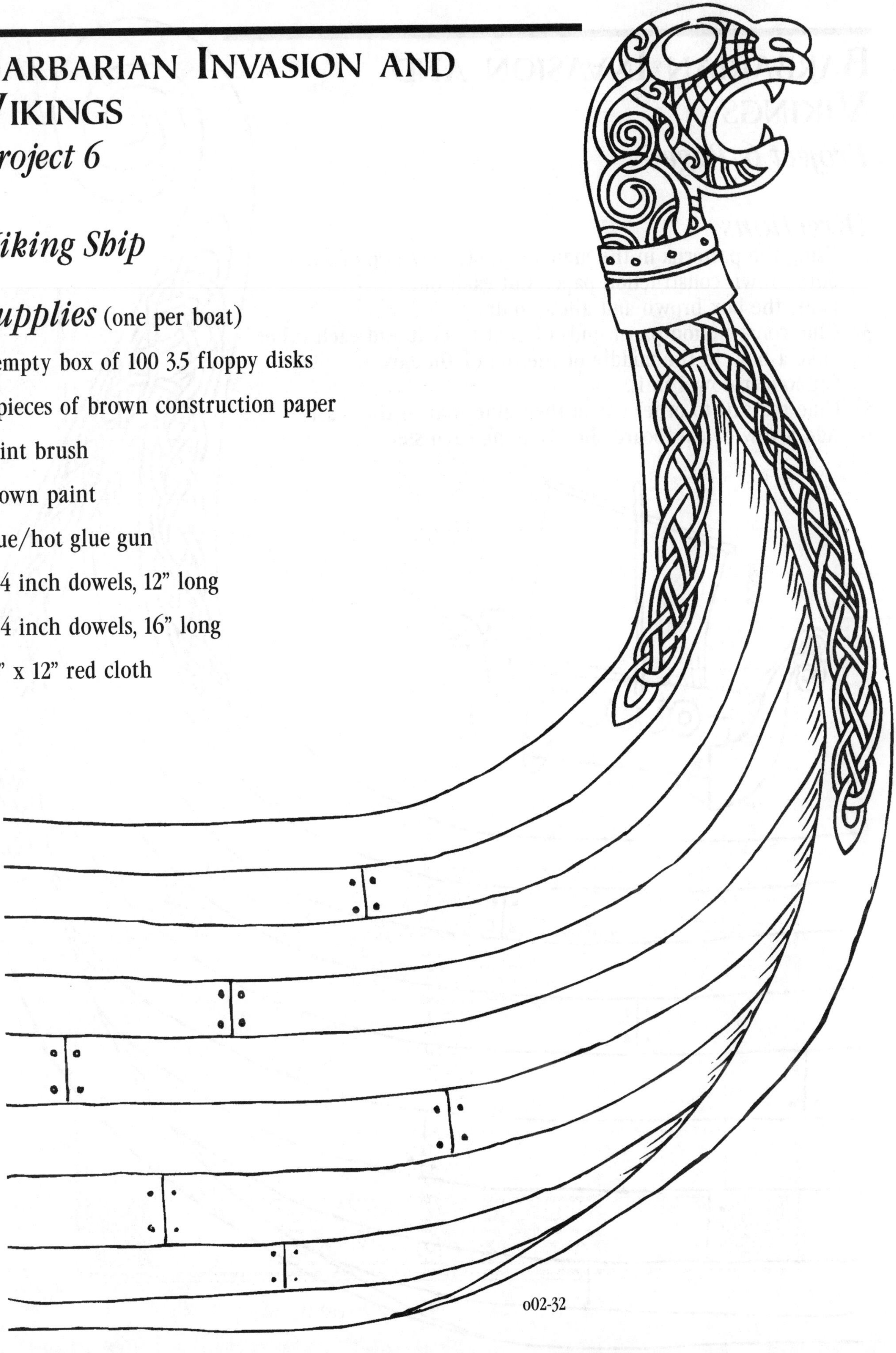

Barbarian Invasion and Vikings

Project 6, Page 2

Directions

1. Using the patterns in the manual, photocopy two of each onto brown construction paper. Cut each out.
2. Paint the box brown and allow to dry.
3. Glue construction paper ends of boat to boat and each other.
4. Poke a hole in the middle of the top of the box and place the longer dowel in it.
5. Glue red sail to other dowel then glue that to the mast.
6. Add a row of cardboard sheilds along each side.

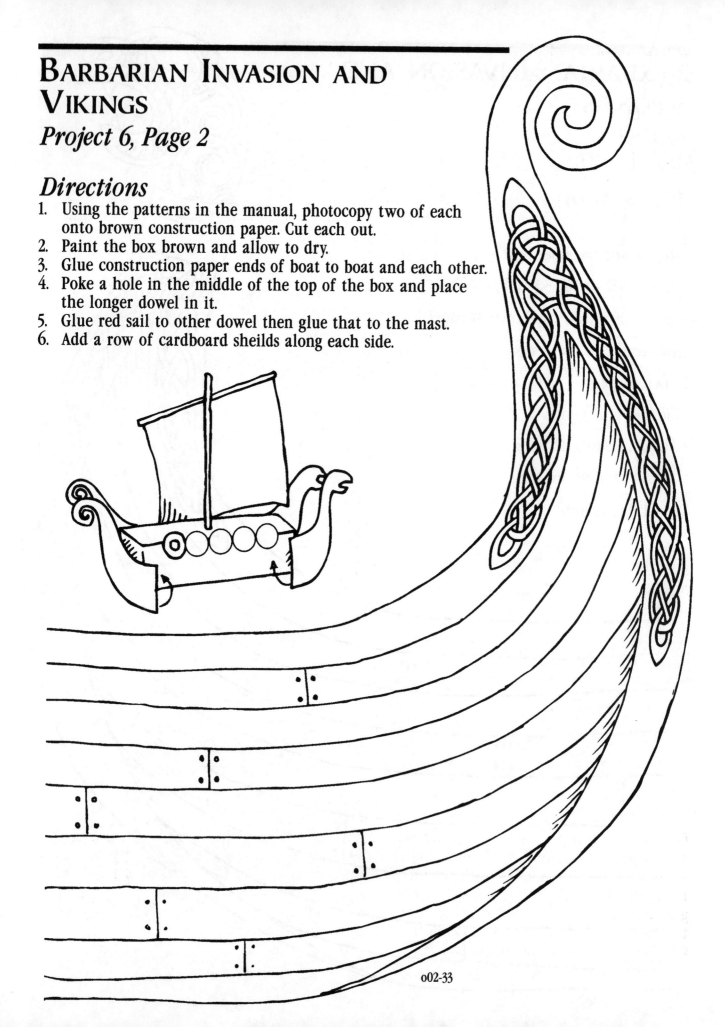

Barbarian Invasion and Vikings

Project 7

Mjolnir *(Thor's Hammer)*

In Norse mythology, Odin was the most powerful, father god. His eldest son, Thor—god of thunder and sky—was the most popular god. He rode through the sky in a brazen chariot drawn by two swift goats, whose hoofs struck sparks from the sky, and the rumble of his chariot made the roar and roll of thunder. Thor wore an iron gauntlet so he could wield his hammer, as it was usually red-hot from creating thunderbolts. So sacred was Mjolnir that the Norse made the sign of the hammer, as they would later make the sign of the Cross, to ward off evil and secure blessings. Many Vikings would wear necklaces with jewelry attached shaped like the hammer of Thor for good luck.

Supplies

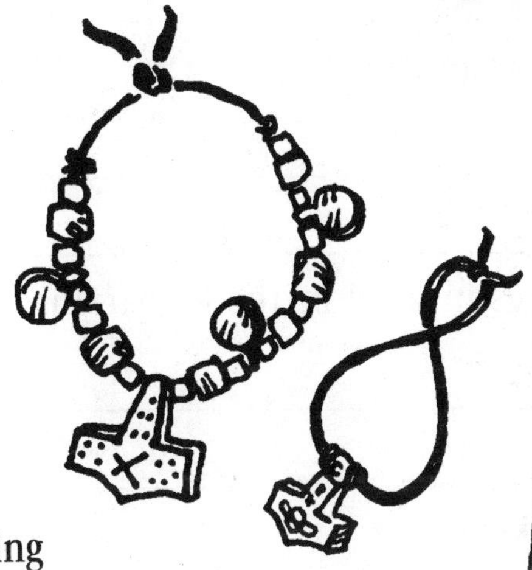

gold foil sheets
embossing tool
leather string
glass and metal beads
glue
cardboard

Most of the above supplies can be purchased at a local craft store. If you have a problem finding the foil or embossing tools they may be ordered from:

Natural Science Industries, Ltd.
910 Orlando Avenue
West Hempstead, N.Y. 11552-3942

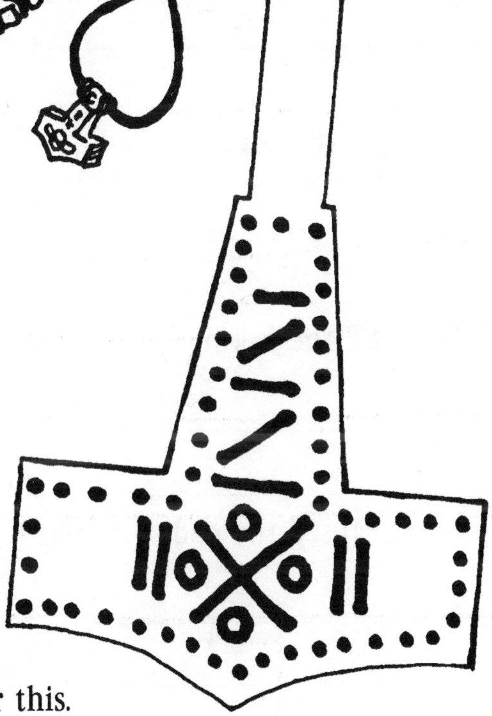

Directions

Using the pattern provided cut out Thor's Hammer from the cardboard. Using the cardboard piece trace the shape onto the foil. The embossing tool may then be used to design shapes onto the foil hammer. Once the design is complete, cut the foil hammer out and glue to the cardboard. String the leather piece through the back of the cardboard and string the beads on after this. Once done tie the string at the end.

Barbarian Invasion and Vikings
Test

1. What is the approximate date of the Barbarian Invasion and Vikings?

2. What is the name of the period when the barbarians and Vikings lived?

3. Describe the personal attributes of the barbarians.

4. Name two barbarian tribes.

5. What empire was invaded by the barbarians?

6. Describe the Vikings.

7. Why did the Vikings ravage the coasts of Europe and America?

8. What caused the end of the influence of barbarians and Vikings?

Barbarian Invasion and Vikings

Test, Page 2

Review

1. In what year did Augustine convert to Christianity?

2. Who was Augustine's mother?

3. What official role did Augustine have in the church?

4. Name two books written by Augustine.

5. Compare Augustine's view on the nature of man to Pelagius' view.

St. Jerome Completes the Vulgate

Worksheet

1. In what year did St. Jerome complete the Vulgate?

2. When was the Old Testament translated from Hebrew to Greek?

3. Why was the New Testament originally written in Greek?

4. Where did St. Jerome live?

5. Was Jerome's translation the first into Latin?

   If, not why did he translate one?

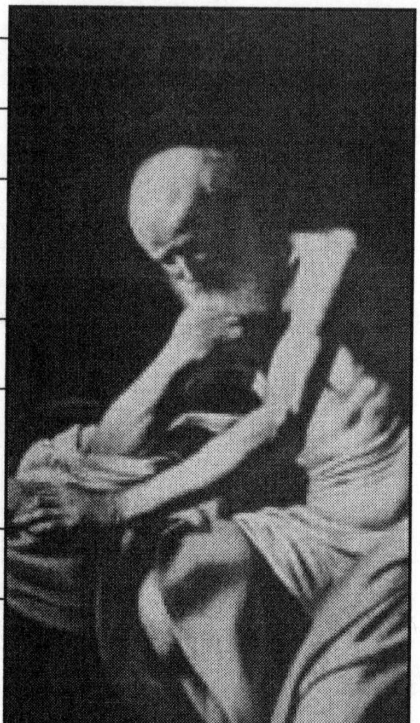

6. What is the Apocrypha?

7. Did Jerome include the Apocrypha?

8. What does "vulgate" mean?

St. Jerome Completes the Vulgate
Project

Psalm 23 (Latin Vulgate Psalm 22)

Below is a section of the Vulgate as Jerome translated it. You may want to go over it with your class or, if your students are capable, translate it.

1 Psalmus David.
Dominus regit me, et nihil mihi deerit:
2 In loco pascuae ibi me collocavit.
Super aquam refectionis educavit me,
3 Animam meam convertit.
Deduxit me super semitas iustitiae,
Propter nomen suum.
4 Nam, et si ambulavero in medio umbrae mortis,
Non timebo mala, quoniam tu mecum es.
Virga tua, et baculus tuus,
Ipsa me consolata sunt.
5 Parasti in conspectu meo mensam,
Adversus eos qui tribulant me;
Impinguasti in oleo caput meum;
Et calix meus inebrians quam praeclarus est!
6 Et misericordia tua subsequetur me
Omnibus diebus vitae meae;
Et ut inhabitem in domo Domini,
In longitudinem dierum.

St. Jerome Completes the Vulgate
Project 2

Research

Go to the library or the internet for information to write a brief paper in your own words on why a lion and/or a skull was often found in paintings of St. Jerome.

St. Jerome Completes the Vulgate

Test

1. In what year did St. Jerome complete the Vulgate?

2. In 200 B.C. the Old Testament was translated from Hebrew into what language? What is this translation of the Bible known as?

3. Why did the New Testament come to us in Greek?

4. Why did St. Jerome find it necessary to translate the Bible into Latin?

5. What is the name for St. Jerome's Latin translation of the Bible? What does this mean?

6. Who was St. Jerome? Where did he live?

St. Jerome Completes the Vulgate
Test, Page 2

Review

1. Describe Augustine's life before he became a Christian.

2. Who were the Donatists?

3. What did Augustine believe man was like even at birth?

4. What historical period coincided with the barbarians and Vikings?

5. What caused the end of the influence of the barbarians and Vikings?

The Council of Chalcedon
Worksheet

1. What was the date of The Council of Chalcedon?

___

___

2. What central question had The Council of Nicea resolved?

___

___

___

3. What question did The Council of Chalcedon primarily address?

___

___

___

___

4. How many bishops covened in this council?

___

___

5. From where did they derive their answers?

___

___

6. What four points did the council affirm?

   a. ___

   b. ___

   c. ___

   d. ___

The Council of Chalcedon
Project

Definition of Chalcedon (451 AD)

Below is the "Definition of Chalcedon." This is the final statement of the council. Define any terms that are unclear. Discuss with your students the meaning and impact of this statement to the controversy it addressed. Several suggested discussion questions follow:

1. Was Jesus part or fully God?
2. Was Jesus part or fully man?
3. Were His two natures (God and human) confused or blended together?
4. Why is it important that Jesus be fully God and fully man without blending together?

Definition of Chalcedon

Following, then, the holy fathers, we unite in teaching all men to confess the one and only Son, our Lord Jesus Christ. This selfsame one is perfect both in deity and in humanness; this selfsame one is also actually God and actually man, with a rational soul (*meaning human soul*) and a body. He is of the same reality as God as far as his deity is concerned and of the same reality as we ourselves as far as his humanness is concerned; thus like us in all respects, sin only excepted. Before time began he was begotten of the Father, in respect of his deity, and now in these "last days," for us and behalf of our salvation, this selfsame one was born of Mary the virgin, who is God-bearer in respect of his humanness.

We also teach that we apprehend this one and only Christ-Son, Lord, only-begotten in two natures; and we do this without confusing the two natures, without transmuting one nature into the other, without dividing them into two separate categories, without contrasting them according to area or function. The distinctiveness of each nature is not nullified by the union. Instead, the "properties" of each nature are conserved and both natures concur in one "person" and in one reality (*hypostasis*). They are not divided or cut into two persons, but are together the one and only and only-begotten Word *(Logos)* of God, the Lord Jesus Christ.

Thus have the prophets of old testified; thus the Lord Jesus Christ himself taught us; thus the Symbol of Fathers (*the Nicene Creed*) has handed down to us.

The Council of Chalcedon
Project 2

Council Fill-In

Fill in the missing portions in the banners below from the church councils.

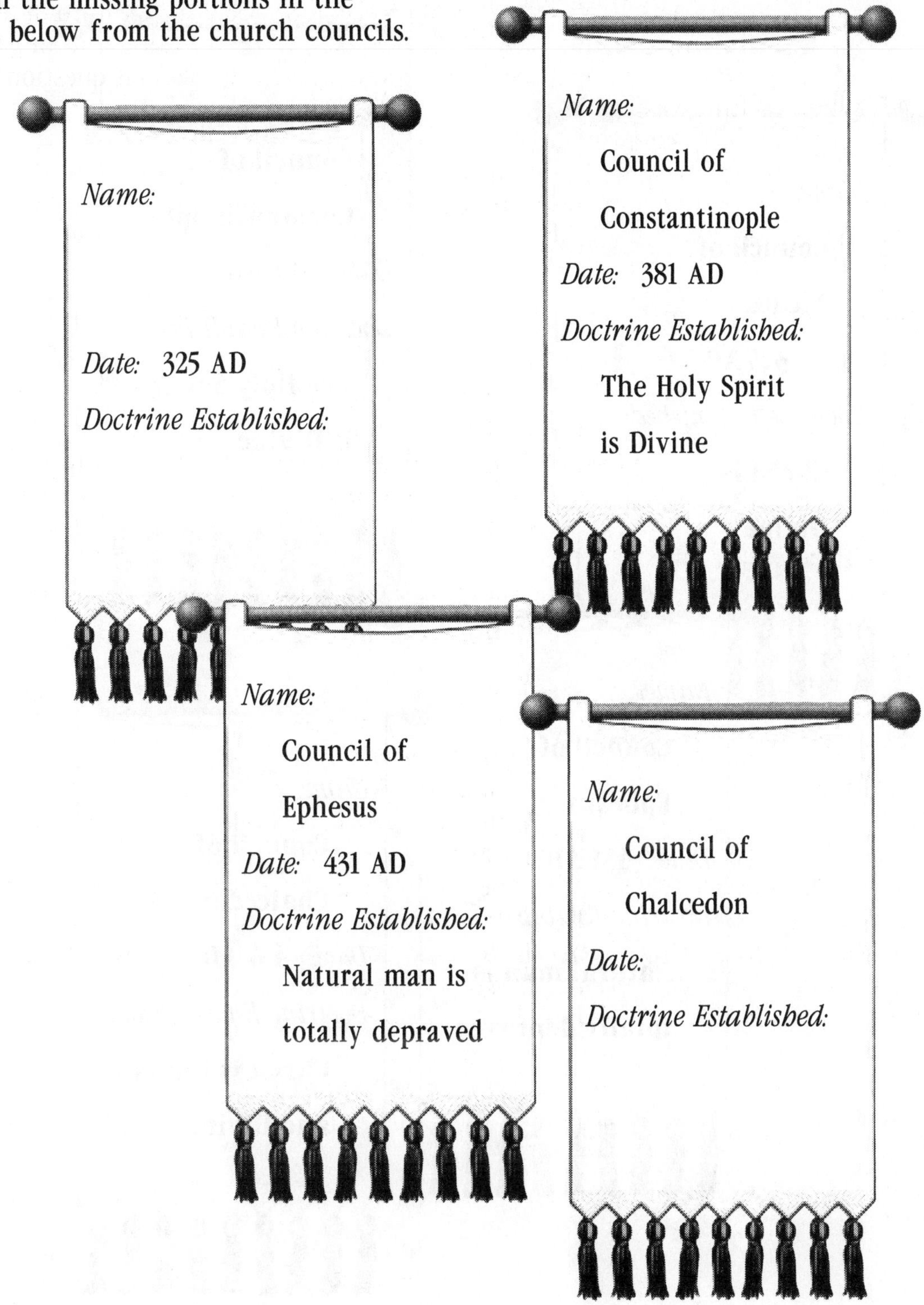

The Council of Chalcedon
Project 2, Page 2

Answer Key

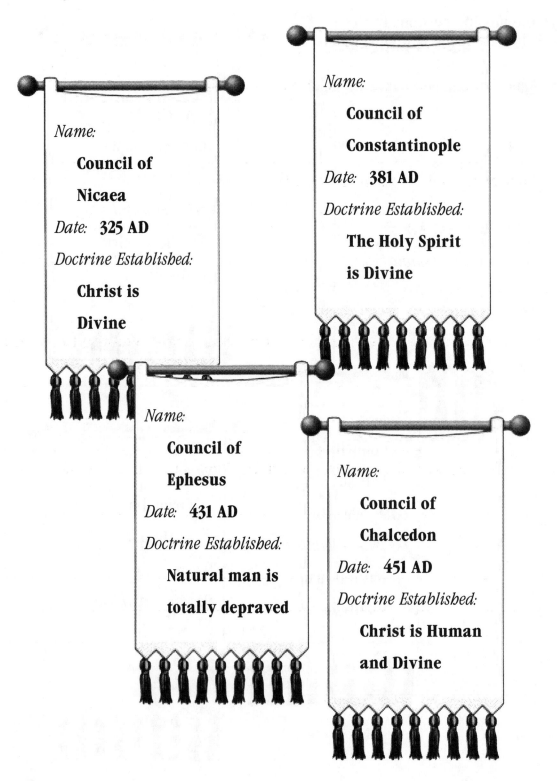

Name:
Council of Nicaea
Date: **325 AD**
Doctrine Established:
Christ is Divine

Name:
Council of Constantinople
Date: **381 AD**
Doctrine Established:
The Holy Spirit is Divine

Name:
Council of Ephesus
Date: **431 AD**
Doctrine Established:
Natural man is totally depraved

Name:
Council of Chalcedon
Date: **451 AD**
Doctrine Established:
Christ is Human and Divine

The Council of Chalcedon
Test

1. What was the date of The Council of Chalcedon?

2. What question did The Council of Chalcedon address?

3. What four points did the Council affirm?

   a.

   b.

   c.

   d.

4. What did the Council consider the source of information for resolving the conflict?

5. How many people were involved in the Council? What title did they hold?

THE COUNCIL OF CHALCEDON
Test

Review

1. What is considered Augustine's greatest work?

2. Describe the barbarians.

3. Name two barbarian tribes.

4. What is the Vulgate?

5. Who translated the Vulgate?

St. Benedict and Monasticism
Worksheet

1. Why did St. Anthony and other Christians move into the desert about the third century?

2. Where does the word "Monk" derive its meaning?

3. Where did monks eventually gather?

4. Who was St. Bendedict?

5. Name the three vows that monks took. Explain them.

6. What became of the monasteries as the Empire and cities declined?

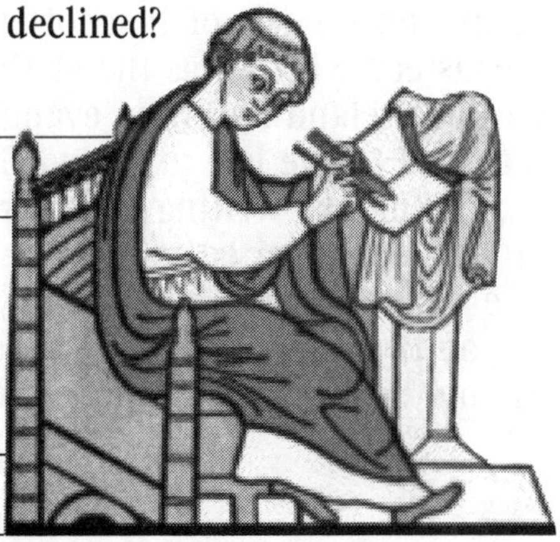

7. How was most of the literature of the ancient world preserved?

St. Benedict and Monasticism
Project

Illuminated Manuscripts

Before the invention of the printing press all the manuscripts or books as we refer to them were copied by hand. It took a great deal of time to produce one book. Because of the hours involved the books also cost a great deal of money. Many of the manuscripts were copied by monks in monasteries. The books may have had as many as 500 pages and were copied by one or more scribes. Monks worked in a special room in the monastery called the *scriptorium*. Manuscripts were copied onto parchment and later onto paper referred to as vellum.

In later years many manuscripts were highly decorated with pictures and designs. In the beginning of many Psalters it was common to have them start with a large initial letter called a "drop cap." The text was written first and a space was left for the large letter. Often gold or silver leaf was used on these initial letters. Because of the expense of the parchment one of the scribes jobs was to place as much writing as possible on the page. He would first measure the page and mark out the area available in which to write. He left a place for the initial letter (or drop cap) and then a different artist would fill in the blank space with *illuminations*. These illuminations were graphic forms that took the form of animals, birds, geometric shapes, grotesque creatures with human heads and animal bodies, and many more.

On the following page are examples of the artwork and writing style found in the Book of Kells, the most famous example of Celtic manuscript art in existence. Now on display in the Library of Trinity College, Ireland, this book is an evangelistary; that is, it contains the four gospels of the New Testament. The Book of Kells was created about 800 A.D., or possibly earlier, by Irish monks and takes its name from the Abbey of Kells where it was kept from the ninth century until 1541. The monastery at Kells was founded in the 6th century by the Irish monk Columcille, which means "Dove of the Church." Columcille, for the love of beautiful manuscripts, illegally copied a psalter belonging to Bishop Finian of Clonard.

When Columcille was found out, King Diarmait ordered the copy returned to Finian. Columcille later mobilized his kinsman to fight Diarmait's army in retaliation. Three hundred and one soldiers were killed over the manuscript which was called *Cathach* (Warrior) ever after. Columcille was exiled as punishment for this course of action. He eventually landed on the isle of Iona, off the coast of present day Scotland, and established a monastery which was the birthplace of Ireland's later zealous evangelizing of barbarous Europe. Ireland had been evangelized nearly one hundred years earlier when Bishop Patrick returned to the Isle to spread God's Word.

The monks writing manuscripts like Cathach, the Book of Durrow, the Book of Kells and others, were limited to just the colors they could make from powdered minerals and the like which yielded white, red, yellow, green, blue, indigo, pink and purple. Enjoy this project as you try your hand as a scribe. Pretend you are an Irish monk in the 6th century, sitting in your small, beehive-shaped hut, copying Scripture to the glory of God.

St. Benedict and Monasticism

Project, Page 2

Supplies

Parchment (1 piece per child)
Calligraphy pens or feather pens (available at craft stores and many museums)
Ink (if using feather pens)
Gold and silver markers
Colored markers (remember, only red, yellow, green, blue, indigo, pink and purple!)
Matches

Instructions

Copy page o05-5 onto parchment paper. Using either a calligraphy or feather pen copy all or part of Psalm 23. Then decorate the white space with "illuminations." Have an adult burn the paper edges to give the page an aged look.

St. Benedict and Monasticism

Project, Page 3

Following are all elements from the Book of Kells that you can utilize for this project. Try to write out the text using the Irish style which looks like this:

abcdefghijklmn
opqrstuvwxyz

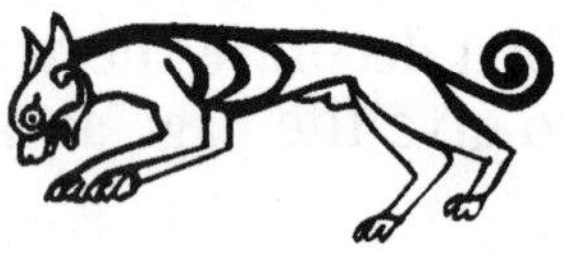

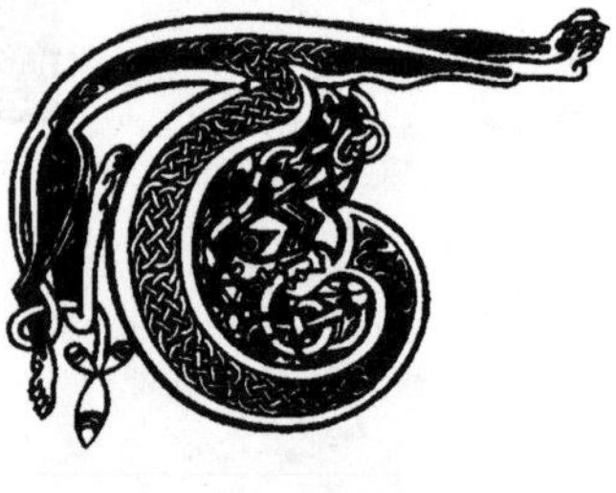

Above: the letter "T"
Left: Symbols for St. Luke and St. John

A PSALM OF DAVID.

St. Benedict and Monasticism
Project 2

Use *The Church In History* to fill in the screens below from the pages indicated.

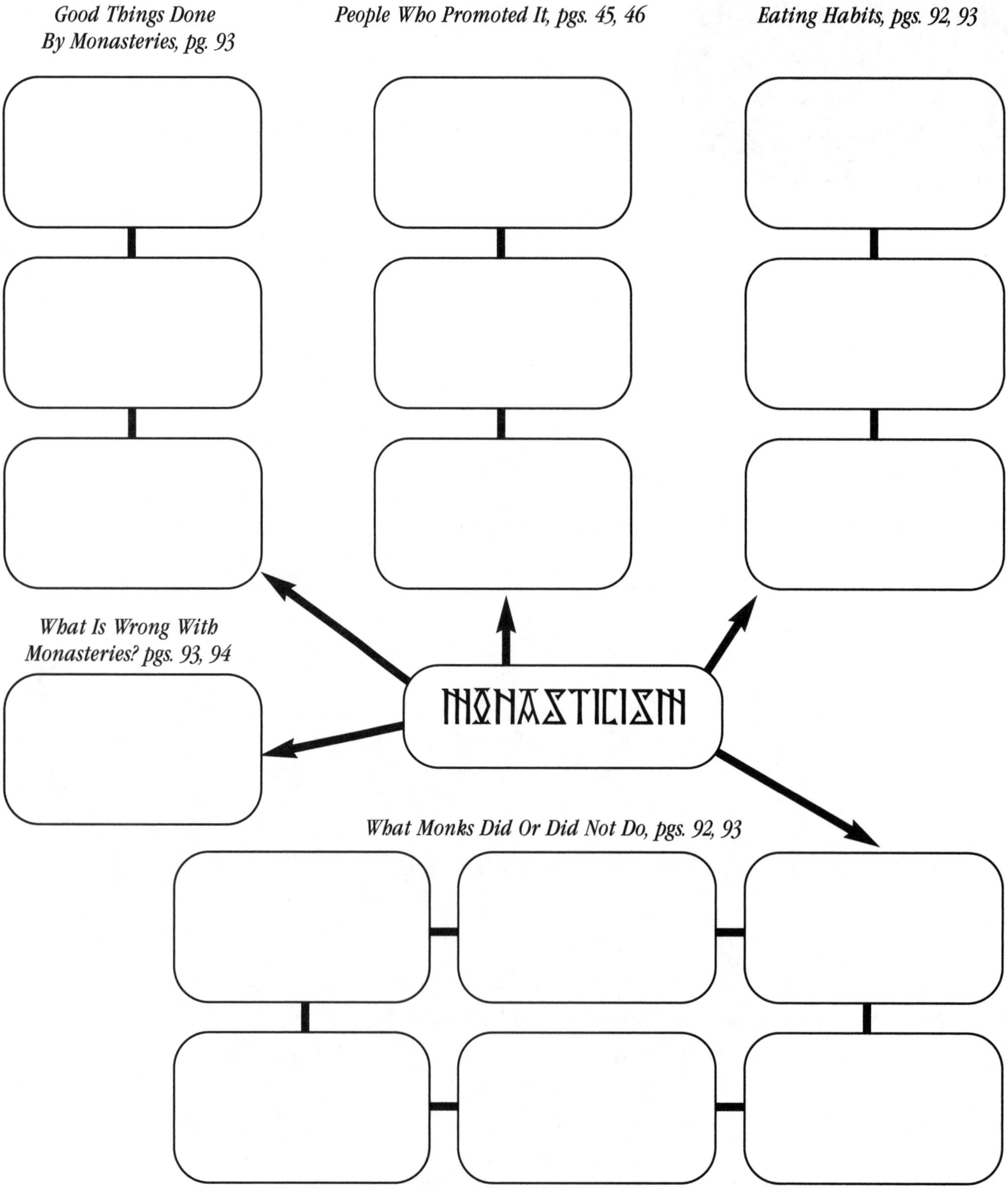

St. Benedict and Monasticism

Test

1. What was the approximate date of St. Benedict and Monasticism?

____

____

2. Why did St. Anthony and other Christians move into the desert around the third century?

____

____

____

3. What were the men referred to as who lived in monasteries?

____

____

4. Who introduced "rules for monasteries" around 540?

____

____

5. List and describe the three vows that monks took?

____

____

____

6. Why did monasteries become the centers of learning?

____

____

7. How was literature from the ancient world preserved?

____

____

____

St. Benedict and Monasticism

Test, Page 2

Review

1. Who was St. Augustine? What did he write?

2. What caused the end of the influence of the barbarians and Vikings?

3. What was the Vulgate? Who wrote it?

4. What question did the Council of Chalcedon resolve?

5. Write in chronological order all the events studied to date. Next to each write the date that corresponds to it.

Justinian the Great
Worksheet

1. What are the dates for the rule of Justinian the Great?

2. When did Justinian conquer to regain most of the Empire that had recently been lost?

3. Where did Justinian build a church? What was its name? What does this name mean?

4. What architectural style was the church Justinian built?

5. With what were Eastern churches usually decorated?

6. What did Justinian try to eliminate?

   How did he go about doing this?

Justinian the Great
Project

Reading and Discussion

In 476, one year before the death of Genseric the Vandal, a Goth named Odoacer became ruler of Italy. He had taken the throne from the handsome boy who had been ruling as Emperor, permitting him to escape and allowing him 6000 gold pieces a year. The Roman Senate, which had once been a courageous and patriotic body of men, decided that there was no longer any Western Empire, and that its rule belonged to the Emperor in the East, whose capital was Constantinople. The Emperor accepted this view, and left Odoacer in Italy to represent him. This event is called the fall of the Western Empire.

In this same year, 476, Theodoric became king of the Ostrogoths, or Goths of the East. The Emperor in the East had hired the Ostrogoths to defend the lower Danube, and Theodoric, a little boy of the royal family, had been sent to Constantinople as a hostage, or pledge, that his people would keep their promises. When Theodoric grew up and became king, the Emperor permitted him to go and drive Odoacer out of Italy. Theodoric started with his army, and with all the rest of his tribe, for they meant not only to drive out Odoacer, but to make their homes in Italy.

There were three fierce battles. Finally, it was agreed that Odoacer and Theodoric should rule with equal powers. Before long, however, Theodoric treacherously murdered Odoacer and became sole ruler of Italy. He meant to rule like the Romans, but more wisely. He chose from the old Roman laws those which he thought just. He broke up the vast estates of the very wealthy and made many small farms, so that much more grain was raised. He built many handsome buildings, and he encouraged his subjects to read and study. The emperors in the East were doing their best to keep back the hordes of Huns and other barbarians, and it really began to seem as if Italy would grow into a powerful, well-governed country with the Goths for its rulers.

That might have come to pass, if a brilliant man named Justinian had not become ruler in the Eastern Empire after the death of Theodoric. His great wish was to bring Italy and Africa into the Empire. Fortunately for him, he had an officer named Belisarius, who was not only a skillful general, but who had the power of making his soldiers eager to follow him. Under his lead, Italy and Africa were regained, the Vandals in Africa were scattered, and the Goths in Italy were hopelessly beaten. Justinian brought together all that was known of the Roman law. It is upon his collection that the governments of the chief countries of Europe are founded. This was necessary, as up until then there had been many rulers and many different rules. The people were confused and Justinian helped to straighten the law out for the people. While he lived, there seemed some hope that the Empire would be mighty again, but as soon as he died, it was the same weak, tottering realm that it had been just before his day.

1. What was the relationship of the barbarians to Justinian? (Help your students to see the chronological relationship of the two.)
2. Discuss the importance of Justinian bringing together all of the known Roman law. Talk about how confusing and chaotic things are when there are not absolutes.

Justinian the Great
Project 2

After Constantine became a Christian, the Christians in Rome came out of the catacombs and built basilicas for churches. Basilicas were long buildings with rows of columns on the inside to hold up the roof. There was a center aisle and an aisle on either side of the center aisle. There was a half circle at the front of the building for an alter and the place for the priest to preach. Originally the Romans used this building style for courthouses or public halls.

The eastern Christians also desired to build churches, but built them in a different way. The kind of buildings they built were called Byzantine. A Byzantine church always had a dome in it. The church also was built in the shape of a Greek Cross, "+". Many times the dome was in the center of the cross. Many of the domes were small until Justinian came to rule. He had his architects build the largest and most beautiful church ever. The name of the church was *Hagia Sophia.* High upon the walls of *Hagia Sophia* were mosaic pictures built with colored pieces of glass and marble set in gold. If one compares Byzantine mosaics with ancient mosaics, one can see the creative power of the peoples' faith. The works of art are of the highest order and they achieved artistic standards as never before.

JUSTINIAN THE GREAT

Project 2, Page 2

Tile Trivets

You may want to try to make a mosaic yourself. Here's how:

Supplies

Pieces of tile (Try a local tile store. They are usually quite willing to give you a box of left over tile.)
Grout
Wood pieces (on which to place the tile)
Tile cutter (small pieces of tile can be broken into interesting shapes. ***Use eye protection*** and a cloth over the tile while shattering with a hammer).

Instructions

Have the students draw a design for their trivet. Keep it simple. Crosses and geometric designs work well. Draw this onto the wood. Have an adult cut the tiles into small pieces.

Have the students choose tiles pieces to "color" in their design.

Glue the tile onto the wood. After this has dried use grout to fill in between the tiles. Wipe tiles clean of excess grout.

Allow to dry.

Should you decide that the above project is too detailed you may also make a mosaic by cutting out 1/4" inch squares of different colored construction paper and glue those to a piece of cardboard.

Justinian the Great
Test

1. What are the dates for the rule of Justinian the Great?

2. When did Justinian conquer to regain most of the Empire that had recently been lost?

3. Who built the *Hagia Sophia*? What does this name mean?

4. What architectural style was the church Justinian built?

5. With what were Eastern churches usually decorated?

6. How did Justinian try to eliminate paganism?

Review

1. In what year did Augustine convert to Christianity?

Justinian the Great
Test, Page 2

2. What official role did Augustine have in the church?

____

____

3. Name two books written by Augustine.

____

____

4. Name two barbarian tribes.

____

____

5. Why did the Vikings ravage the coasts of Europe and America?

____

____

____

Mohammed and Islam

Worksheet

1. What did Mohammed found (begin)?

2. When and where was Mohammed born?

3. What was Mohammed's education?

4. Who was Khadjiah?

5. Describe the vision that Mohammed claimed to have.

6. What does *Islam* mean?

7. Who was Mohammed's first convert to Islam?

Mohammed and Islam
Worksheet, Page 2

8. Why did Mohammed flee to Medina in 622?

____

____

9. Of what does Mohammed's flight to Medina mark the beginning?

____

____

____

10. Muslims confess that there is one __________ and ____________________ is his prophet.

11. List the five things that followers of Islam must do.

a. ____

b. ____

c. ____

d. ____

e. ____

12. What is the Koran?

____

____

____

13. How did Islam spread throughout the world?

____

____

____

____

MOHAMMED AND ISLAM
Project

Reading and Discussion

This story is about a man named Mohammed. He was born in Mecca in Arabia, and he became so famous when he was a man that the people who knew him as a child fancied that many wonderful things had happened to him when he was small. It was said that the sheep bowed to him as he passed by, and that even the moon stooped from her place in the heavens to do him honor. While he was in the house of his nurse, so the legend says, her well never dried and her pastures were always fresh and green.

The little boy soon lost both father and mother, and was brought up in the house of his uncle. He must have been a most lovable boy, for every one seems to have been kind to him. This uncle held an office of great honor, he was guardian of a certain black stone which, it was said, the angel Gabriel had given to Abraham. The stone was built into the outer wall of the Kaaba, a little square temple which the Arabians looked upon as especially holy. Most of them were worshipers of idols, and the Kaaba was the home of enough idols to provide a different one for every day in the year. Throngs of pilgrims journeyed to Mecca to kiss the stone and worship in the Kaaba; and the boy must have heard marvelous tales of the strange places from which they came. His uncle was a merchant and used to go with caravans to Syria and elsewhere to get goods. When Mohammed was twelve years old, he begged earnestly to be allowed to go with him. The uncle said "No." Then the boy pleaded, "But, my uncle, who will take care of me when you are gone?" The tender-hearted man could not refuse any longer, and Mohammed went on his first journey.

After this, he always traveled with his uncle, and when the uncle went out to help his tribe fight another tribe, Mohammed became the uncle's armor-bearer. He learned about life in a caravan, and about buying and selling goods, and while he was hardly more than a boy, he was often employed by merchants to go on such trips as their agent. At length he was engaged by a wealthy widow named Kadijah to manage the large business which the death of her husband had left in her charge. She became more and more pleased with the young man, and after a while she sent a trusty slave to offer him her hand. He was surprised, but not at all unwilling, and soon there was a generous wedding feast with music and dancing. The house was open to all who chose to come, and a camel was killed that its flesh might be given to the poor.

Mohammed thought much about religious questions. He came to believe that his people were wrong in worshipping idols, and that there was only one true god. He used to go to a cavern a few miles from Mecca to pray and meditate. One month in every year he gave up entirely to this. After a while, he began to have strange dreams and visions. In one of these he thought the angel Gabriel held before him a silken cloth on which there was golden writing, and bade him read it. "But I do not know how to read," replied Mohammed. "Read, in the name of the Most High," said the angel; and suddenly the power to read the letters came to him, and he found the writings were commands of god. Then the angel declared, "Thou art the prophet of god." Mohammed told Kadijah of his vision, and she believed that the angel had really come to him. After a little, he began to preach wherever people would listen. A few believed in him, but most people only laughed at his story.

Mohammed and Islam

Project, Page 2

Still he kept on preaching, and after a while, although he had but few followers in Mecca, there were many in Medina who had come to believe that he was the prophet of god. He decided that it was best for him to go to them, and in the year 622 he and a few friends escaped from their enemies in Mecca and went to Medina. This is called the Hegira, or flight. To this day Mohammedans do not count the years from the birth of Christ, but from the Hegira.

As soon as the prophet was in Medina, his followers began to build a mosque, or place for prayer, in which he might preach. They made the walls of earth and brick. The pillars were the trunks of palm trees, and the roof was formed of their branches with a thatch of leaves. He decided that his disciples should be called to prayer five times a day, and after all these centuries the call, or muezzin, is still heard in the East from some minaret of each mosque, —"God is great. There is no god but god. Mohammed is the apostle of god. Come to prayers. Come to prayers." At dawn the crier adds, "Prayer is better than sleep." Every true Mussulman, as followers of Mohammed are called, is bound to obey this rule of prayer, and as he prays, he must turn his face toward Mecca. He is also commanded to make at least one pilgrimage to Mecca before he dies, and to kiss the sacred black stone. It is still in the wall of the Kaaba, but the Kaaba itself is now within a mosque so large that it will hold 35,000 persons.

It is probable that Mohammed never learned to read or write, but his followers jotted down his words on bits of palm leaves or skins or even the shoulder-blades of animals, and many of them they learned by heart. After the death of the prophet, the califs, as his successors were called, collected these sayings and arranged them in a book called the Koran, which is the sacred volume of the Mussulmans.

For a long while, Mohammed preached peace and gentleness and charity, and he won many followers. Then he came to believe that if people would not obey his teachings, it was right to makewar upon them. He marched against Mecca with a large army of his disciples, and soon captured it. After a time, either by preaching or by fighting, the Mohammedans, or Mussulmans, became the rulers of all Arabia. After the death of their prophet, they continued their conquests. They overcame Syria, Persia, Egypt, northern Africa, and Spain. A little later they swarmed over the Pyrenees Mountains, and pushed on as far north as Tours. In 732, just one hundred years after the death of Mohammed, the Mohammedans and the Franks met in battle on the plain of Tours, and after a terrible combat the Mohammedans were so completely overwhelmed that they retreated toward Spain and never again tried to conquer the land of the Franks.

After each student has read the above, discuss the life of Mohammed. Several suggested discussion questions follow:

1. Why was *god* not capitalized in the above reading?
2. How do we know that Mohammed's vision was not true?
3. Are there practitioners of Islam today? If so, where can they be found?

Mohammed and Islam
Project 2

Comparison of Religions

Look up the verses in the table and contrast the requirements of Islam with the blessings of Christianity. You may wish to teach the students to use a concordance so they can research the Word of God.

Islam	Christianity
Pray five times a day, facing Mecca	Ephesians 6:18, 1 Thessalonians 5:17, Hebrews 4:16
Give required alms	Matthew 23:23, Luke 11:39-41
Fast from dawn to dusk for one month each year	Matthew 6:16-17, Psalm 35:13
Travel to Mecca on a pilgrimage once in a lifetime	John 4:19-24

Middle Ages, Reformation and Renaissance

Project 3

The Rise of Islam and the Birth of Europe

I

Even though most of Europe remained in Christian hands, the rise of Islam was one of the most important events in the history of Europe. Before the Muslim invasions, the most important division in the Mediterranean world was between the Latin-speaking west and the Greek-speaking east. Afterwards, the most important division was between Christian Europe and the Muslim empire. Before-hand, Europe was just a vague, geographic expression. Afterwards, it was a whole new civilization. It was "Christendom", the world of Christianity. Before-hand, close cultural and commercial relations between all of the lands of the Mediterranean sea was normal. Afterwards, the hostility between the Islamic and Christian worlds caused this interconnected world to be divided up between two warring camps.

II

Or perhaps, it was between three worlds; the rivalry between the Latin west and the Greek east didn't end. Of these three regions that now divided the old Roman World, Latin Christendom was perhaps the poorest. Aside from Italy itself and a few cities in Southern France, almost all of the great old cities and trade centers of the Roman Empire were now a part of the Islamic or Byzantine (Eastern Roman) empires. Even most of Spain fell into Muslim hands and even after the Muslims were stopped by the Franks at Tours, the West was subjected to more invasions by the Vikings from the North and the Magyars from the East. Now that they no longer had the wealth of the Mediterranean on which to draw strength, they had to fall back on their own resources.

III

The time from the end of the Muslim invasions until the end of the Viking invasions (c. 700-1000 AD) was a very trying time for Western Europe, but in spite of it all, Western civilization actually grew and flourished during this period. One of the most important reasons for this was an improvement in, of all things, agriculture. The Roman style of agriculture only worked very well in the warm and wet Mediterranean climate. During this period, however, better plows and horse harnesses allowed the northern Europeans to successfully farm areas that the Romans hadn't been able to farm very well. Since, back then, agriculture was the foundation of all civilizations, this made a world of difference. In fact, by the end of the Middle Ages, Northern Europe was wealthier and produced more crops than Mediterranean Europe. Another important technological change was in ship-building. The types of ships that the Phoenicians, Greeks and Roman had used in the Mediterranean didn't always work very well in the rough Atlantic Ocean. Improving on the ship-building and sea-faring skills of the Vikings, northern Europeans eventually built impressive new trading cities on the Atlantic Ocean. Thrown back on their own resources, Latin Christendom eventually built a whole new civilization on a whole new economic basis.

Vocabulary

1. *vague:* ______________________________

____

2. *geographic:* ______________________________

____

3. *civilization:* ______________________________

____

4. *cultural:* ______________________________

____

5. *commercial:* ______________________________

____

6. *hostility:* ______________________________

____

7. *interconnected:* ______________________________

____

8. *agriculture:* ______________________________

____

9. *technological:* ______________________________

____

Key Word Outline:

I ____________________

1. ____________________
2. ____________________
3. ____________________
4. ____________________
5. ____________________
6. ____________________
7. ____________________

II ____________________

1. ____________________
2. ____________________
3. ____________________
4. ____________________
5. ____________________

III ____________________

1. ____________________
2. ____________________
3. ____________________
4. ____________________
5. ____________________
6. ____________________
7. ____________________

8. ______________________________

9. ______________________________

10. ______________________________

11. ______________________________

Middle Ages, Reformation and Renaissance

Project 3, Page 5

Answers

Vocabulary

1. *vague:* poorly defined
2. *geographic:* having to do with the mapping of the earth
3. *civilization:* a place characterized by a common lifestyle and way of seeing the world
4. *cultural:* having to do with the ideas, practices and beliefs that tie a civilization together
5. *commercial:* relating to money or trade
6. *hostility:* intense rivalry and/or dislike
7. *interconnected:* tied together
8. *agriculture:* the art of growing crops and herding animals
9. *technological:* relating to material know-how

Key Word Outline:

I Christendom, Before and After Islam
1. Rise, Islam, important
2. Before, division, Latin-Greek
3. After, division, Christian-Muslim
4. Before, geographic, expression
5. After, new, civilization
6. Before, close, relations
7. After, hostility, divided

II Christendom's Predicament
1. Perhaps, three, worlds
2. Latin, poorest
3. Cities, now, Islamic/Byzantine
4. After, Vikings, Magyars
5. Fall back, own, resources

III Christendom Rises to the Challenge
1. Trying, time, 700-100
2. Reasons, flourished ?
3. One, agriculture
4. Roman, Mediterranean, climate
5. Plows, harness, farm
6. Agriculture, foundation, difference
7. End, wealthier, crops
8. Another, ship-building
9. Type, didn't, rough
10. Improving, on, skills
11. Built, new, civilization

MOHAMMED AND ISLAM
Test

1. Write a summary about Mohammed. Include where he was born, in what year, what he did for a living, and describe his education.

2. Who did Mohammed marry? How did he meet her?

3. Write a summary about Mohammed's vision. What did this vision cause?

4. Define Islam.

Mohammed and Islam

Test, Page 2

5. Who do Muslims believe is god's prophet?

6. What are the five things to which a Muslim must adhere?

7. How did Islam spread throughout the world?

Review

1. Who was Augustine's mother? What impact did she have upon him?

2. What was the name of the historic period when the barbarians and Vikings lived?

3. Why was the New Testament originally written in Greek?

4. Who was St. Benedict?

5. Write in chronological order all the events listed to date.

CHARLES MARTEL, PEPIN THE SHORT, AND CHARLEMAGNE

Worksheet

1. Who was Charles Martel?

____

____

2. Who was Martel's son? How did he become king? Why was this significant?

____

____

____

3. What was Charlemagne's relationship to Martel?

____

____

4. In ________ Charlemagne was made ____________________ by the Pope.

5. What three things did Charlemagne wish to establish in his empire?

____

____

____

6. Of what did Charlemagne's empire consist?

____

____

7. What was Charlemagne's favorite book?

____

____

____

____

Charles Martel, Pepin the Short, and Charlemagne

Project

Reading and Discussion

The Christmas Crowning of Charlemagne

About twelve hundred years ago, thousands of Saracens, who were among the followers of Mohammed, crossed the narrow strait from Africa into Spain. The world was then coming out of those centuries of ignorance and fear which are known as the Dark Ages. The dark-skinned people—Arabs and Africans—who followed Mohammed, went about converting people by making them prostrate themselves with their faces turned toward the East and repeat the Mohammedan creed. Those who refused to bow down and repeat this creed were killed. Ofcourse everyone was very much afraid of missionaries who used such methods as these, and large parts of Asia and Africa had come under Mohammedan control. When they reached the shores of Spain, they thought they were going to convert and conquer Europe, too.

The Saracens marched north through Spain and into the country of the Franks, whose great-great-great-grandchildren are the French people of to-day. Here the victory of the invaders ceased to be so easy, for they were met by a certain Duke Charles, who beat them in a great battle near Tours and drove them back. For his bravery in saving Europe from these dark-skinned enemies, Duke Charles was named Martel, the Franks' word for "hammer."

Charles the Hammer had a son, Pepin, who was called the Short, because he was not a tall man. But though he was small, Pepin had a big, brave heart. He fought for his country against the Lombards, a savage people in North Italy, and he was rewarded for his valor and success by being made king of the Franks.

When Pepin was crowned by the Pope, he had a son Charles, twelve years old. This Charles was so ambitious that, even while a boy, he began to dream of conquering other nations, and becoming king not only of France but of other lands as well. All through his boyhood he dreamed of what he would do if he were king. It was not many years after his father's death, when he became king in fact, before Charles Martel's grandson had conquered so many nations in the south and so many savage tribes in the north of Europe that he became a king of kings, or emperor, and received the title of Charle"*magne,*" which means Charles the Great.

Perhaps the best thing that Charlemagne ever did was to keep Alcuin, a scholar from Britain, at his court as a trusted friend and teacher. In those days such men in other kings'

Charles Martel, Pepin the Short, and Charlemagne

Project, Page 2

palaces were merely chaplains or religious teachers, but Alcuin taught the king, the queen, and the princes grammar, spelling, arithmetic, and other common branches. This Palace School proved to be such a good thing that the emperor ordered that not only any child of a nobleman, but even of the poorest peasant, could come to it if the boy showed talent for learning. The books in the Palace School were printed very slowly with a pen, sometimes in bright inks and gold. As there were no public libraries in those days, Alcuin searched the world for books for his pupils. These parchments were rare and very costly. Instead of Charles's children going to school, the Palace School went with the children, as the emperor moved from place to place and from palace to palace.

Charlemagne's armies were led by brave knights called *paladins.* The foremost of these paladins were Roland and Oliver, who fought in combats and tournaments. They were both of heroic size, eight feet tall, and performed the same feats, so that one could not be distinguished from the other. A story is told of these two having fought five days on an island in the River Rhine without either of them gaining the least advantage over the other; so now, when two men are equal in some great struggle, people exclaim—"A Roland for an Oliver!" Roland, also called Orlando, was the chief hero, and Oliver seems to have been his reflection or shadow. Roland was a nephew of Charlemagne. He is described in the "Song of Roland" as having a wonderful horse, a miraculous saber, and a magic horn, which he blew so that it could be heard thirty miles. The greatest story told of him is that he commanded the rear guard of Charlemagne's army as they were returning from Spain through a pass in the Pyrenees Mountains. Set upon by 100,000 Saracens, Roland blew his magic horn so that his uncle the emperor heard it eight miles away.

In the advancing guard with Charlemagne, however, lurked an evil genius, who told the anxious emperor that Roland's horn was not a signal of distress, but that his nephew was hunting stags in the mountains. Roland fought until the 100,000 Saracens were slain, and he had only fifty of his 20,000 soldiers left. Then 50,000 more Saracens came out of the mountains and killed the brave paladin and his fifty men. While Roland was dying of his wounds, this legend goes on, he threw his magic sword into a poisoned stream. Another version of the story is that Roland died of starvation while trying to find his way, wounded and alone, through the mountains to catch up with the army.

Charlemagne and his valiant paladins rode and fought in all parts of Europe, beating the savage Germans beyond the Rhine, and conquering tribes and peoples all over Europe almost as far as Constantinople, the great capital of the Eastern Empire. At last the dream

Charles Martel, Pepin the Short, and Charlemagne

Project, Page 3

of the twelve year-old lad at his father's crowning came true, when Charlemagne himself was crowned at Rome, the city of the Caesars, as Emperor of the Western World, on Christmas Day, in the year of our Lord 800.

It is written that the crowning of Charlemagne was prepared as a surprise to him by the Pope and his people in Rome. While Charles and his sons were kneeling before a shrine very early on that Christmas morning, Pope Leo appeared in the great church with a crown of gold set with many precious gems, and placed it on the head of the kneeling king, thus proclaiming him Emperor of the Western World. In an instant the Pope, the cardinals, the priests, and the people rose from their knees and chanted these words:

"To Charles the Augustus, crowned of God, the great and pacific emperor, long life and victory!"

Charlemagne was a wise and good emperor who did many things to help his people. He built a lighthouse at Boulogne to guide ships to port, encouraged farming and made wise laws. He was kind to scholars and his favorite recreation was talking to them. He spoke several languages very well and wrote a great deal. Among his writings were a grammar book, poems in Latin and many letters.

Discussion

After reading the above discuss the following questions as a class:

1. Who did Charles Martel defeat at the Battle of Tours?

2. How did Pepin the Short become the king of the Franks?

3. What was unusual about peasant children being allowed to attend the palace school?

4. Have the children retell the story of Roland.

5. Why was Charles called Charlemagne? What does Charlemagne mean?

6. Describe Charles' coronation.

7. List some of Charlemagne's accomplishments.

CHARLES MARTEL, PEPIN THE SHORT, AND CHARLEMAGNE

Project 2

Map

The map below is a picture of the extent of Charlemagne's empire at his death. During his reign he conquered so much territory that his kingdom was twice as large as it was when he received it from Pepin his father. Charlemagne's victories united much of Europe, bringing an end to the fighing among these warring tribes.

Locate the territories he took from the Lombards. Color each on the map with a colored pencil. Using a modern day map determine what present countries these lands are now.

When Charlegmagne conquered the Saxons, they were still worshiping the pagan gods of the barbarians such as Woden and Thor. Charlemagne and his people, the Franks, were a Christian nation who forced those he conquered to become Christians. Those who refused were put to death. Discuss the effectiveness of this type of evangelism.

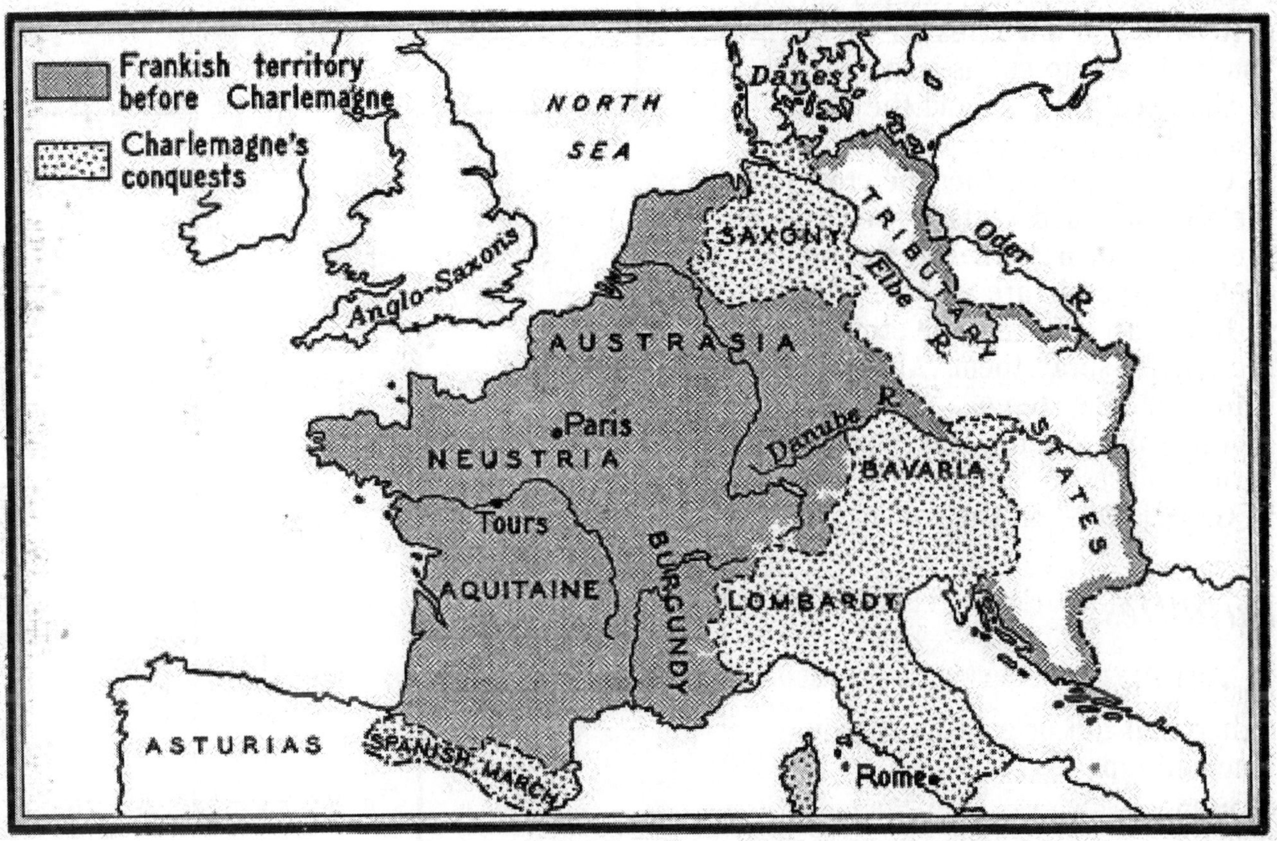

Charles Martel, Pepin the Short, and Charlemagne

Project 3

Making Charlemagne's Crown

Directions

Before starting, decide if you want to use gold foil for your crowns, or gold paint. If you decide you would like to use foil, glue it onto the poster board prior to step number one. If you are using gold spray paint, the crowns may be painted after they are assembled.

1. Using the patterns provided cut one pattern A, and one cross for each crown. You will need to cut as many pattern B's as you need to fit around the child's head.
2. Glue or tape together the crown using the tabs provided. Attach the cross in the middle of pattern A at the top. (Refer to the picture.)
3. If you are painting the crowns, this is the time to spray them. Allow to dry before starting step 4.
4. Using black paint, dab the crown in various places to "antique" the crown.
5. Glue "jewels" on the crown.

Supplies

poster board
either gold foil or gold spray pain
glue and tape
scissors
pencil
plastic jewels (these can be found at any craft store)
black paint (to antique)
sponge or towels (to dab on paint)

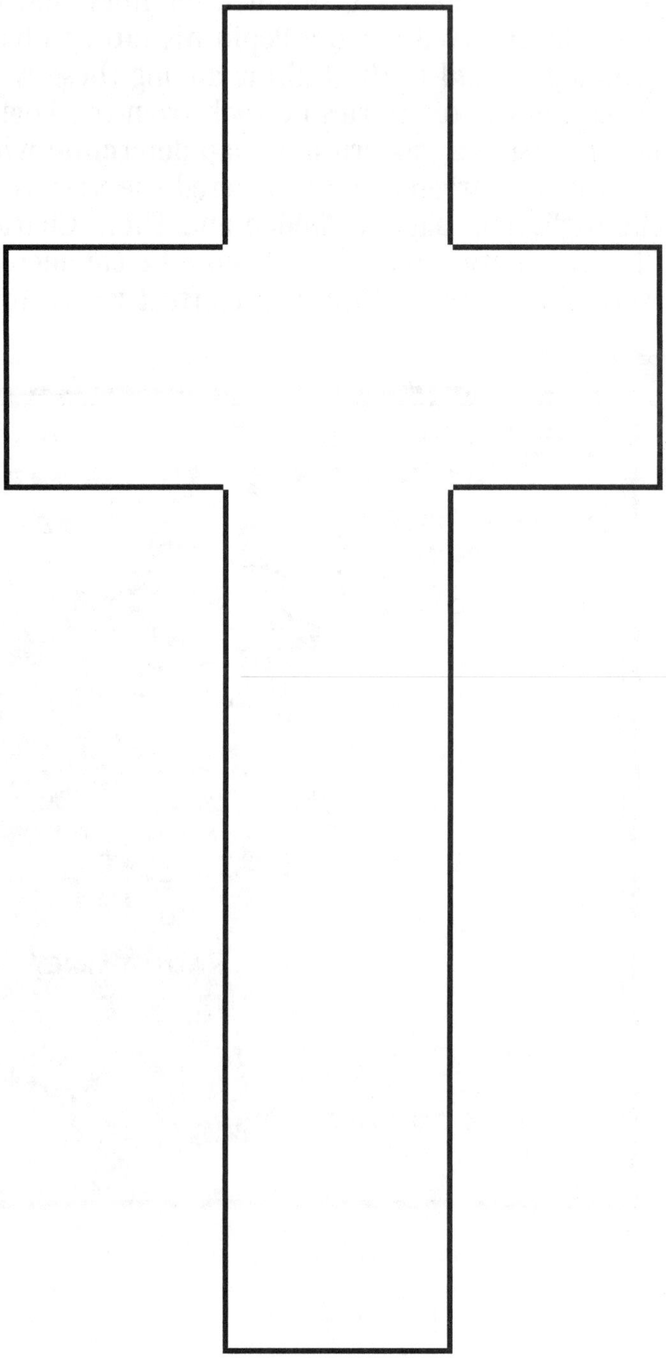

Charles Martel, Pepin the Short, and Charlemagne

Project 3, Page 2

Pattern A

Charles Martel, Pepin the Short, and Charlemagne

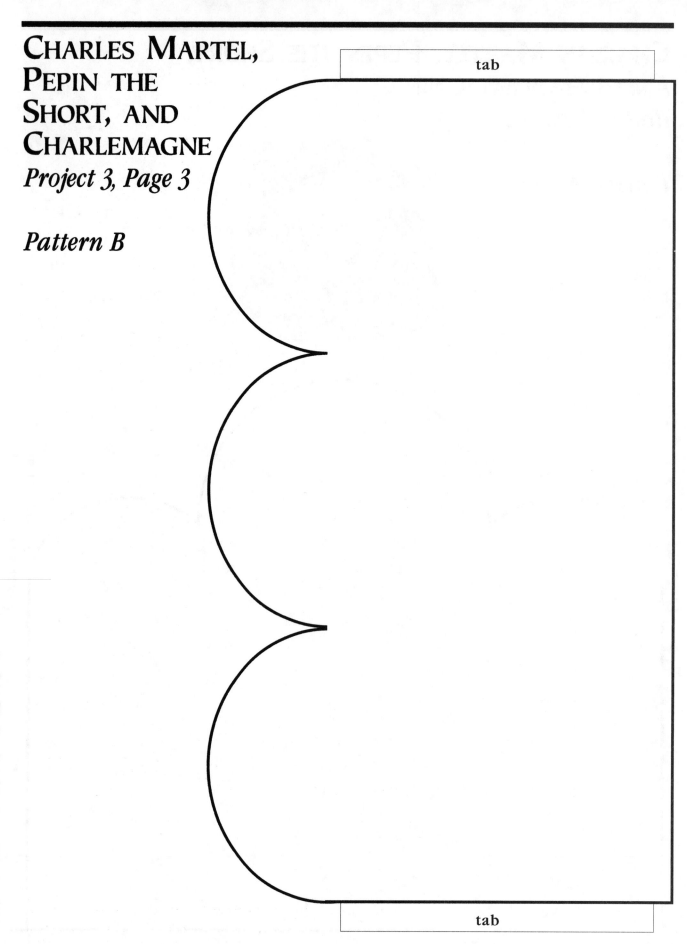

Project 3, Page 3

Pattern B

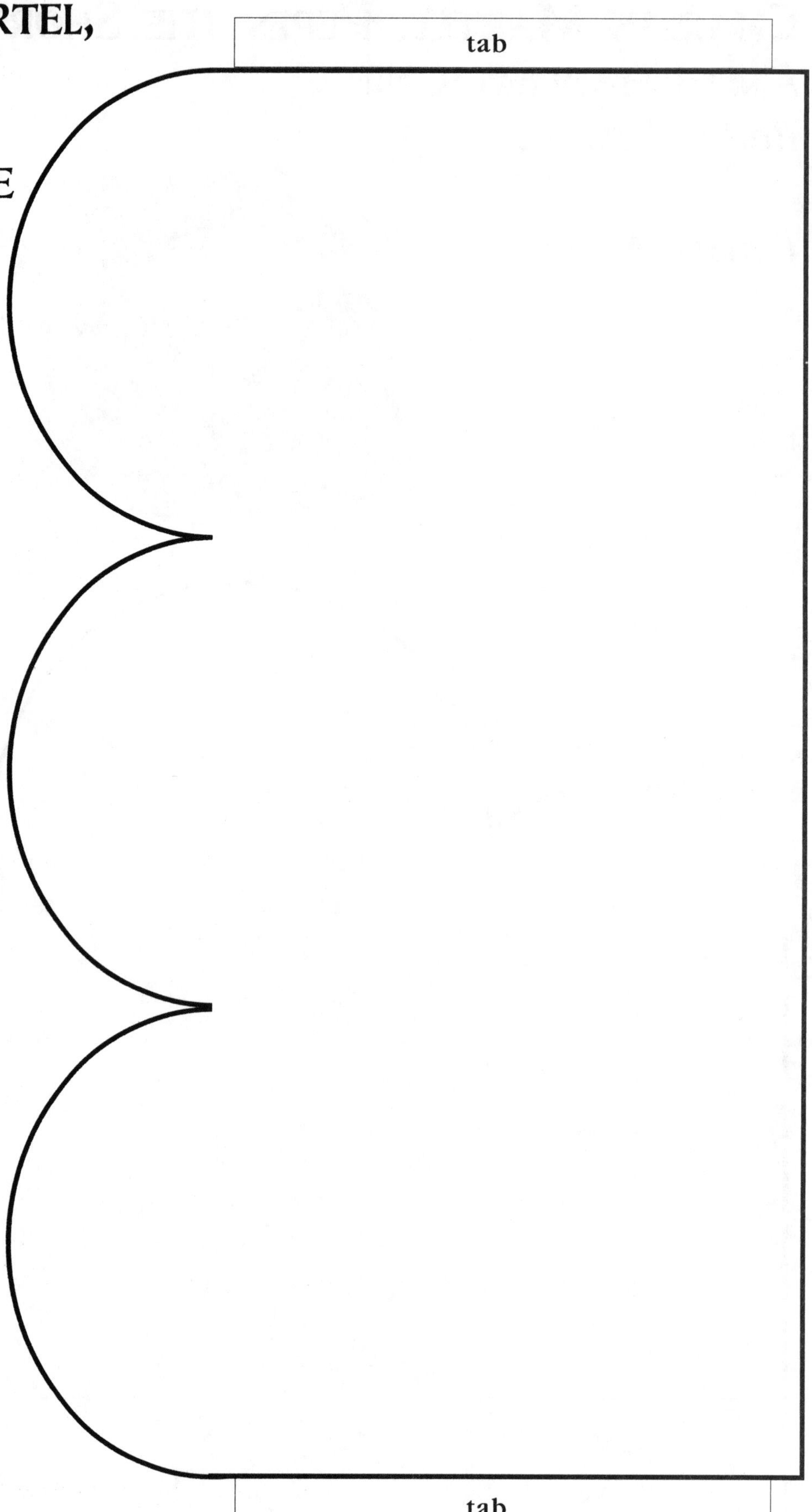

Charles Martel, Pepin the Short, and Charlemagne

Test

1. What are the dates of Charles Martel, Pepin the Short, and Charlemagne?

2. Who was the practical leader of the Franks?

3. How did Pepin the Short become king? What is significant about this?

4. Who came to rule after Pepin? What office did the Pope bestow on this person?

5. What three things did the ruler in question number 4 want to establish?

6. What countries did Charlemagne's empire include?

Charles Martel, Pepin the Short, and Charlemagne
Test, Page 2

Review

1. Who baptized Augustine? When?

2. Describe what the barbarians were like.

3. What four points did the Council of Chalcedon affirm?

   a.

   b.

   c.

   d.

4. How was most of the literature of the ancient world preserved?

5. On the back of this paper list the events studied to date in chronological order.

Alfred the Great

Worksheet

1. Over what kingdom did Alfred the Great rule?

2. Who tried to take over Alfred's kingdom in 865? What was the outcome?

3. What city did Alfred capture in 886?

4. What happened to Tryggvesson, King of Norway, as he led the Viking raids in England? What did this event in his life cause to happen in the lives of others?

5. The Danes almost destroyed _______________ and _______________ in England.

6. What two things did Alfred the Great do that helped reestablish the kingdom of England?

ALFRED THE GREAT
Project

Reading, Discussion and Web

ALFRED, THE GREATEST OF THE SAXON KINGS

Over one thousand years ago, the king of the West Saxons on the island of Britain, now England, had four sons. Alfred, the youngest of these, was his father's favorite. When this boy was only five, his royal father sent him to Rome to be confirmed by the Pope. After Alfred came back his queen-mother died, and the father made a pilgrimage, or religious journey, to Rome, taking young Prince Alfred, with many court gentlemen, soldiers, and servants.

On their way the king and his train were given a royal welcome by the king of France. Alfred's father fell in love with the beautiful young daughter of the French King, and asked her hand in marriage. Her father consented, so the royal wedding took place on the Saxon king's return from Rome.

Alfred's new mother soon became very fond of him. Young as he was, he had learned to play the harp. But when he was twelve years old, Alfred had not been taught to read. Saxon kings and princes thought most kinds of learning were for priests and lawyers. When gentlemen made contracts or signed law papers, they did not write their names, but "set their signs and seals thereunto," as is done today in legal documents. All the books were written on parchment in Latin.

One day Alfred saw his French stepmother reading a roll of parchment on which Latin words were printed by hand in many colors. As the lad admired it, the queen told him she would make him a present of the scroll as soon as he learned to read and understand it. He went right out and coaxed a monk (or priest) to teach him Latin, and he soon became the happy owner of the beautiful parchment.

Learning to read opened a new world to Prince Alfred. He wrote verses and songs for his harp, and began to compose both words and music of hymns to be sung in the cathedral near his father's palace.

When Alfred was fourteen his father died. Each of his brothers became king, one after another, and died within a few years.

Alfred was twenty-two when the last brother died and left him to be king. Some rough people, called the Danes, from the north countries across the sea, had landed on the island of Britain, and the Saxons were compelled to give battle to them so as not to be killed or made slaves to those rough Northmen. So Alfred had to fight to keep on being king. When he began to reign, he ruled like all the other kings he had known. His father and brothers had treated the people as if they were made only to work and pay their way, like cattle, so Alfred did the same at first.

The fierce Danes kept coming over in larger numbers. In a hard-fought battle, Alfred was defeated and most of the army was slain. Fleeing for his life, the young king found a hiding place in the hut of a swineherd, a man who tends hogs. This man knew who Alfred was, but kept the king's secret from his wife, who thought the stranger was a poor soldier from the Saxon army

Many stories are told of what the king did while he lived in the hut of this swineherd.

ALFRED THE GREAT
Project, Page 2

These tales have changed so much, all the hundreds of years which have passed since Alfred's time, that they are called legends. The best known of these is the story of the king and the cakes. Once when the housewife was going out to do some work, she asked him, while he was fixing his bow and arrows, to mind the cakes she had left baking in the ashes of the fireplace. The distracted king's mind was on higher things than coarse meal cakes. When the woman came in she found them burning. She was so angry that she called Alfred a good-for-nothing beggar, and added that if he could not pay for what she gave him to eat, he ought at least to look after her cakes a little while.

Alfred had the good sense to see his own conduct through the poor woman's eyes. So, instead of being angry or telling her who he was, he said gently, "I am sorry I was so careless. I will try not to forget again."

"A soft answer turneth away wrath," Alfred had read in the roll of Proverbs in his Latin Bible. It may have been during the long months he spent in the home of this shepherd that the humbled king decided to translate the best parts of the Bible into the Saxon language so that the people could read it.

Another story is that Alfred stayed in the hut alone while the family were away fishing. He had only a loaf of bread to last until their return. A beggar came and asked for bread. Alfred broke his little loaf in two, gave the man half, and ate his half with the beggar. The swineherd returned that day with fish enough for a family feast. In the night the beggar of the day before appeared, as an angel, to the captive king, and said that God had seen how Alfred had humbled his heart so that he was now fitted to rule his people wisely and well.

The Danish army was now encamped not far from the king's hiding place. Encouraged by the vision of the shining pilgrim, Alfred started out to see for himself how strong the enemy was and what they were going to do. So he disguised himself as a wandering musician, playing a harp. He played and sang for the Danish soldiers, and was soon taken before their fierce leader, like David, with his harp, before King Saul. The Danes were so pleased with him and his music that they asked him to stay with them. As soon as he had found out all he wanted to know, he took up his harp and left the camp of the enemy. The Danes invited him to come again.

Hurrying back to the swineherd's hut, Alfred sent word to the leaders among his people that he was alive and ready to go on with the war against the Danes. The people believed their brave young king was dead.

The Saxon chiefs came at once and knelt to King Alfred. When the poor woman realized who her guest was, she fell on her knees and begged him to forgive all she had said to him. Alfred lifted her tenderly from the ground, and told her he would reward her and her loyal husband when he was safe on the throne again.

The Danish army was astonished, early one morning, to hear three trumpet blasts, and to see a great army of Saxon soldiers marching to meet them, led by that wandering minstrel! Of course, the Saxons gained the victory and made the Danes promise not to come and attack them again. They agreed, but did not keep their word long. After that, instead of waiting for the Danes to land in Britain, King Alfred fitted up a fleet of ships so that he

Alfred the Great
Project, Page 3

could go out and fight them on the sea. This has been called "the beginning of the British navy."

Then Alfred improved the years of peace by making laws which allowed the people more rights and privileges. He invented a simple clock of candles, by which the people could tell the time of day. He rebuilt the towns that had been destroyed in the war and trained his people not only to fight but to till their farms. He made wise laws and did much to educate his subjects by having books translated from Latin into Anglo-Saxon, the language of the Saxons. Best of all, he translated the Bible into the language of the people. Because of all the acts which taught the people how to make their lives better and happier he is known as Alfred the Great. In one of his histories, King Alfred wrote what he tried to do in his own life: "My will was to live worthily as long as I lived and, after my life, to leave to them that should come after, my memory in good works."

After reading *Alfred, The Greatest of the Saxon Kings*, discuss as a class the difference between a legend and truth. Then on the next page draw a picture of five important events or contributions Alfred the Great made to society during his life.

ALFRED THE GREAT
Project, Page 4

Alfred the Great
Test

1. Where was Alfred the Great king?

2. Who were the Danes? What did they have to do with Alfred the Great?

3. In 886 what did Alfred unify? How did he accomplish this?

4. Who was Tryggvesson? What happened to him during the Viking raids?

5. What did the Danes nearly destroy in England?

6. How did Alfred the Great help to reestablish the kingdom of England after warring with the Danes?

ALFRED THE GREAT
Test, Page 2

Review

1. Name two books that St. Augustine wrote?

2. Describe the Vikings.

3. Why did St. Jerome find it necessary to translate the Bible into Latin?

4. Who do Muslim's believe is god's prophet?

5. Write in chronological order all events listed to date. Include dates.

OTTO I AND THE HOLY ROMAN EMPIRE
Worksheet

1. In what year did Otto I become King of Germany?

2. What did Pope John XII ask of Otto I?

3. Who controlled the Church at this time? How?

4. What were vassals?

5. What did many Dukes of Germany try to do to Otto I?

6. How did Otto I become King of Italy?

7. What happened to Otto I on February 2, 962?
   Why was this important?

OTTO I AND THE HOLY ROMAN EMPIRE
Worksheet, Page 2

8. What was the Treaty of Verdum?

____

____

____

____

9. From _______ until _______, when Napoleon rose to power the Holy Roman Empire remained distinctly ___________.

Ring Seal of
Otto the Great

Otto I and the Holy Roman Empire

Project

Mapping

Recently, we talked about Charlemagne's rule. After his death the empire of Charlemagne passed to his only legitimate son, a weak ruler who had difficulty enough in keeping it intact. After the latter's death the empire was divided among Charlemagne's three grandsons, though only one could hold the imperial title. Disputes which soon arose about the inheritance found a temporary settlement in a treaty concluded at Verdun (843). Lothair, the oldest brother, received North Italy and a narrow strip of land along the valleys of the Rhine and the Rhone, between the North Sea and the Mediterranean. Louis and Charles, the other brothers received kingdoms lying to the east and west, respectively, of Lothair's territory. These arrangements have historical importance, because they foreshadowed the future map of western Europe. The East Frankish kingdom of Louis, inhabited almost entirely by Germans, was to develop into modern Germany. The West Frankish kingdom of Charles, inhabited mainly by descendants of Romanized Gauls, was to become modern France. Lothair's kingdom, however, never became one national state. A part of it now belongs to the kingdom of Italy, and another part survives as Belgium, Holland, Luxembourg, and Switzerland.

The imperial idea was revived about one hundred and fifty years after Charlemagne's death, by an able German ruler, Otto I, often called Otto the Great. Otto led his armies across the Alps, went to Rome, and had the pope crown him as Roman emperor (962). Otto's dominions were considerably smaller than Charlemagne's, since they included only Germany and North Italy. Nevertheless, Otto and the emperors who followed him asserted vast claims to sovereignty in Europe, as the heirs of Charlemagne and, through him, of Constantine and Augustus. The new empire came subsequently to be styled the Holy Roman Empire, the word *Holy* in its title expressing its intimate connection with the Papacy. It lived on in some measure for more than eight hundred years and did not quite disappear from European politics until the opening of the nineteenth century.

The successors of Otto the Great constantly interfered in the affairs of Italy in order to secure the Italian crown and the imperial title. They treated that country as a conquered province which had no right to a national life and an independent government under its own rulers. At the same time, they neglected their German possessions and failed to keep their powerful territorial lords in subjection. Consequently, neither Italy nor Germany became a united state, such as was formed in England, France, Spain, and other countries during the later Middle Ages.

Instructions

Depending on the age and ability of the students, on the map on the following page have them either:

- Color the Western Roman Empire and the Roman Empire in the East
- Label and color the kingdoms of Lothair, Louis, and Charles
- Outline the empire of Otto I to demonstrate the land he reunited.

OTTO I AND THE HOLY ROMAN EMPIRE
Project, Page 2

Europe in the Age of Otto the Great—962 A.D.

Otto I and the Holy Roman Empire
Test

1. What were the dates for Otto I and the Holy Roman Empire?

2. In what year did Otto I become King of Germany?

3. During this time period who strongly influenced the decision of who would become Pope?

4. What did Otto I do to the German dukes who tried to act independently of him?

5. Who became King of Italy in 951? How did this occur?

6. What act caused the reuniting of the Empire in the West?

7. How long did the Holy Roman Empire stay distinctly German?

Otto I and the Holy Roman Empire

Test, Page 2

Review

1. What role/titles did Augustine hold in the church?

2. Who was St. Jerome? Where did he live?

3. What question did the Council of Chalcedon address?

4. List the three vows taken by Benedictine Monks.

5. List the events studied to date in chronological order.

The East-West Schism

Worksheet

1. What is the date of the East-West Schism?

____

____

2. What groups divided in the first major division in the Church? When did it occur?

____

____

3. What was the specific incident that purportedly caused the schism in 1054?

____

____

4. What were the two main issues of controversy in the Church that led to its split?

____

____

5. What were the Western Church's positions on the above issues?

____

____

6. What were the Eastern Church's positions on the above issues?

____

____

7. What two branches of the Christian church exist today as a result of this split?

____

____

____

____

THE EAST-WEST SCHISM
Project

Church Differences

Using information from the card and the resources mentioned on it, list the differences below between the Western and Eastern churches.

THE CHURCH UNITED

[the East-West Schism occurs in 1054]

EASTERN CHURCH (Eastern Orthodox)	WESTERN CHURCH (Roman Catholic)

The East-West Schism

Project 2

The Pope the Patriarch and the Schism

I

Though the Western Roman Empire fell in the 5th Century, the Eastern empire survived for another thousand years. It is often called the Byzantine Empire, because its capital had formerly been known as Byzantium. It guarded the straits of Bosporus, running between Greece and Asia Minor. Constantine had noticed its strategic location, rebuilt it and renamed it Constantinople. As soon as it became an important capital city, the emperor decided that it needed to have its own patriarch.

II

Now a patriarch is a sort of very important bishop, ranking above other bishops and exercising authority over them. In those days the hierarchy was bishop, then archbishop, then metropolitan bishop, then patriarch. At first there were only four patriarchs. They were the patriarch of Rome, who was also called the pope, Jerusalem, Antioch, the chief city of Syria, and Alexandria, the chief city of Egypt. Though the patriarch of Rome claimed to be above the others, the others didn't generally agree. The four original patriarchs didn't really like the idea of a fifth being created at the emperor's behest, but he was the emperor; he got his way.

III

Ironically, the Patriarch of Constantinople would eventually become the most important religious leader in the East after the fall of the western empire. There were various reasons for this. First, after the fall of the western empire, Constantinople was the only one that was still the capital of a great empire. Second, because of various controversies, heresies and schisms there were often more than one man claiming to be the "real" patriarch of Antioch or Alexandria. Finally, after the Islamic invasions, Alexandria, Jerusalem, and often Antioch, were in enemy territory, and so declined in importance in the church.

IV

While the Pope in Rome continued to claim to be the head of the whole church, the patriarch started to claim to be the "ecumenical patriarch", the "first among equals" of all the patriarchs. At the same time, the Latin-speaking western church and the Greek-speaking eastern church grew more and more different in their ceremonies, government and doctrine. Over 500 years there had actually been many controversies, disagreements and schisms between them, along with some reconciliations. The final break between the two halves of the church occurred, however, in 1054.

The East-West Schism

Project 2, Page 2

Vocabulary

1. *survived:* ______________________________
2. *strait:* ______________________________
3. *strategic:* ______________________________
4. *hierarchy:* ______________________________
5. *metropolitan:* ______________________________
6. *behest:* ______________________________
7. *controversies:* ______________________________
8. *heresies:* ______________________________
9. *schisms:* ______________________________
10. *ecumenical:* ______________________________

The East-West Schism
Project 2, Page 3

11. *ceremonies:* ____________________

12. *doctrine:* ____________________

13. *reconciliation:* ____________________

Key Word Outline

I ____________________

1 ____________________
2 ____________________
3 ____________________
4 ____________________

II ____________________

1 ____________________
2 ____________________
3 ____________________
4 ____________________
5 ____________________
6 ____________________

THE EAST-WEST SCHISM
Project 2, Page 4

III ______________________________

1 ______________________________

2 ______________________________

3 ______________________________

4 ______________________________

5 ______________________________

IV ______________________________

1 ______________________________

2 ______________________________

3 ______________________________

4 ______________________________

The East-West Schism

Project 2, Page 5

Answers

Vocabulary

1. *survived:* remained alive
2. *strait:* a passage connecting two large bodies of water
3. *strategic:* having great military or economic value
4. *hierarchy:* a structure of authority
5. *metropolitan:* having to do with a large city
6. *behest:* will or command
7. *controversies:* intense disagreements
8. *heresies:* beliefs inconsistent with orthodoxy
9. *schisms:* splits in the church
10. *ecumenical:* relating to the whole church
11. *ceremonies:* a set of required formal acts
12. *doctrine:* a consistent set of beliefs
13. *reconciliation:* a repairing of relationships

Key Word Outline

I. Constantinople and the Eastern Empire
1. Eastern, empire, survived
2. Called, Byzantium, capital
3. guarded, straits, Bosporus
4. Important, emperor, patriarch

II. Patriarchs, Old and New
1. Patriarch, above, bishops
2. Hierarchy, archbishop, metropolitan
3. First, only, four
4. Jerusalem, Antioch, Alexandria
5. Rome, claimed, above
6. Fifth, created, behest

III. The Rise of Constantinople's Patriarch
1. Constantinople, most, important
2. Reasons
3. Still, capital
4. Controversies, heresies, schisms
5. Enemy, territory, declined

IV.The Great Schism
1. Pope, ecumenical, patriarch
2. Western, eastern, different
3. 500 years, controversies
4.Final break, 1054

The East-West Schism
Test

1. When did the East-West Schism occur?

2. What event finally caused the schism to occur?

3. What were the two main differences in the Church at this time?

4. What position did the Western Church take on these issues?

5. What position did the Eastern Church take on these issues?

6. What two Churches resulted from the above split?

THE EAST-WEST SCHISM
Test, Page 2

Review

1. Who was the founder of Islam? Where was he born? What did he do for a living before starting Islam?

2. What caused the end of the influence of barbarians and Vikings?

3. What two things did Alfred the Great do that helped reestablish the Kingdom of England?

4. What four points did the Council of Chalcedon affirm?

5. Write in chronological order all the events studied to date. Next to each one write the date associated with it.

The Feudal System
Worksheet

1. What was the feudal system?

2. During what time period was this system the predominant form of social government?

3. Who gave land to the vassals in return for military service?

   What did the vassals do in turn?

4. Who were the freemen?

5. Who owned the serfs?

6. How did this system serve European culture?

7. How did the feudal system end?

THE FEUDAL SYSTEM
Project

Life in the Feudal System

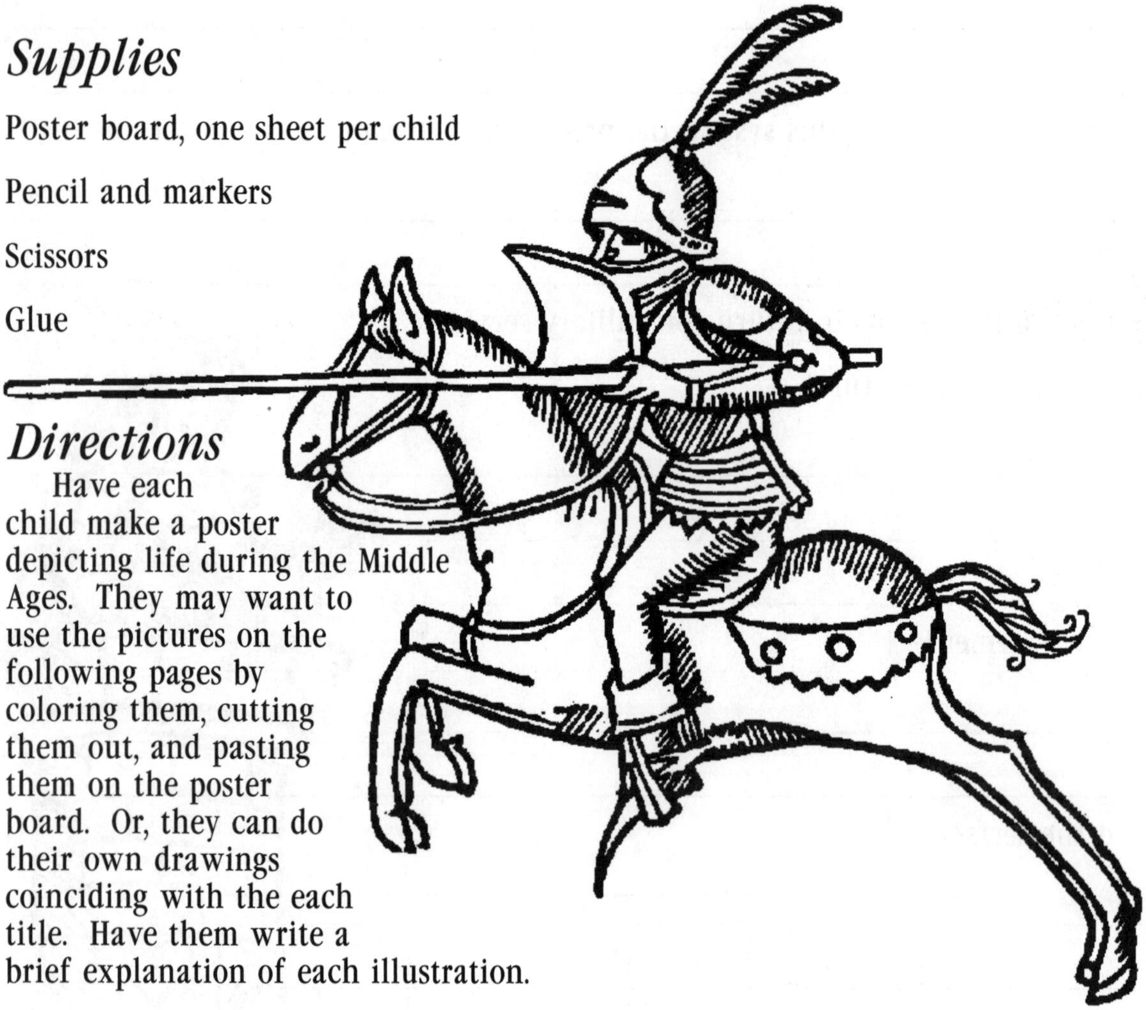

Supplies

Poster board, one sheet per child

Pencil and markers

Scissors

Glue

Directions

Have each child make a poster depicting life during the Middle Ages. They may want to use the pictures on the following pages by coloring them, cutting them out, and pasting them on the poster board. Or, they can do their own drawings coinciding with the each title. Have them write a brief explanation of each illustration.

THE FEUDAL SYSTEM

king

sub-vassal

vassal

THE FEUDAL SYSTEM
Project, Page 3

serf

knight

freeman

THE FEUDAL SYSTEM

Project 2

Heraldry

Shields were used by knights during the Middle Ages. It has been said that they began to decorate them in order to be recognized. When knights went into battle or tournaments, their faces could not be seen as they were covered by a helmet. The decorated shield allowed others to know their identity.

Over time a standardized system known as *heraldry* developed. Heraldry had a strict set of rules, based on symbols and colors. The *coat of arms* as it came to be known was passed on to his eldest son. Other sons could use the same coat of arms by placing a symbol on it depicting their birth order. Each symbol had a meaning that was understood by all.

The symbols on the next page are all from actual heraldic designs. This project can be tied into a literaure project on C.S.Lewis' *Chronicles of Narnia* by having the student place the rampant lion from the next page on the shield in red over a green field in keeping with Narnia's flag.

Making Your Own Coat of Arms

Materials

1/4" plywood or poster board cut to twice the size of the pattern

Paint or markers

Pencil

Examples from books (library, internet, etc.)

Directions

Cut one shield per child.

Allow each student to first draw the outline with pencil and have them explain their symbols.

Make corrections, as necessary.

Have them color the shield.

The Feudal System

Project 2, Page 2

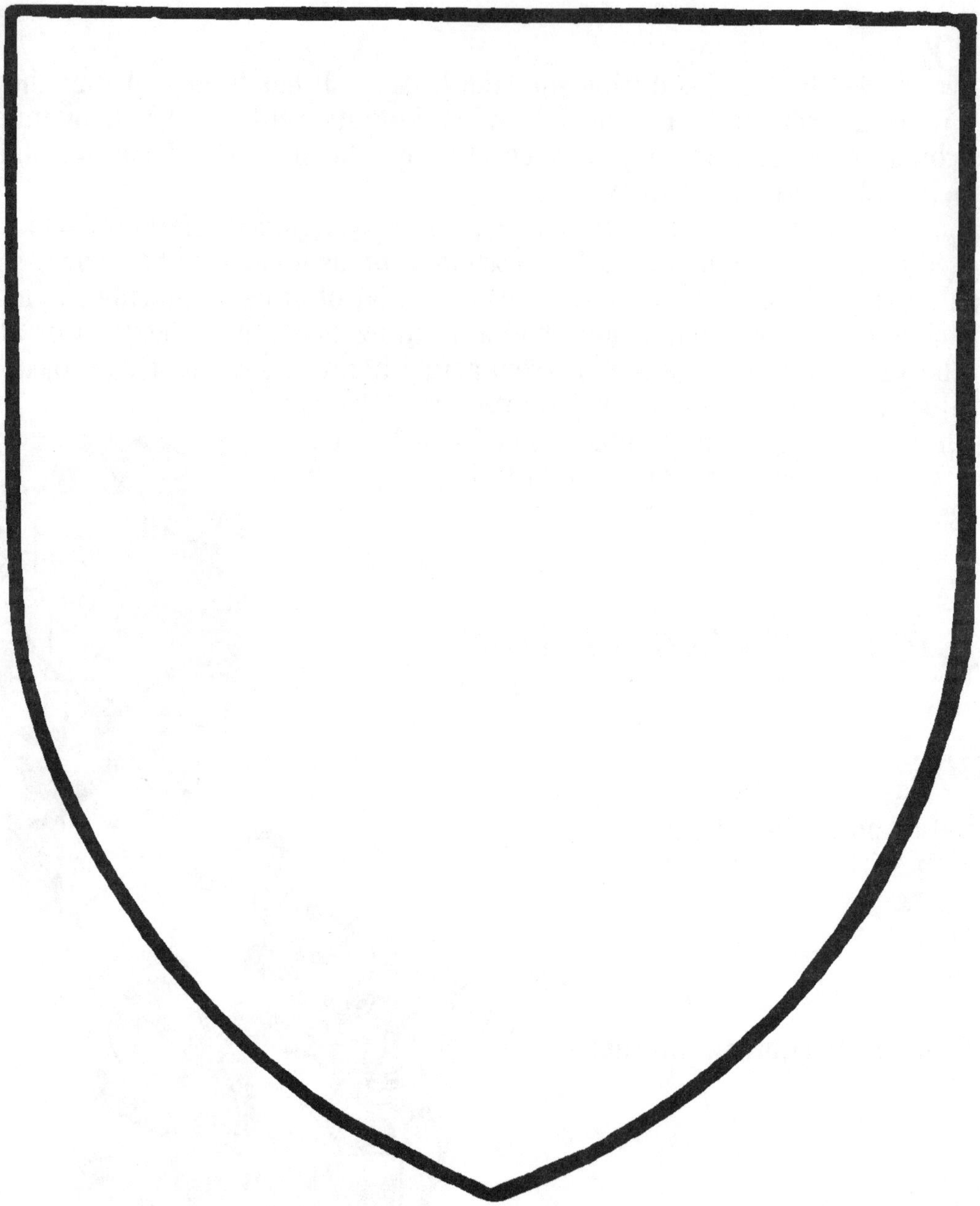

The Feudal System
Project 3

Making a Model Castle

The outward mark of feudalism was the castle, where the lord resided and from which he ruled his fief. Defense formed the primary purpose of the castle. Until the introduction of gunpowder and cannon, the only siege weapons employed were those known in ancient times. They included machines for hurling heavy stones and iron bolts, battering rams, and movable towers, from which the besiegers crossed over to the walls. Such engines could best be used on firm, level ground. Consequently, a castle would often be erected on a high cliff or hill, or on an island, or in the center of a swamp. A castle without such natural defenses would be surrounded by a deep ditch (the "moat"), usually filled with water. If the besiegers could not batter down or undermine the massive walls, they adopted the slower method of a blockade and tried to starve the garrison into surrendering. Ordinarily, however, a well-built, well-provisioned castle was impregnable.

A visitor to a castle crossed the drawbridge over the moat and approached the narrow doorway, which was protected by a tower on each side. If he was admitted, the iron grating ("portcullis") rose slowly on its creaking pulleys. The heavy, wooden doors swung open, and he found himself in the courtyard, commanded by the great central tower ("keep"), where the lord and his family lived, especially in time of war. At the summit of the keep rose a platform whence a sentinel surveyed the country far and wide; below, two stories underground, lay the prison, dark, damp, and dirty. As the visitor walked about the courtyard, he came upon the hall, used as the lord's residence in time of peace, the armory, the chapel, the kitchens, and the stables. A spacious castle might contain all the buildings necessary for the support of the lord's servants and soldiers.

Materials

Cardboard boxes
Milk cartons
Cardboard
Construction paper
String
Scissors
Glue
Markers
Gray tempera paint
(combine white and black if necessary)
Sand

Castle video or book by Macauley could help.

Directions

Before beginning to build your castle, study the next page. Use this as a reference when building your castle.

1. Start with a large cardboard base for each castle.
2. Use a large box for the castle keep. Attach paper towel rolls or milk cartons for the towers.
3. Use card board to cut the castle walls. Notch them at the top.
4. Cut a gate and drawbridge from cardboard also.
5. Use clay to create a moat.
6. After all pieces are in place mix paint and sand together. Mix about 2 cups of paint to 1/2 cup sand, and then paint the entire castle.

The Feudal System

Project 3, Page 2

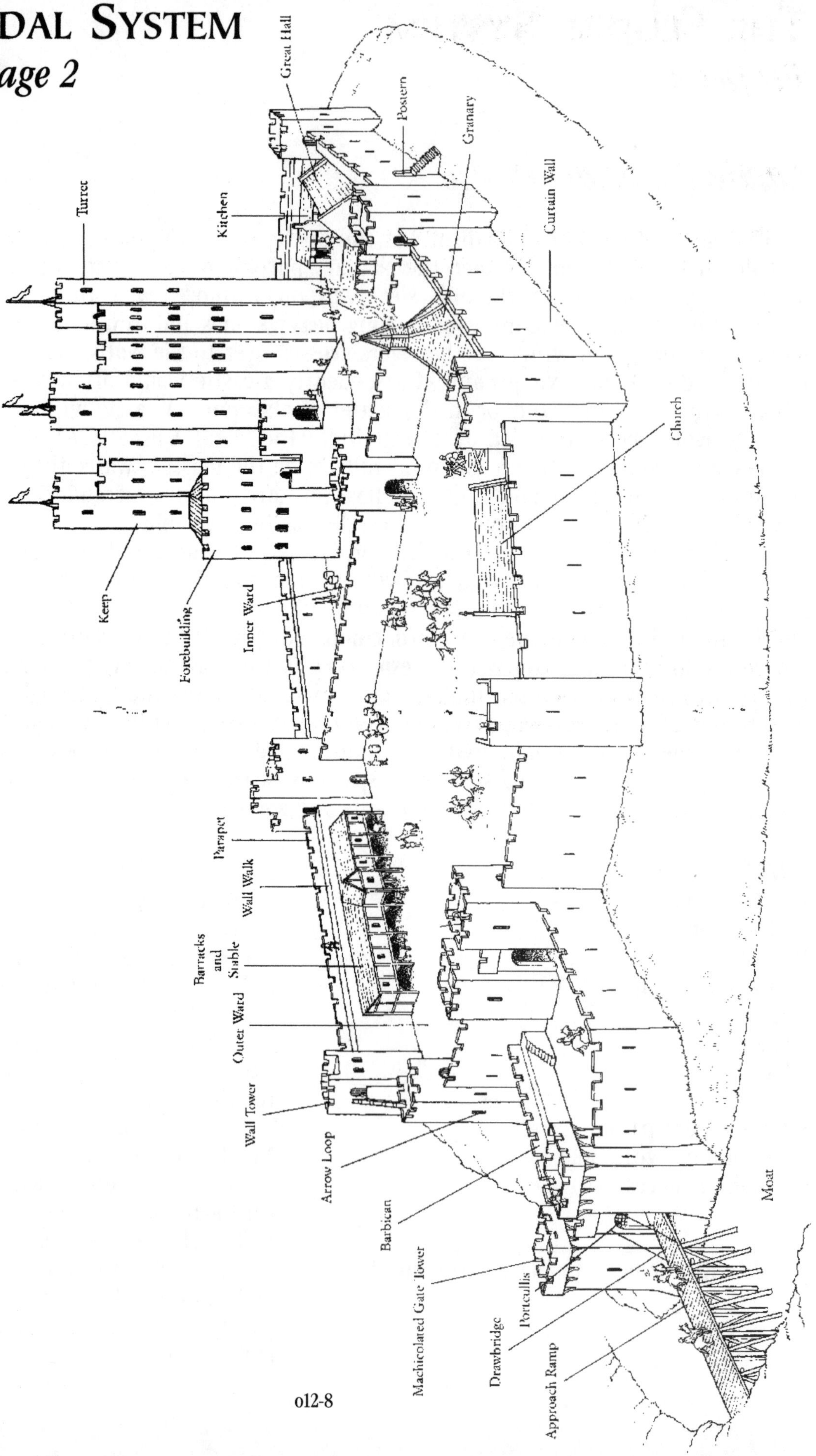

THE FEUDAL SYSTEM
Project 4

Castle Report

Each student can learn about and report on one of the more well known castles. Use the following list to get started.

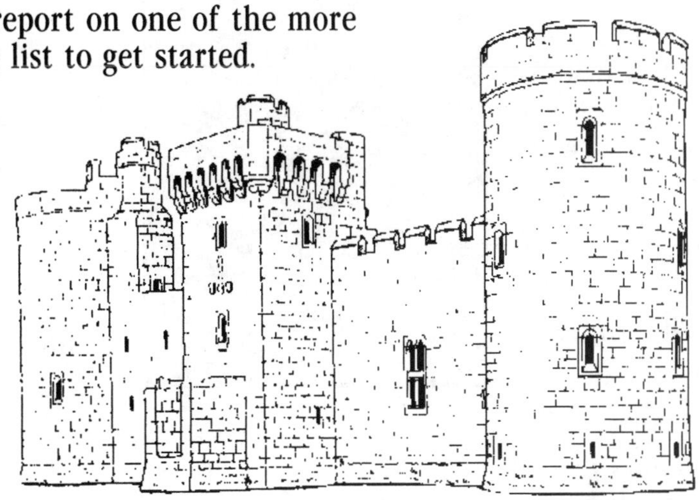

- WHITE TOWER
- NEUSCHWANSTEIN
- ALCAZAR
- PICKERING
- CHATEAU DU MOULIN
- LINDERHOF

Try to find who built the castle and when, distinguishing features, and a drawing. Use the internet (web hint-check this site: http://fox.nstn.ca/~tmonk/castle/castle.html), encyclopedias, magazines and library books. You may know someone who has visited a castle. They may have slides, photos, and more.

The Feudal System
Project 5—A Medieval Feast

A fun way to conclude your study of the feudal system is to host a medieval feast. The Lord and Lady of a manor would have had great feasts which would have included things such as these...

Menu

Trenchers *(basically pocket-less pita bread. Stale trenchers were used as plates.)*
Beef or Lamb Stew
Fruit *(apples, grapes, pears)*
Desert *(pudding or cake)*
Drink *(water or grape juice)*

Recipes—

Trenchers (8-10 trenchers)

2 cups flour
2 t. baking powder
1/4 cup shortening
1/2 tsp. salt
3/4 cup milk

Using a fork, cut shortening into flour, baking powder, and salt to make coarse crumbs. Make a well in the crumb mixture and pour in milk. Stir with a fork until mixed, but don't over stir. Divide into 8-10 pieces, depending on size desired. Knead each piece 12 times. Roll to about 1/4 inch thick and form into a round "plate". Bake at 450 degrees for 10-12 minutes.

Beef Stew (8 servings)

2 lbs. Stew beef
2 8 oz. Jars of onion or beef gravy
salt pepper
herbs: thyme, rosemary, oregano (start with small amounts)
1 small onion, cut in wedges large enough to "pick out"

Stew all ingredients in a crock pot about 3 hours on high, or until meat is tender.

Wassail (serves 8)

1 1/2 quarts apple cider
2 cups cranberry juice
1/2 cup brown sugar
1/2 cup sugar
3 sticks cinnamon
1/2 tsp. ginger
1/2 tsp allspice
1/4 tsp ground mace
2 large oranges cut into eigths and pierced with cloves

Pour all the above ingredients except oranges into a large crock pot. Cover and cook on high one hour. Stir as necessary. Turn heat down to medium and cook for at least four hours. During the last hour add oranges.

Decorations

Paint a scene as though looking out a castle window onto a large sheet. Use sponge "bricks" and several shades of paint to add realism.

Entertainment

Play Chess, Nine Men's Morris, marbles and horseshoes. You may have some "troubadours" who can entertain.

The Feudal System

Project 6–Serf for a Day

Draw names to assign initial roles of:

KING

VASSAL

LESSER NOBLES

KNIGHTS

FREEMEN

SERFS

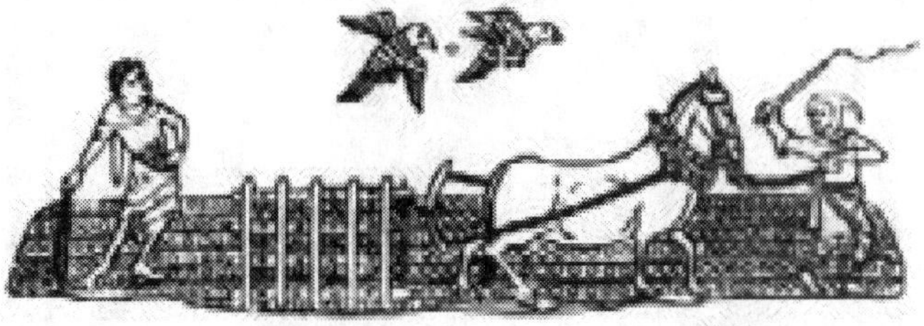

Everyone moves down the ladder one step until serfdom, then it is a rapid rise to kingship. You may wish to have several vassals so you can depict how a serf is loyal to his lord, but not necessarily to other lords. Give out play money and land deeds (see next page). Students should render acts of service and give tribute to their lord. Lords should grant land and protection to their vassal, etc. You should probably assign times and places where the Serf for a Day is in effect.

After spending several days role playing, discuss the arbitrariness of the system and the benefits and disadvantages.

Money

THE FEUDAL SYSTEM
Project 6, Page 3

Deed

DEED

this propertee belongeth to ye godly man, his lordship—

____

in great appryshiation for his grace loaning such gift to—

____

taxes, fees, and armed service shall be returned whenever such is called for.

THE FEUDAL SYSTEM
Project 7–Literature Unit

King Arthur and His Knights of the Round Table–Study Guide

Begin reading this book as soon as your study of the feudal system starts. It will probably take 30 days to complete the reading and testing for King Arthur. This is a wonderful book with important themes. The reading and enjoyment of this book is worthy of your class time. Before beginning, discuss the setting, author, illustrator, characters, genre, and the theme. Students can copy the information for their own King Arthur notebook. A three prong pocket folder can be used for the notebook. Use the sheet provided to fill in the notebook pages. Comprehension questions may be answered on these sheets. Do not feel that you must answer all the questions, but choose those that you wish. Students can draw a cover illustration on a blank sheet of paper and, when they are satisfied with the illustration, glue it to the folder.

Setting
Use maps of Britain to identify the setting. Most references have a modern name. Identify the time setting. The end of the Realm is about 454 years after the crucifixion of Christ.

Author
Read the Author's Note. List the resources Roger Lancelyn Green used to write this edition. Read the last paragraph of the Author's Note to determine why Green used so many different sources. Name several fairy tales that have been retold over and over again.

Illustrator and copyright.
Use the copyright page to find the illustrator's name and copyright date.

Characters
List some of the important characters. For the characters of Arthur, Merlin, Launcelot, and Percivale. You may wish to keep an ongoing list of character qualities.

Genre
Discuss the meaning of nonfiction and fiction. If you wish to be more specific, discuss fantasy, historical fiction, and fables.

Theme
The theme for this edition of King Arthur is summarized by Green in the Author's Note. "I have endeavored to make each adventure a part of one fixed pattern–Arthur's kingdom, the Realm of Logres, the model of chivalry and right striving against the barbarism and evil which surrounded and at length engulfed it." Define chivalry, barbarism, and engulfed. As you read the book, call the theme of chivalry versus barbarism to attention as often as necessary.

THE FEUDAL SYSTEM

Project, Page 2—Literature Unit

King Arthur and His Knights of the Round Table—Study Guide

Vocabulary

There are many new words in King Arthur for most children. The understanding of King Arthur will be greatly enhanced with a knowledge of the vocabulary words listed for each chapter. In the first few chapters there are many words but the list becomes more manageable in the remaining chapters. Use 13 pieces of notebook paper folded in half top to bottom for a glossary. On each half of the page write a letter of the alphabet. Students will record each vocabulary word and its definition in the glossary. Most of the words are used several times so this should be a ready reference while reading. The vocabulary, questions and activities are divided into Chapters for ease of use. Vocabulary should be defined before the day's reading and checked for accuracy in context. If there is time after the reading, students can copy the sentence where each vocabulary word occurs, check the definition of the word, and write an original sentence using the word. As students answer the comprehension questions, encourage them to use supporting quotes from the book. All answers should be complete sentences.

The Feudal System
Project, Page 3—Literature Unit

King Arthur and His Knights of the Round Table—Study Guide

Book One Chapter One
Vocabulary

enchanter	nunnery
magic	wretched
Archbishop	murmur
anvil	breadth
tournament	pavilion
jousting	lodgings
jests	stile
solemn	oath
hilt	scabbard
bade	seneschal
Pentecost	homage
squire	slain
vengeance	avenge
smote	wroth
churls	hermitage
samite	questing

Activities and Comprehension Questions

· Make a family tree for Arthur.
· Salt Dough Anvils

Salt Dough Recipe
1 Ω c. salt
4 c. flour
1 Ω c. water
1 t. alum (if you do not plan to bake the clay)

Mix dry ingredients, then gradually add the water. When the dough forms a ball, begin to knead. Add more water if the dough is too crumbly. Use salt dough to make an anvil with a sword sticking out. Use a pencil to carve the words on the anvil. If desired, bake at 300 degrees F. Small creations take about 30 minutes.

· Find words from the chapter to describe Arthur.
· What character flaw nearly gets Arthur killed?
· Does Arthur learn his lesson? Use quotes from the chapter to support your answer.
· Draw pictures showing how Arthur obtains his swords.

Book One Chapter Two
Vocabulary

mantle	realm
damsel	penance
naught	dolorous
fate	lamented
abide	portcullis
swoon	

Activities and Comprehension Questions

· Describe Balyn's misfortunes.
· What misdeeds does Garlon commit?
· Why does King Pelles seek to avenge Garlon's death?
· Draw a picture of the room at Castle Carbonek with the Spear and Cup.
· What happened when Balyn struck King Pelles?
· Describe the death of Balyn.

The Feudal System
Project, Page 4—Literature Unit

King Arthur and His Knights of the Round Table—Study Guide

Book One Chapter Three
Vocabulary

bounty	strife
siege	perilous
hart	brachet
cur	boon
priory	vanquished
palfrey	manor
penance	succor
chivalry	

Activities and Comprehension Questions

- How does Arthur achieve peace throughout Britain?
- Locate Camelot, now Winchester, on a map.
- Merlin tells Arthur what will happen if he marries Guinevere, but what is Arthur's response?
- What causes strife among Arthur's knights?
- Draw a picture of the wedding of Arthur and Guinevere.
- Describe the Round Table and its seats.
- What is the Siege Perilous?
- What is the first quest of the Round Table?
- Match the knight with the quest.

Gawain	The quest for the Brachet
Tor	The quest for the White Hart
King Pellinore	The quest to bring Lady Nimue back to Camelot

- Copy the oath of the Round Table and decorate the page.
- To where does Merlin go?

Book One Chapter Four
Vocabulary

hawthorn	barque
bulwarks	dismal
lamented	craven
cleft	wiles
vainly	fiend
mantle	perforce

Activities and Comprehension Questions

- Draw Merlin's resting place.
- Who is Morgana le Fay?
- Describe Morgana le Fay.
- Who does King Arthur battle?
- Why does Arthur not fair well?
- What defense does Morgana le Fay give when caught attempting to murder her husband?
- How does the Lady Nimue twice save Arthur's life?

Book Two Chapter One
Vocabulary

minstrels	jerkin
dire	tarry
valour	Yule-tide
festal	girt
mire	palisade
trestles	comely
hind	jest
chamberlain	wheedle

Project, Page 5—Literature Unit

King Arthur and His Knights of the Round Table—Study Guide

blithe
sluggard
oratory
absolved
chid
scythe
tryst
renown

Activities and Comprehension Questions

· Draw the Green Knight.
· What is the bargain between the Green Knight and Gawain?
· What is the bargain between the castle lord and Gawain?
· Does Gawain keep his bargains?
· Who is the Green Knight?
· Who sent the Green Knight on his quest?

Book Two Chapter Two
Vocabulary

litter
behest
traversed
lych-gate
boughs
array
porter
writhe
lunes

Activities and Comprehension Questions

· What miracle does Launcelot perform?
· Draw the tree and glue shields to it.
· How does Launcelot escape Morgana le Fay?
· Describe Launcelot, use examples to support your description.
· What does it mean that Launcelot crossed himself when he spoke with Allewes?
· Relate the trick Sir Launcelot played with Sir Kay's armor.
· How was Launcelot's reputation established, by boasting or deeds?

Book Two Chapter Three
Vocabulary

stalwart
fie
tallow
rail
lineage
vulgar
scullion
knave
wanes

Activities and Comprehension Questions

· Who is Beaumains?
· Draw pictures of the knights that Beaumains conquers.
· What color knight would you wish to be? Draw yourself in your chosen color and with an appropriate setting.
· How does Beaumains treat the Lady Linnet even with her railing at him?
· Think of a motto for Beaumains.

Book Two Chapter Four
Vocabulary

lay
moored
lair
braggart
vitals
espied
fosterling
wooed
seneschal
devour
vaunting
dregs

Activities and Comprehension Questions

· Locate Cornwall on the map.
· Why does Arthur seek to fill the seats by the Siege Perilous?
· Draw a picture of the clue to Marhault's slayer.

The Feudal System
Project, Project 6—Literature Unit

King Arthur and His Knights of the Round Table—Study Guide

- Tramtris is Tristram scrambled. Scramble your name to disguise it.
- What plan does King Mark have to make peace with Ireland?
- How does Iseult the Fair discover Tramtris is Tristram?
- What causes Tristram to fall in love with Iseult?
- How does Tristram die?
- Draw the rose trees intertwined.

Book Two Chapter Five
Vocabulary

cavalcade	parapet
pensively	frugal
rooks	daws
tarry	chastise
insolence	girths
four-score	bier

Activities and Comprehension Questions

- How do Enid's harsh words nearly cause the death of Geraint?
- Find 3 Bible verses dealing with harsh words.

Book Two Chapter Six
Vocabulary

carrion	pomp
mirth	loathly
moor	tremulous

Activities and Comprehension Questions

- According to the old woman, what is the thing women most desire? Do you agree or disagree and why?
- How does Sir Gawain show his honor for the Lady Ragnell? How is he rewarded?
- Who does the author suggest are Percivale's parents?

Book Two Chapter Seven
Vocabulary

bower	draught
foliage	bracken
sombre (somber)	procession
grail	cromlech

Activities and Comprehension Questions

- Where does the true worth of knighthood lay?
- What words of wisdom does Percivale's mother leave him with?
- What does Sir Gonemans teach Percivale?
- Draw a picture of the Procession of the Grail.
- Where does the Lady Blanchefleur live?
- What does Blanchefleur tell Percivale about the fall of Logres and the Quest of the Grail?

Book Two Chapter Eight
Vocabulary

redress	blithe
rent	guile
wits	

The Feudal System
Project, Project 7—Literature Unit

King Arthur and His Knights of the Round Table—Study Guide

Activities and Comprehension Questions

- How does the evil concerning Launcelot and Guinevere creep in?
- Look up Joseph of Arimethea in Matthew 27:57-60, Mark 15:42-46, John 19:38, and Luke 23:50-53.
- What wicked plan does Elaine carry out to win Launcelot?
- What happens to Launcelot because he is shamed?
- Why can Launcelot not touch the grail, even though in earthly matters he is the best knight?

Book Three Chapter One
Vocabulary

minster

Activities and Comprehension Questions

- What is the date given on the Siege Perilous?
- Who is Galahad's father?
- Whose seat is the Siege Perilous?

Book Three Chapter Two
Vocabulary

chivalry prowess

Activities and Comprehension Questions

- What is the history of Galahad's new shield?
- Who is Galahad to trust?
- Draw the Enchanted Ship.

Book Three Chapter Three
Vocabulary

recluse temptations

Activities and Comprehension Questions

- What temptations does Percivale overcome?

Book Three Chapter Four
Vocabulary

felon trespass

Activities and Comprehension Questions

- How does the hermit say to reach the Grail?
- What temptations does Sir Bors overcome?
- Why did Sir Lionel seek to kill his brother and the monk?

Book Three Chapter Five
Vocabulary

feeble

Activities and Comprehension Questions

- Who is on the ship when it departs?
- What does Dindrane, Percivale's sister, do for the ill maiden?
- What is the maiden's punishment for the castle custom?

The Feudal System
Project, Page 8—Literature Unit

King Arthur and His Knights of the Round Table—Study Guide

Book Three Chapter Six
Vocabulary

bridle	absolution
sacrament	

Activities and Comprehension Questions

· Why does Sir Hector fail to achieve the Quest of the Holy Grail?
· What is Hector's interpretation of the extinguished candles?

Sun Catcher Candlesticks
Use markers to draw candlesticks with seven candles on clear plastic lids from deli containers. With a hole punch, make a hole in the top rim. Thread string through the hole and hang the catchers near a window.

· Discuss who is the giver of absolution.
· Summarize what it means to be moderate and to speak only in due season.
· In small groups, prepare a skit of the scene in the castle hall and act out the procession of the Grail to the Grail Room. Each group can perform the skit for the class.
· How does Gawain remove the curse from the castle and wastelands?

Book Three Chapter Seven
Activities and Comprehension Questions

· What was Naciens' punishment for sinning against Joseph of Arimethea?
· How does Galahad heal King Pelles' dolorous stroke?
· What is Blanchefleur's test of who is to be her husband and the next king of Carbonek?
· What happens when Galahad's life is accomplished?
· Does Sir Launcelot learn from his failure to achieve the Quest of the Holy Grail?

Book Four Chapter One
Vocabulary

pilgrimage	archers
strive	dissension
groveled	a-maying (You will need to use the context.)

Activities and Comprehension Questions

· What changes take place in Logres after the quest of the holy grail?
· How does Arthur know the passing of Logres is very near?
· What trickery does Melligraunce attempt against Launcelot?
· What plan do Guinevere and Launcelot make in the queen's garden?

Book Four Chapter Two
Vocabulary

civil war	slanders
conspirators	smock
truce	sunder
mischief	lament
fortified	

The Feudal System

Project, Page 9—Literature Unit

King Arthur and His Knights of the Round Table—Study Guide

Activities and Comprehension Questions

· What punishment is Guinevere sentenced to for her betrayal of Arthur?
· Does Gawain react moderately towards Launcelot as Naciens told him to?
· Where does Launcelot go after the first peace with Arthur?
· What does Mordred attempt in Arthur's absence?
· What does the Archbishop mean by bell, book, and candle?
· How does Sir Gawain die?

Book Three Chapter Three
Vocabulary

harrying
ominous
feint
adder
doleful

Activities and Comprehension Questions

· What people are invading Britain, taking advantage of the war between Mordred and Arthur?
· What warning does Sir Gawain give Arthur in Arthur's vision?
· What happens to start the battle?
· What command does Arthur give Sir Bedivere concerning Excalibur?
· Draw the scene when Sir Bedivere throws the sword into the lake.
· When will Arthur come again?

Epilogue
Vocabulary

heathen

Activities and Comprehension Questions

· Where is Guinevere when Launcelot seeks King Arthur?
· Draw the hazel tree on one page and cut out a small cave entrance. On a second page, draw the cave scene. Staple or glue the hazel tree on top of the cave scene.
· Make up a quest for King Arthur and His Knights of the Round Table.

The Feudal System

Project—Literature Unit

King Arthur and His Knights of the Round Table

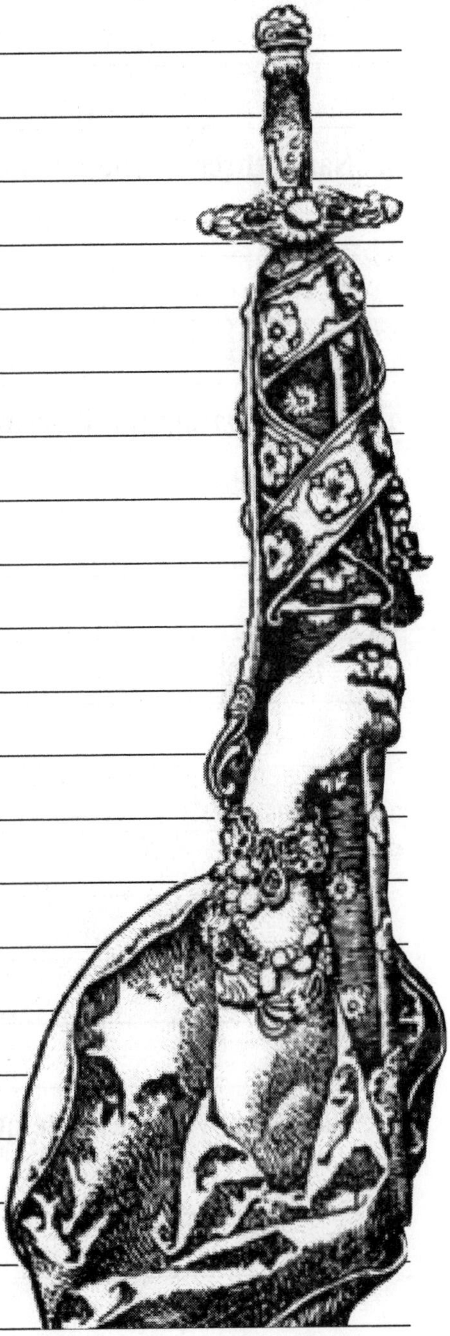

THE FEUDAL SYSTEM

Test—King Arthur and His Knights of the Round Table

1. Who wrote King Arthur and His Knights of the Round Table?

2. Is King Arthur fiction or nonfiction?

3. Name three of the main characters.

4. Write a paragraph describing one of the main characters.

5. What was your favorite quest?

THE FEUDAL SYSTEM
Test

1. What were the dates when the feudal system was in place?

2. What was the feudal system and what purpose did it serve?

3. Fill in the hierarchy of the feudal system below.

4. When did the feudal system end? What caused it to end?

THE FEUDAL SYSTEM
Test, Page 2

Review

1. Name two books that Augustine wrote.

2. Who introduced the rules for monasteries around 540?

3. How did Justinian the Great form his code of law?

4. Write a summary about Mohammed's vision. What did this vision cause?

5. Write in chronological order all the events studied to date.

WILLIAM THE CONQUEROR AND THE BATTLE OF HASTINGS

Worksheet

1. What was the date of "William the Conqueror and the Battle of Hastings?"

2. What did the French king give the Norsemen at the time that Alfred the Great gave the Danes part of England?

3. What was the religion of the Danes and the Norsemen?

4. What was the problem with their understanding of Christianity?

5. William was a Duke. What did he desire to be? How did he accomplish this?

William the Conqueror and the Battle of Hastings

Project

How William of Normandy Conquered a Kingdom

When the first son was born to Robert, Duke of Normandy, and Arlette, the daughter of a tanner, the nurse laid the day-old baby on the straw carpet of the castle. In those days most of the floors of the houses, whether huts or castles, were of earth or stone, covered with straw which could be cleared out, as from a modern stable, to allow fresh straw to be laid down. When placed on the floor in his little blanket, Baby William reached out and clutched some of the straws so tightly in his small pink fists that one of those who noticed smiled and said, "He will take fast hold on everything he lays his hands on when he grows up."

When William was seven, Duke Robert, his father, being about to make the voyage to the Holy Land, called some of his nobles together and said, "I am resolved to journey to the place where our Lord Christ died and was buried. But because I know this journey is full of dangers, I would have it settled who should be duke if I should die."

The nobles and knights took an oath that they would stand by his son William and not let any one keep him from being duke of Normandy. Then Duke Robert sailed away and died during the long voyage.

William was away hunting in a Norman forest when his faithful fool (as they called a sort of clown kept by a king to amuse the court) broke in where he lay asleep and shouted, "Fly, or you will never leave here a living man!" The young duke jumped up, dressed in haste, and mounted his horse, riding through the forest in the moonlight and fording rivers till he came to the castle of a friend who was sure to be faithful to him. This knight and his three sons rode with William to his own castle.

It turned out that a number of the Norman lords who had taken the oath to satisfy Duke Robert were now declaring that they would not serve under the low-born grandson of a tanner. The fool had learned that they were plotting rebellion and the death of his young master.

William, who was now twenty years old, gathered an army of loyal knights and men, and waged fierce warfare against the traitors, who retreated within the walls of a Norman town. The young duke soon captured the town, and proved to these rebels, as well as to the men of the neighboring kingdom of France, that the grandson of a tanner might be a greater general than the son of a king. At the beginning of a great battle of brave knights against braver knights, a champion of heroic size came out

William the Conqueror and the Battle of Hastings

Project, Page 2

from the ranks of the enemy and threw down his gauntlet, or glove, challenging any knight of Normandy to come and fight him with the sword. William himself took up the gauntlet, and drove his sword through an open place in the big knight's armor, so that he fell dead from his horse.

Then, like the Philistines of old when David slew their giant, the Duke's enemies fled in all directions. Many of them were slain in battle, others while running away were cut down by the battle-axes of Norman knights, and many more perished in the flooded river.

Those were brutal days, when people thought that whatever a great king or noble might do was all right if he only had the power to put it through. An example of such high-handed dealing is William's conquest of England. He had once paid a visit to Edward the Confessor, the priestly king of England. The duke claimed, on his return to Normandy, that Edward had promised to leave the kingdom to him, as a relative. It happened that Harold, an English earl, was shipwrecked on the coast of Normandy. William seized Harold, shut him up in prison, and kept him there until he promised to do his best to make William King of England at the death of Edward.

Two years later, when Edward the Confessor died, it was found that in spite of his promise to William he had advised in his will that Harold be elected king by the @#%*!?~$, an assembly of English freemen. This body of men took the good old king's advice, chose Harold king, and saw that he was crowned at once. Harold excused himself for breaking his word to William because King Edward had decided in his favor instead of William's, and because the oath he had made had been forced from him while he was a prisoner.

William, however, was very angry when he heard that Harold had allowed himself to be crowned king of England. Getting together as large an army as he could in Normandy, he sailed across the Channel. In leaping ashore from his boat, he tripped and fell forward with his hands upon the ground. Realizing that his soldiers would think this a bad sign, he clutched both hands full of earth, and rising he held them up, exclaiming, "See, I have taken possession of this land of England."

The Normans took position in the village of Hastings. Harold went into camp on top of Senlac hill, now called Battle, about six miles from Hastings, and dug trenches around it. Here a great battle began at four o'clock in the morning of the 14th of October, 1066. In advance of the Norman lines rode a knight in armor, bearing the duke's colors, singing the Song of Roland, the great paladin in the army of Charlemagne, who had lived and fought nearly three hundred years before. It was a brave combat, with many knights and nobles on each side. The, Norman found the Englishman a foeman worthy of his steel.

The Saxons, entrenched on Battle Hill, held their ground so well that William saw he could not gain the day unless he drew them away from that point of vantage. So he ordered a retreat, and the honest Saxons chased the flying Normans, expecting to catch and

WILLIAM THE CONQUEROR AND THE BATTLE OF HASTINGS

Project, Page 3

slay them. But to their great surprise, the Normans turned and fought harder than before. Harold was killed by an arrow shot into his eyes. The Saxon army, without a commander, was thrown into confusion, and thus the day was won by strategy. William, Duke of Normandy, became William the Conqueror of England.

No one now had a better claim to the throne of England than William. He was crowned in the new Westminster Abbey, on Christmas Day, 1066, and took his proud place in history as William the First of England. He had to fight four years longer to break down all opposition from the northern counties. In rewarding the Norman knights and nobles who had helped him gain possession of England, the king gave them great estates scattered over the kingdom. William brought to the island many scholars and bishops, and did much to establish the Church in England. Though he had been rough and cruel, he was both shrewd and wise in proving his own rights and in strengthening his kingdom.

William ruled England with a strong hand for twenty-one years. He forbade the buying and selling of slaves, yet he reduced the Saxon farmers to serfs almost as low as slaves. He ordered a record like a census made, and a survey of the kingdom which was recorded in what is called the Domesday Book.

It was terribly hard for the good, honest Anglo-Saxon people to see the Normans move into their homes and force them to work like slaves on the very places they themselves had owned. But the Normans had the power and the Saxons could not help themselves. For hundreds of years the Normans spoke the French language, and the Saxons, the English. The very names of the meats on your table at home are signs of the Norman Conquest, nearly nine hundred years ago. The animals in the pastures and stables of England were called by the names the Saxons gave them– cow, calf, sheep, swine. But the meats of those animals when cooked and served upon the tables of the masters are still known by the Norman French names, as beef (Norman name for cow), veal (Norman for calf), mutton (Norman for sheep), pork (Norman for hog or swine) Milk is a Saxon word, but cream is from the French, because the Saxons had to milk the cows and drink only milk, while they served their Norman lords the cream.

The Norman traits of keenness, tact, and worldly wisdom have been mingling for many centuries with the honest, sturdy integrity of the Anglo-Saxons. Little by little, as the races grew together, the nobles became less haughty and cruel and the poorer people were lifted out of their poverty. But it took many centuries for men to learn the lesson that

"Kind hearts are more than coronets, and simple faith more than Norman blood."

On the following pages illustrate the life of William the Conqueror, titleing each frame.

William the Conqueror and the Battle of Hastings

Project, Page 4

William the Conqueror and the Battle of Hastings

Project, Page 5

William the Conqueror and the Battle of Hastings

Project 2

Bayeaux Tapestry

The Bayeaux Tapestry illustrates the events leading up to and through the Battle of Hastings. It is not a true woven tapestry, but rather like an embroidered cartoon with Latin text. View pictures of the Tapestry in a book. Measure out its 230 foot length, it will amaze you! The Bayeaux Tapestry is on display in Bayeaux, France. It is amazingly well preserved. An interesting web site is www.cablenet.net/pages/book/index.htm. You may wish to have your students paint and display a few of the scenes of the Tapestry.

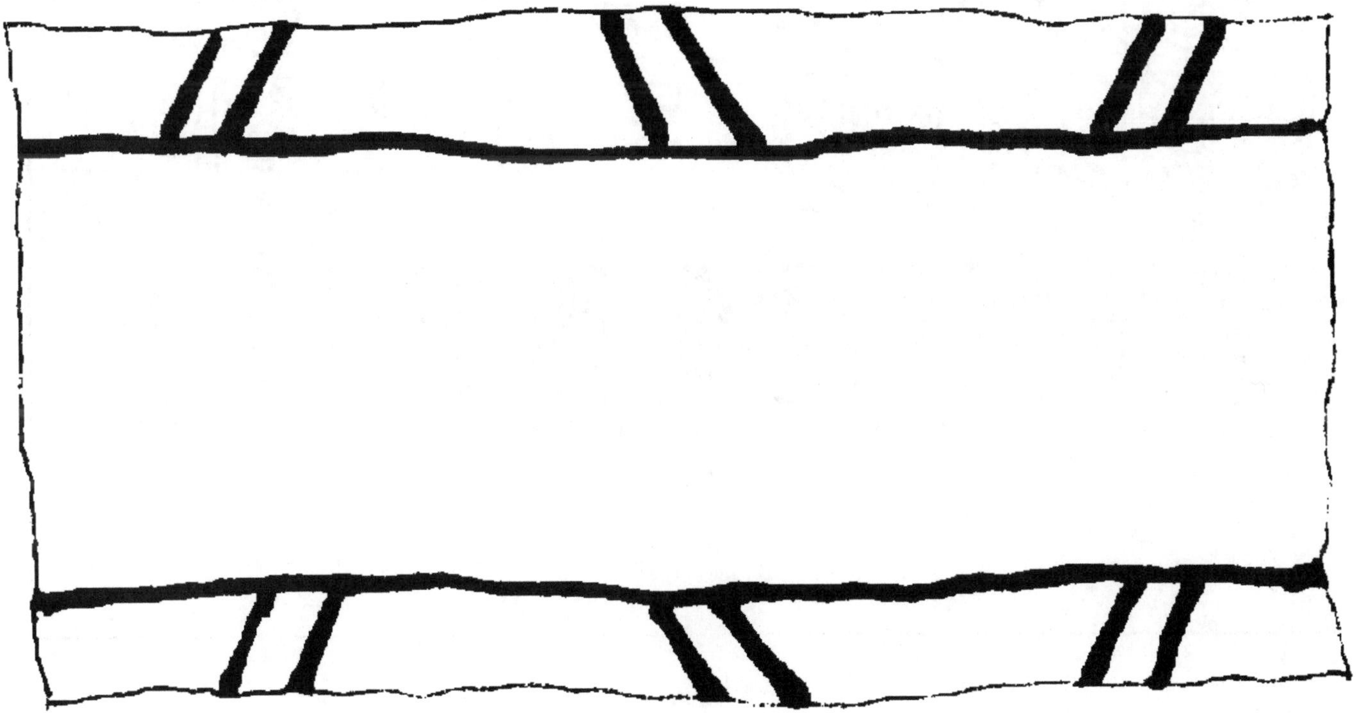

William the Conqueror and the Battle of Hastings
Project 3

Domesday Book

William the Conqueror ordered the creation of the Domesday Book. It was a detailed listing of the property and the people of his kingdom. Each student can make a small Domesday Book of their property at school. The covers can be made using from the graphic below.

Create a list of lasting influences of the Norman invasion of England, for example the Tower of London, castle design, and language. Students can research further and write a paragraph on one for display on a poster or bulletin board.

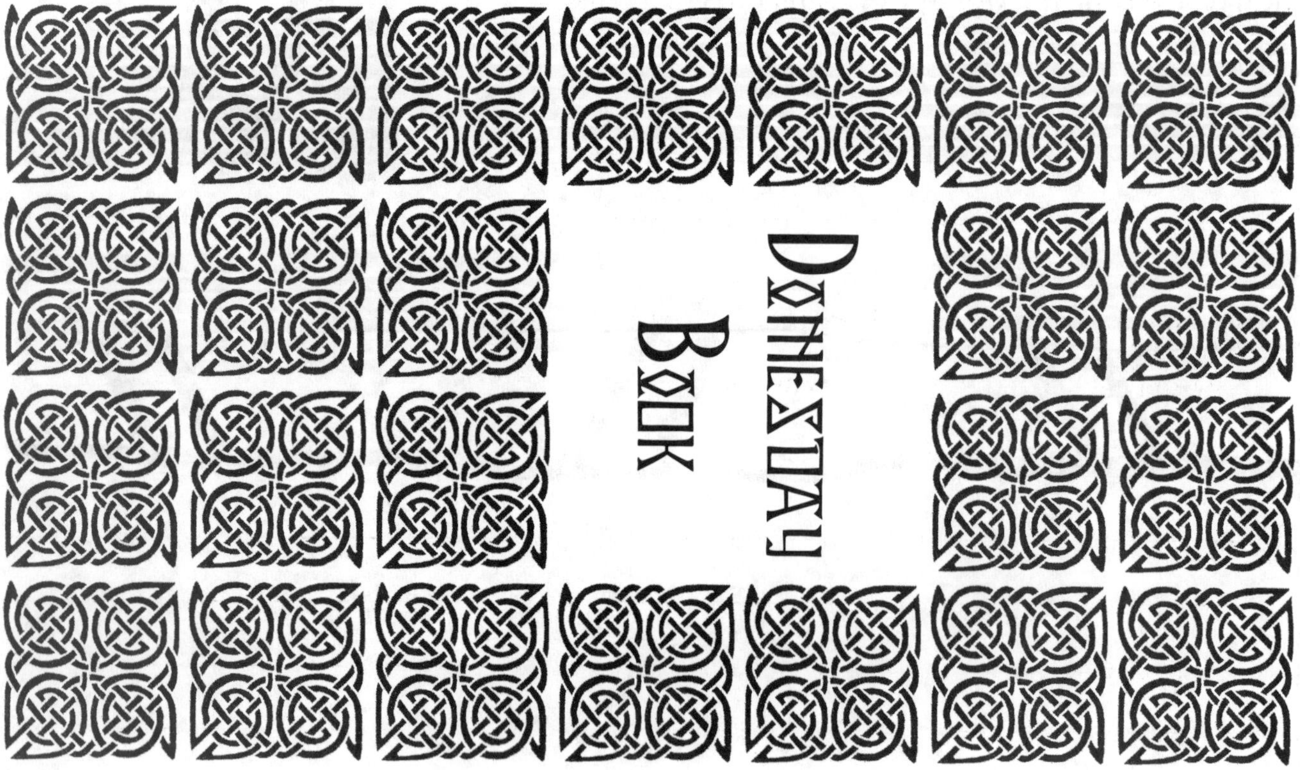

William the Conqueror and the Battle of Hastings

Test

1. What is the date of "William the Conqueror and the Battle of Hastings?"

2. When the French king gave the Norsemen part of France called Normandy, what did Alfred the Great give the Danes?

3. What religion did both groups adopt? What was the problem with it?

4. William the Conqueror decided that he wanted to be king of England. How did he accomplish this? When was he crowned king?

William the Conqueror and the Battle of Hastings

Test, Page 2

Review

1. What did Justinian the Great build in Constantinople? What is the name of the building?

   What was its architectural style?

2. What are three things to which a Muslim must adhere?

3. Who came to rule after Pepin the Short?

   What office did the Pope bestow on this person?

4. Who were the Danes? What did they have to do with Alfred the Great?

5. List in chronological order the events studied to date.

   Next to each one place the appropriate dates.

Cathedrals in Europe

Worksheet

1. Define the word *cathedra.*

____

____

2. For what area is the bishop responsible?

____

____

____

3. A cathedral church can be any _______ or __________,
   but it is often a large ________ church.

4. What was the style referred to of most buildings?

____

____

5. What was the Gothic style? Where did it originate?

____

____

6. How long did many of the craftsmen work on these churches?

____

____

7. List three things common to a Gothic style cathedral.

____

____

____

8. Where is the largest cathedral? How long did it take to build?

____

____

Cathedrals in Europe

Project

Cathedral Architecture

On the following five pages you will find detailed information about Gothic Cathedrals. Please discuss these in detail with your class. There is also a stained glass window for them to color. If you run this off on transparency film and then have the students color it with permanent markers you will have a wonderful stained glass effect. These are fun to hang in a window for display.

The book *Cathedral* by David Macaulay is by far the best source on cathedrals that we have found. This is a great book to read aloud to your students over the week that you cover this card. *Cathedral* is also available as a video.

The first project is a character presentation of cathedral information. The teacher, or a volunteer, should act out the part of the master builder's apprentice.
The apprentice can explain the marvels of Gothic Cathedrals in a memorable way. Appropriate pictures should be used in the presentation whenever possible.

Cross Section of Amiens Cathedral

A, vaulting; B, ribs; C, flying buttresses; D, buttresses;
E, low windows; F, clerestory

Cathedrals in Europe
Project 2

Apprenticeship

Cathedral building began in Saint Denis, France around 1150 AD. Cathedrals became the focus of city life. Often they were built to house relics, which were bits of bone, wood, etc. said to have belonged to a saint. A cathedral could require 100 years to complete.

Master Builder's Apprentice

Good day to you! Are you the new apprentices? You there with the muscles, you look like a stone mason and you with the keen eyesight, you should be a glass cutter. My master, the master builder of this great and beautiful cathedral, has been working on this building for nearly 50 years, and we still have lots more to accomplish. There is lots of work to do you know! As you can see, I have an organizational chart of who is currently employed to build this cathedral. Each of these craftsmen has a workshop with apprentice. So, you can each find a master to be apprenticed to.

master builder

carpenter | blacksmith | roofer

mortar maker | mason | quarryman | stone cutter

sculptor | glass maker

We want this cathedral to be the most beautiful Gothic cathedral anywhere, so we teach our workers a little about Gothic architecture. To be truly Gothic, a building must be delicate and glass-filled with harmony, stability, and height. A worshipper should have a sense of God's greatness and order. You will notice in this floor plan, Gothic cathedrals are usually in the shape of a cross.

A thick walled foundation is laid first. The walls go about 25 feet below the ground and are thickest at the bottom. Each stone used to build the cathedral is carefully measured, cut, and marked by the stone cutters so the stone mason will know where the stone is to be placed. The master mason continually checks to be sure the wall is level horizontally and plumb vertically. The only way to have straight walls is to start straight and stay straight

Cathedrals in Europe

Project 2, Page 2

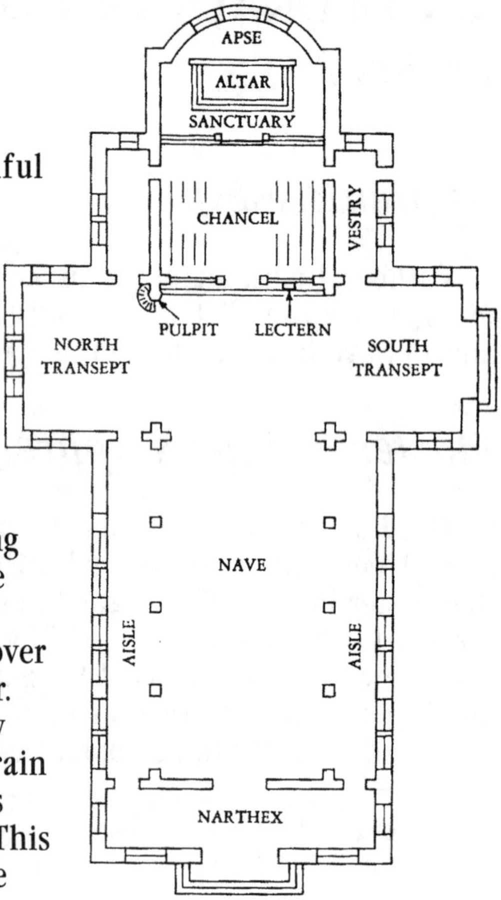

with each stone. Because we want to have lots of beautiful windows, we have made the sections of wall as small as possible. We can fill in the space between the piers with tracery, which is the stone frame work for windows.

Many people are amazed at how tall the roof is and how small the walls can be in comparison. This is accomplished by using buttresses. The flying buttress relieves downward pressure on the piers from the vault, or ceiling. This helps the weight to be spread out. Sometimes builders have gone a little too far with making the walls smaller and the wall has caved in, but we have learned from these experiences.

The roof is made of triangular trusses. Lead sheets cover the wooden frame to protect the wood from bad weather. To keep water from settling on the roof or wearing away the foundation, a drainage system has to be installed. Drain pipes and gutters are made from lead. Also stone masons carve stone gutters and down spouts for the buttresses. This is one of the fun jobs for the sculptors. They often carve the downspouts to look like frightening creatures. They make the water drain out of the creatures' mouths. Some believe they will scare away evil spirits. The name gargoyle has become attached to these wild-looking, carved downspouts because they gargle when it rains.

The ceilings are an amazing bit of engineering. After the walls are in place, wooden models of the roof arches are made and hoisted up into position. Cut stones are laid on the wooden ribs and mortared into place on the arches. Then a layer of wood is put in to join the arches. The wood is covered with mortar and stones and finally with concrete. When the concrete hardens, the wood is removed and voila- a stone roof.

Most new workers think they would like to work on the stained glass windows. It is an interesting process. The glass is made from beechwood ash and washed sand that is melted. The vivid colors come from adding different metals to the molten glass. Glass blowers scoop out a ball of molten glass, blow it up like a balloon, then spin it on the end until it is a flat disc. The disc, after being allowed to cool, is cut into the pieces needed. The pieces are joined together with lead. Windows as high as 60 feet can be made using reinforcing bars. The windows of our cathedrals, like many cathedral windows, will show different scenes from the Bible. Almost no one owns a Bible, and many commoners couldn't read it anyway. In the windows, we can tell Bible stories in pictures. One of my favorite window designs is the large, round window, known as a Rose window. You can always tell a great Gothic cathedral by its great heights, flying buttresses, and the rose window of stained glass.

Now that you know so much about Gothic architecture, you should be ready to choose which craftsman you want to be apprenticed to.

Cathedrals in Europe
Project 3

Stained Glass Window

Photocopy this window design of the Madonna and Child (Bourges Cathedral c. 1220) on transparency film and then color with permanent markers.

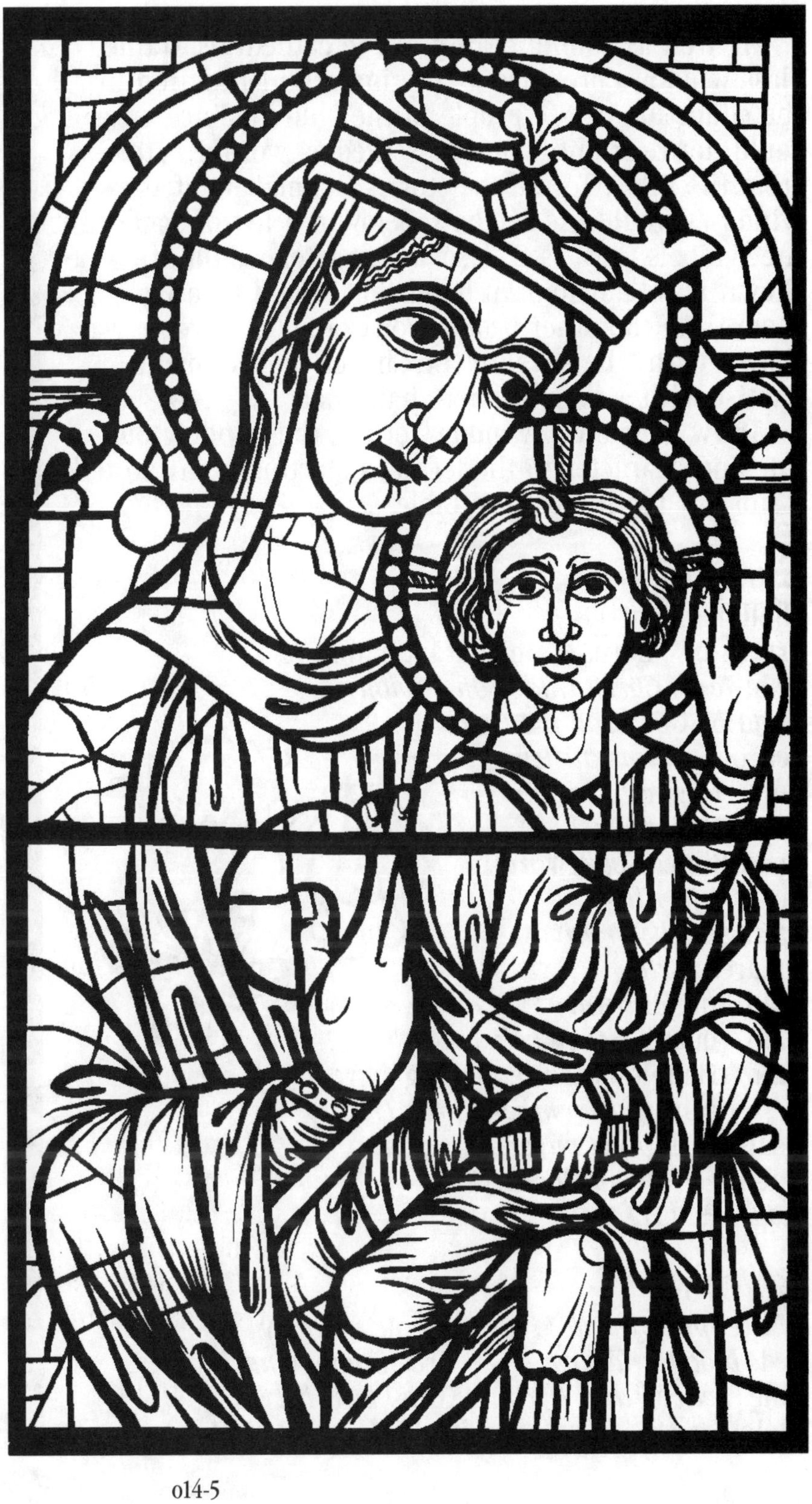

Cathedrals in Europe
Project 3, Page 2

Do-It-Yourself Stained Glass Window

As well as adding beauty to the cathedrals, stained glass windows provided a very important function in the education of the people in the church. Since most could not read, the windows served as wordless stories from the Bible. To tell the stories the makers of the windows would use symbols. Below is a list of some of the symbols they used. Also, a character would often be shown with a symbol in hand that would identify them from the other people. For example, St. Peter was shown with "the keys" to the Church and John the Baptist with a rough camel's hair coat.

Draw your own "window" or use the window outline and character to the left as a starting point, to tell a story or truth from the Bible.

Symbols—

Shell: baptism
Crown of Thorns/Lamb/Grape vines: *Jesus*
Fish: *Jesus Christ God's Son Saviour*
Hand of God: *God the Father*
Peacock: *immortality*
Butterfly: *resurrection*
Dove: *Holy Spirit*
Open Bible: *God's Word*
Circle: *eternity*
Triangle: *the Trinity*
Square: *earth*
Halo/round: *saint*
Halo/square: *living believer*
Halo/triangle or circle, having a cross within it: *a member of the Trinity*
Noah's Ark: *the Church*
Anchor: *Hope in Christ*
Stag: *(Ps 42:1) piety*

Colors—

White: *purity and joy*
Red: *blood and love*
Blue: *heaven and truth*
Violet: *truth*
Purple: *royalty*
Green: *hope and life*
Gray: *humility*
Gold: *heavenly light*

Cathedrals in Europe

Test

1. What is the approximate date of cathedrals in Europe?

2. What is the seat of authority for a bishop?

3. What is a diocese?

4. What is usually true about a cathedral?

5. What building style was derived from Rome?

6. What new building style came out of Northern Europe?

7. List three characteristics of the church above, in question number six.

Cathedrals in Europe
Test, Page 2

8. How long did many men work on the cathedrals?

9. Where is the largest cathedral?

Review

1. What is the name of the period when the barbarians and Vikings lived?

2. In 200 B.C. the Old Testament was translated from Hebrew into what known language?
   What is this translation of the Bible known as?

3. Why did the New Testament come to us in Greek?

4. Why did monasteries become centers of learning?

5. List in chronological order all the events studied to date.
   Next to each place the appropriate date.

The Crusades
Worksheet

1. What were the approximate dates of the Crusades?

2. What is the meaning of *Deus Vult! Deus Vult*?

3. Who was intent on motivating the people to reclaim Jerusalem from the Muslims?

4. List the five reasons that people were willing to go on the Crusades?

5. What happened on the First Crusade?

6. What happened on the Second Crusade?

THE CRUSADES

Worksheet, Page 2

7. What was the cause of and what occurred on the Third Crusade?

8. How many Crusades were there? Which ones met with success?

9. Which was the most tragic of all the Crusades? What was the outcome of this Crusade?

10. Why did the idea of the Crusades finally die out?

THE CRUSADES

Project

Postcard From the Holy Lands

Choose one of the Crusades to research further. Pretend you are a knight on that crusade and write a postcard home. Describe where you are, who the leaders are, what your objective is, tell if you have been successful, and when you will return home. Draw a picture on the front of your postcard or use the following graphics.

Shown left to right: Crusaders under siege, Fortified city in the Holy Land, Guarded Tower, and Jerusalem

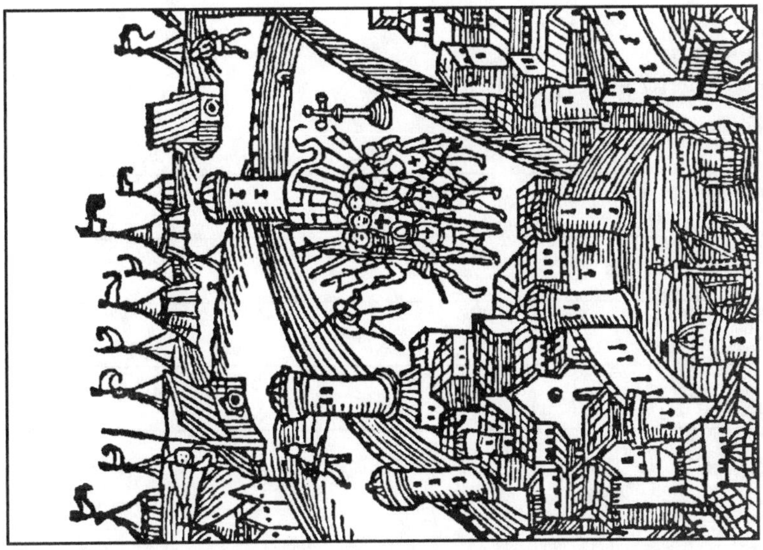

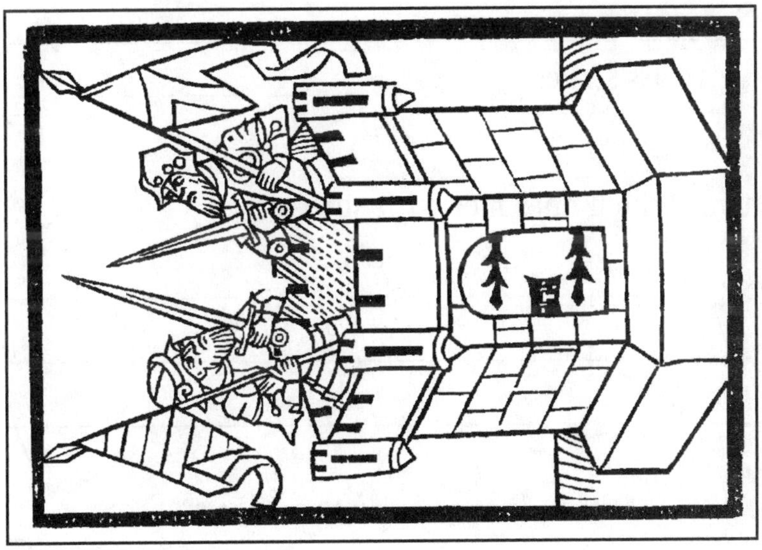

THE CRUSADES
Test

1. What were the approximate dates of the Crusades?

____

____

2. What is the meaning of *Deus Vult! Deus Vult?*

____

____

3. Pope Urban was intent on motivating the people to reclaim ________________ from the Muslims.

4. List five reasons that people were willing to go on the Crusades.

____

____

____

____

____

5. What occurred on the first Crusade?

____

____

6. The Second Crusade was launched to give assistance to the ________________ in Jerusalem.

7. In total, how many Crusades were there? Which ones met with success?

____

____

____

The Crusades

Test, Page 2

8. Which was the most tragic of all the Crusades? What was the outcome of this Crusade?

9. Why did the idea of the Crusades finally die out?

Review

1. What is the feudal system?

2. What two Churches resulted from the East-West Schism?

3. Over what kingdom did Alfred the Great rule?

4. What is the Koran?

5. List in chronological order those events studied to date. Next to each, place the approximate date.

St. Francis of Assisi
Worksheet

1. In what year and where was St. Francis born?

2. What was the occupation of St. Francis' father?

3. What caused St. Francis' conversion?

4. What command of Christ did St. Francis try to follow literally?

5. What were his followers called and how did they live?

6. When did Pope Honorius officially recognize the community?

   As what did they become known?

7. What did St. Francis require of his monks?

ST. FRANCIS OF ASSISI

Worksheet, Page 2

8. St. Francis loved __________ and is said to have preached even to the ____________ and ___________.

9. To what foreign country did St. Francis travel to preach?

____

____

____

St. Francis of Assisi
Project

Prayers of St. Francis

Read and discuss the following prayers of St. Francis....

St. Francis of Assisi's prayer in praise of God given to Brother Leo:

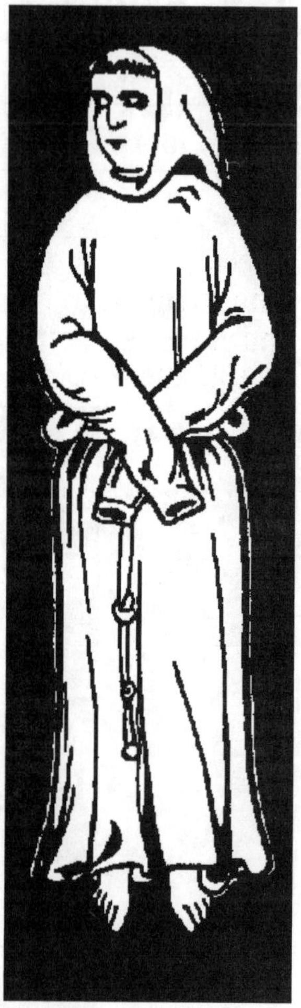

You are holy, Lord, the only God,
and Your deeds are wonderful.
You are strong.
You are great.
You are the Most High.
You are Almighty.
You, Holy Father are King of heaven and earth.
You are Three and One, Lord God, all Good.
You are Good, all Good, supreme Good,
Lord God, living and true.
You are love. You are wisdom.
You are humility. You are endurance.
You are rest. You are peace.
You are joy and gladness.
You are justice and moderation.
You are all our riches, and You suffice for us.
You are beauty.
You are gentleness.
You are our protector.
You are our guardian and defender.
You are our courage. You are our haven and our hope.
You are our faith, our great consolation.
You are our eternal life, Great and Wonderful Lord,
God Almighty, Merciful Saviour.

St. Francis of Assisi

Project, Page 2

Canticle of Brother Sun and Sister Moon of St. Francis of Assisi:

Most High, all powerful, all good Lord,
All praise is Yours, all glory, all honour and all blessings.
To you alone, Most High, do they belong,
and no mortal lips are worthy to pronounce Your Name.

Praised be You my Lord with all Your creatures,
especially Sir Brother Sun,
Who is the day through whom You give us light.
And he is beautiful and radiant with great splendour,
Of You Most High, he bears the likeness.

Praised be You, my Lord, through Sister Moon and the stars,
In the heavens you have made them bright, precious and fair.

Praised be You, my Lord, through Brothers Wind and Air,
And fair and stormy, all weather's moods,
by which You cherish all that You have made.

Praised be You my Lord through Sister Water,
So useful, humble, precious and pure.

St. Francis of Assisi

Test

1. What are the dates of St. Francis of Assisi?

2. Where was St. Francis born? What did his father do for a living?

3. What did God use in St. Francis' life to bring him to conversion?

4. What command of Christ did St. Francis try to literally follow?

5. What monastic order was named after him?

6. How did those in the order treat the poor?

7. What was an unusual fact about St. Francis' preaching?

8. In what other country did St. Francis preach?

St. Francis of Assisi

Test, Page 2

Review

1. What is the name of the seat of authority for a bishop?

2. How many crusades were there in total?

3. Name the three vows the Benedictine monks took?

4. How did Justinian the Great try to eliminate the remains of paganism?

5. List in chronological order all the cards studied to date.

The Magna Carta
Worksheet

1. What was the date of the Magna Carta?

____

____

2. Who became king of England when Richard the Lionhearted died? What did the people think of him?

____

____

____

3. What are two reasons that the English subjects rebelled against the king in question two?

____

____

4. What was the Magna Carta and when was it signed?

____

____

5. List three guarantees in the Magna Carta? To whom were they guaranteed?

____

____

____

6. The Magna Carta did much to establish ____________ ____________ as we know them ____________.

The Magna Carta

Project

Reading and Letter to the Pope

Less than two hundred years after the reign of William the Conqueror one of his descendants, King John, sat upon the throne of England. He was an exceedingly bad ruler. He stole, he told lies, and he put innocent people in prison. If he wanted money, he simply demanded it of any persons who had it, and if they refused to give it, he did not hesitate to torture them till they yielded. Men who had committed crime and deserved to be punished he would set free if they could raise enough money to make him a present. If two men disagreed, and brought their difficulty before him for trial, he would decide in favor of the one who had made him the larger gift. Sometimes, for some very small offense, he would demand money of a poor man who had only a horse and cart with which to earn his living, and if the man had no friends to bribe the king, his horse and cart were sold to help fit the royal treasury. King John was even believed to have murdered a nephew, the young Prince Arthur, who had a claim to the throne.

John ruled not only England, but also the duchy of Normandy, which had descended to him from William the Conqueror. As Normandy was a fief of France, Philip, King of France, called upon his vassal John, to account for the death of the prince. John refused to appear. Then Philip took away nearly all his French possessions. That loss made his income much smaller. Moreover, the cost of carrying on the government had increased. There was, then, some reason for his constant need of money, even though there was so little excuse for his manner of obtaining it.

When the archbishop of Canterbury died, there was a dispute about who should succeed him. The pope was appealed to, and he bade the monks of Canterbury name a good, upright man named Stephen Langton to take his place. This choice did not please the king, therefore he seized the monastery and its revenues and banished the monks. For six years John resisted the pope and refused to allow Langton to become archbishop. Finally he became afraid that he was going to die, and then he yielded most meekly. He even went to Langton to beg for absolution, or the pardon of the church. "When you promise to obey the laws of the land to treat your people justly, I will absolve you," replied the archbishop.

The Magna Carta
Project, Page 2

John was always ready to make a promise, but he never kept it unless convenient. He promised what the archbishop asked but, as might have been expected, he soon broke his word.

Now, next to the king, the barons were the most powerful men of the kingdom; but they did not know what to do. Fortunately, the archbishop knew. He called the baron together, and read them what had been the law of the land since a short time before the death of William the Conqueror. Then the barons understood what their rights were, and they took a solemn oath to defend them. "But we will wait for one year," they said. "The king may do better." They waited a year; then they waited till Christmas. The king had not improved, and the barons went to him and asked him to repeat the promises that he had made to the archbishop. John was insolent at first, but when he saw that the barons were in earnest he became very meek, and said that what they asked was important, to be sure, but also difficult, and he should need a little time before making the agreement. By Easter he should be able to satisfy them. The barons did not believe him, and so, when Easter came, they brought to the appointed place a large body of armed followers. After a while John sent to ask what it was the the barons insisted upon having. Then bold, dignified Stephen Langton read aloud to him from a parchment such articles as these: "A free man shall not be fined for a small offense, except in proportion to the gravity of the offense." "No free man shall be imprisioned or banished except by the lawful judgement of his equals, or by the law of the land."

John grew more and more angry as these were read. When the archbishop went on to read other articles declaring that the king must not take bribes or impose taxes without the consent of his council, or body of advisers, and finally read one giving the barons the right to elect twenty-five of their number to keep watch over him and seize his castles if he did not keep his promise. Then John went into a furious passion. "I will never grant liberties that would make me a slave," he declared.

Nevertheless, John had to yield. There was a famous green meadow with low hills on one side and the River Thames on the other. Its name of Runnymede, or Meadow of Council, was given it long before William the Conqueror landed in England, because there the Saxons used to hold their councils. To this meadow the barons and their army marched from London. Then out of a strong fortress that rose near at hand, and across the drawbridge that swung over the moat, rode the angry and sulky ruler of England. He signed the parchment, either in the meadow or on an island in the river, and then he went back to his palace. He gnashed his teeth, and shrieked, and rolled on the floor like a madman, but the barons were hard at work seeing to it that many copies of this parchment were made and sent over the land to be read aloud in the churches.

This parchment was the famous Magna Carta, or Great Charter, signed in 1215. The barons were then the most powerful men of the kingdom, and they saw to it that as long as he lived the king kept his word. About fifty years later, not only the barons but representatives of the towns were admitted to the council. This was the beginning of the English Parliament. Now, if a king ruled unjustly, he must account, not only to the barons, but to the whole people. From that day to this, no ruler had ever been able to remain on the throne of England who had not kept the promises that King John was obliged to make that June day at Runnymede.

The Magna Carta
Project 2, Page 3

After reading the previous information about King John and the Magna Carta, use this page to write a letter to the pope. Pretend that you are a baron who has suffered a terrible injustice at the hand of King John and you want this made known to the pope. Remember to include all the details of your story as the pope would be interested in these.

The Magna Carta
Test

1. Who was King John? What did the people think about him and why?

2. What disagreement did King John have with the pope?

3. What was the Magna Carta? On what date was it signed and by whom?

4. List three rights granted in the Magna Carta.

5. What influence has the Magna Carta had on us today?

THE MAGNA CARTA
Test, Page 2

Review

1. List the five reasons that people generally went on the crusades.

2. What are the four things that Muslims must do in their lifetime?

3. Name a book that St. Augustine wrote.

4. Who was at the top of the hierarchy in the feudal system?

5. List in chronological order all the events covered to date. Next to each place the appropriate date.

St. Thomas Aquinas
Worksheet

1. What are the dates for St. Thomas Aquinas?

____

____

2. Where was St. Dominic born and in what year?

____

____

3. Who was the leader of the Order of Preachers? What did they preach against?

____

____

4. What gifts did the Order of Preachers believe to be necessary in order to preach?

____

____

5. What was another name for the Order of Preachers?

____

____

6. Unlike some orders, the Order of Preachers was to move into the ___________ not to remain in _______________.

7. How did Thomas Aquinas' family feel when he joined the Dominican Order?

____

____

8. What was different about the way Aquinas sought to express Christian revelation?

____

____

____

St. Thomas Aquinas

Worksheet. Page 2

9. What is the title of Aquinas' greatest work and what does it entail?

____

____

____

____

____

10. Why was the above work never finished by Aquinas?

____

____

____

St. Thomas Aquinas

Project

Reading and Timeline

Because there are many dates and places involved in this reading, make a timeline of St. Thomas' life and follow his travels on a map. Define any words in bold.

Saint Thomas Aquinas, a Dominican theologian, was born Thomas d'Aquino, the son of a baron, in his family's castle at Roccasecca, central Italy, in 1224 or 1225.

At about the age of five, Thomas was placed by his parents in the Benedictine monastery at Monte Cassino. His uncle had been abbot of the monastery, and his family had similar ambitions for Thomas.

When Monte Cassino became the scene of a battle between papal and imperial troops, however, Thomas withdrew and enrolled at the University of Naples in November of 1239, where he stayed until April of 1244. There he came into contact with members of the Dominican order and, against the opposition of his family, became a Dominican friar in late April of 1244. Shortly after, in May of 1244, his family intervened forcibly, having him abducted and detained thereafter at Roccasecca. His mother tried to persuade Thomas for more than a year to give up his membership in the Dominican order. Failing to persuade him, Thomas was allowed to return to his order in July or August of 1245.

He then went north to study for his novitiate till 1248, after which he came under the guidance of Albert the Great at Cologne until the Fall of 1252, during which time (1250/51) he was ordained a priest. From the Fall of 1252 to the Spring of 1259, Thomas taught at the Dominican house of studies in Paris. It was during this time that he lectured on the *Sentences of Peter Lombard.* Between March 3 and June 17 of 1256, he was incepted as a master of theology, and was regent master in theology at Paris until 1259, during which time that he began his *Summa Contra Gentiles.*

1259 found Aquinas leaving Paris for Naples, where he stayed until the Fall of 1261 as head of the Dominican house of studies. From September of that same year to September of 1265, Aquinas was at Orvieto as a lector, where he completed the *Summa Contra Gentiles.* After a time at Rome in 1265 and Viterbo in 1267 (his great work, the *Summa Theologiae* was begun in 1266), he took up his second Parisian regency from January of 1269 to 1272. This was followed by his assignment to Naples in 1272 as regent of theology. December 6, 1273 saw the cessation of his writing and a dramatic increase in meditation and devotion.

While going north to attend the Council of Lyon, Thomas injured his head, fell ill and died in the Cistercian abbey of Fossanova on March 7, 1274.

St. Thomas Aquinas

Project, Page 2—Timeline

1220

1275

St. Thomas Aquinas

Project 2

Verbum Supernum

Verbum Supernum was written by St. Thomas Aquinas (1225-1274) in honor of Jesus in the Blessed Sacrament. In addition to Verbum Supernum, St. Thomas also wrote *Adoro Te Devote, Lauda Sion, Pange Lingua,* and *Sacris Solemniis* at the specific request of Pope Urban IV (1261-1264) for the then newly instituted Feast of Corpus Christi in 1264. It is used as a hymn at Lauds (Morning Prayer) on Corpus Christi. The last two stanzas are the text for the hymn *O Salutaris Hostia.* Following is the Latin version. The English translation is on the next page.

Verbum supernum prodiens,
Nec Patris linquens dexteram,
Ad opus suum exiens,
Venit ad vitae vesperam.

In mortem a discipulo,
Suis tradendus aemulis,
Prius in vitae ferculo,
Se tradidit discipulis.

Quibus sub bina specie,
Carnem dedit et sanguinem;
Ut duplicis substantiae
Totum cibaret hominem.

Se nascens dedit socium,
Convescens in edulium,
Se moriens in pretium,
Se regnans dat in praemium.

O salutaris hostia
Quae caeli pandis ostium
Bella premunt hostilia;
Da robur, fer auxilium.

Uni trinoque Domino
Sit sempiterna gloria:
Qui vitam sine termino
Nobis donet in patria. Amen.

St. Thomas Aquinas

Project 3

The Word of God

After reading the prayer on the left and studying the Latin version, the original language in which it was written, answer the questions on the right hand side of the page. They correspond with each verse.

The Word of God proceeding forth,
Yet not leaving the Father's side,
Went forth upon His work on earth
And reached at length life's eventide.

1. To whom does the "Word of God" refer?

By false disciple to be given
To foemen for His Blood athirst,
Himself, the living Bread from heaven,
He gave to His disciples first.

2. Name the false disciple.

To them He gave, in twofold kind,
His very Flesh, His very Blood:
Of twofold substance are we made,
And He would freely be our Food.

3. To what does giving flesh and blood refer?

By birth our fellowman was He,
Our Food while seated at the board;
He died, our ransomer to be;
He ever reigns, our great reward.

4. What is meant by "Our Food while seated at the board" mean?

O saving Victim, opening wide
The gate of heaven to all us below:
Our foes press on from every side;
Your aid supply, Your strength bestow.

5. To whom does "O saving Victim" refer?

To Your great Name be endless praise,
Immortal Godhead, One in Three!
O grant us endless length of days
With You in our true country. Amen.

6. What common name is given to the term "Three" as used here?

St. Thomas Aquinas
Test

1. What are the dates for St. Thomas Aquinas?

____

____

____

2. St. Dominic and his associates preached against ____________ and realized the need to use ________________ gifts in preaching.

3. When Thomas Aquinas joined the Dominican Order what did his family think?

____

____

____

4. What method did Aquinas use to express Christian revelation?

____

____

____

5. What is Aquinas' greatest work and what is it about?

____

____

____

6. What reason did Aquinas give for never finishing the above book?

____

____

____

____

St. Thomas Aquinas

Test, Page 2

Review

1. What four things did the Council of Chalcedon affirm?

2. What did Pelagius teach? Is this true?

3. Describe the barbarians.

4. For what is St. Jerome known?

5. List in chronological order all the events studied to date.

   Next to each one write the appropriate date.

Marco Polo
Worksheet

1. Who was the grandfather of Kublai Khan?

2. What kingdom did he inherit and where did he make his capital?

3. What was unique about the city of Venice?

4. What was the "Silk Road?"

5. What was the occupation of Marco Polo's father? How did this cause young Polo to come into contact with Kublai Khan?

6. What offer did Kublai Khan give to Marco Polo's father?

7. What is The Travels Of Marco Polo about?

Marco Polo
Project

In the days of Marco Polo, Venice was one of the richest and most powerful cities in Europe, and nowhere else, perhaps, could one see so many magnificent palaces and churches. Venice had shrewd merchants, daring sailors, and many ships, and it was chiefly through the enormous trade which she had built up with the East that she had grown so wealthy.

Among the most enterprising of the Venetian merchants were the father and uncle of Marco Polo. Indeed, when Marco was a little boy, he used to hear stories of his father and his uncle that must have seemed to him almost like fairy tales. "They went away from Venice to make a voyage to Constantinople," the little boy's friends said, "and in Constantinople they bought a great quantity of rich jewelry. We think they must have gone into the unknown countries of Asia to trade, perhaps even to China, where the great khan lives."

When the boy was about fourteen, his father came home, and then he had stories to tell indeed. He had gone far into Asia, had sold the jewelry brought from Constantinople, had been at the court of the great Kublai Khan, ruler of China, and now he and his brother had come back to Italy with a message from the khan to the pope. He showed the boy the khan's golden tablets which he had given to the brothers. The royal cipher was engraved upon them and a command that wherever in the khan's domain the brothers might go, his subjects should receive them with honor and should provide them with whatever they needed. The brothers were going back to China, and now the boy was happy, for his father promised that he might go with them.

Then they made the long, leisurely journey from Venice to Constantinople, and across Asia to China. They traveled through fertile valleys and sandy deserts, over stony mountains and through gloomy passes. They saw strange birds and fruits and peoples. They visited handsome cities, and lonely tribes that had no settled homes. It was a slow journey. In one place the sickness of the young Marco delayed them for many months. Sometimes they had to wait for company before they could venture through dangerous countries. Once they had to go far out of their way to avoid passing through a region where two tribes were waging war. At length they came within forty miles of the home of the great Kublai Khan, ruler of China. Here they were met by a large escort, sent out by the khan, and were brought into the city with every mark of honor that could be shown them.

The khan took a strong liking to the young Marco, and gave him a position in the royal household. The young man put on the Chinese dress, adopted the Chinese manners and customs, and learned the four languages that were most used in the country. The khan was delighted with him and often gave him a golden tablet and sent him off on a journey so that on his return be could describe to him the wonderful things that he had seen. Marco's father and uncle were also given positions in the khan's service, and by his generosity they soon became exceedingly wealthy.

China was not home, however, even after they had lived in that country for many years,

MARCO POLO
Project, Page 2

and they longed to see their own Venice. They begged the khan to allow them to return. "But why?" he asked. "It is a dangerous journey; you might lose your lives. Do you want money or jewels? I will give you twice as much as you now have; but I care for you too much to let you go away from me." Without the khan's tablets, the journey would be impossible; and the Polos began to fear they would never see their home again.

Some months before this the ruler of Persia had sent an embassy to beg that a granddaughter of the Great Khan might become his wife. The princess and a long suite of honor set off for Persia; but the way lay through a country that was at war, and they had to return. The Persian ambassadors, however, had been away from Persia three years, and they did not dare to remain longer at the Chinese court. Just then, Marco Polo arrived from a voyage to some of the islands off the coast. The idea occurred to the ambassadors that they might take ship and go by water to the Persian Gulf at less expense and with greater safety than by the overland way. They talked with the Polos, and found that they would be only too glad to go with them. Then they begged the khan to allow the three Venetians, who were experienced sailors, to escort them. The khan was not pleased, but he finally yielded. He gave the Polos his golden tablets, loaded them down with presents of jewels, and they and the ambassadors and the fair young princess sailed away with a fleet of fourteen vessels furnished with stores and provisions for two years. It was twenty-one months before they came to Persia. The Polos rested a year in the leisurely fashion of those days, then returned, not to China, but to Venice, having been absent twenty-four years.

THE COURT OF KUBLAI KHAN

At Venice there had been rumors long before that the famous travelers were dead. They were, of course, greatly changed, and they spoke Italian rather stiffly and queerly. It was hard to believe that these foreign looking men in their long, rough Tartar coats could be the members of the wealthy family of Polo. They had some trouble in getting possession of their own palace, and even after they had succeeded, many thought they were impostors. The story is told that to convince these doubting friends, they invited them to a magnificent banquet. After the feast, the coarse, threadbare coats were brought in and quickly ripped open. There rolled out such a store of rubies and emeralds and diamonds and sapphires as the bewildered guests had never seen. The whole room blazed and sparkled with them. For the sake of safety on the dangerous journey the Polos had brought their immense wealth in this form. Then the guests were convinced that the three men were not impostors, and they were treated with the utmost respect.

War broke out between Venice and Genoa, and Marco Polo was put in command of a warship. He was taken prisoner by the Genoese and it was while he was in prison that he dictated to a gentleman of Genoa the stories of his travels. All Genoa became interested, and their famous prisoner was soon set free. Copies of his book in manuscript w,-nt everywhere. Some doubted its truth, and when the author was on his deathbed, they begged him to take back the parts of it that they thought must be exaggerated. "There is no exaggeration in the book," he declared. "On the contrary, I have not told half the amazing things that I saw with my own eyes."

Chapter 17

OF THE QUANTITY OF GAME TAKEN AND SENT TO THE COURT DURING THE WINTER MONTHS

At the season when the Great Khan resides in the capital of Cathay, which is during the three months of December, January, and February, at which time the cold is excessive, he gives orders for general hunting parties to take place in all the countries within, forty days' journey of the court.

The governors of districts are required to send all sorts of game of the larger kind, such as wild boars, stags, fallow deer, roebucks, and bears, which are taken in the following manner:All persons possessed of land in the province repair to the places where these animals are to be found, and proceed to enclose them within a circle, when they are killed, partly with dogs, but chiefly by shooting them with arrows. Such of them as are intended for his Majesty's use are first gutted and then forwarded on carriages, in large quantities, by those who reside within thirty stages of the capital. Those, in fact, who are at the distance of forty stages, do not, on account of the length of the journey, send the carcases, but only the skins, some dressed and others raw, to be made use of for the service of the army as his Majesty may judge proper.

Chapter 18

OF LEOPARDS AND LYNXES USED FOR HUNTING DEER OF LIONS HABITUATED TO THE CHASE OF VARIOUS ANIMALS AND OF EAGLES TAUGHT TO SEIZE WOLVES

The Great Khan has many leopards and lynxes kept for the purpose of chasing deer, and also many lions which are larger than the Babylonian lions, have good skins and of a handsome colorbeing streaked on the sides, with white, black, and red stripes. They are active in seizing boars, wild oxen and asses, bears, stags, roebucks, and other beasts that are the objects of sport. It is an admirable sight, when the lion is let loose in pursuit of the animal, to observe the savage eagerness and speed with which he overtakes it. His Majesty has them conveyed for this purpose, in cages placed upon cars, and along with them is

Marco Polo
Project, Page 4

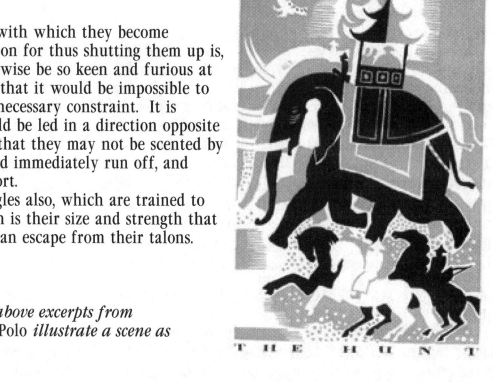

confined a little dog, with which they become familiarized. The reason for thus shutting them up is, that they would otherwise be so keen and furious at the sight of the game that it would be impossible to keep them under the necessary constraint. It is proper that they should be led in a direction opposite to the wind, in order that they may not be scented by the game, which would immediately run off, and offer no chance of sport.

His Majesty has eagles also, which are trained to catch wolves, and such is their size and strength that none, however large, can escape from their talons.

After reading the above excerpts from The Travels of Marco Polo *illustrate a scene as described by Polo.*

Middle Ages, Reformation and Renaissance
Project 2

The Nomads of the Heartland and the Mongol Empire

I

When Marco Polo traveled to China, he found it to be ruled by the Mongols, a group of people that had originally been nomadic wanderers. The Mongols were not the first nomads from Central Asia to have a dramatic impact on world history, however. In fact, periodic invasions out of Central Asia is one of the most important themes of world history. Why did it occur over and over again. First, it must be noted that the lifestyle of the nomads made them natural warriors. They practically lived on horseback and learned to hunt with the bow from their horses from an early age. Thus, two of the most difficult skills of warfare, riding and shooting, were just a part of life for them. Settled civilizations, where most of the people were farmers or artisans didn't have this advantage. Second, the nomads inhabited the "heartland" of Eurasia. If you look on a map, you will notice that Europe and Asia are really just one big landmass and that in its center are thousands and thousands of miles of open plains, called "steppes", which are perfect for the nomads. All of the great civilizations of Europe and Asia where located around the "rim" of this "heartland". Any time any of the great civilizations grew weak, the nomads could, if they had a strong leader to organize them, sweep down and pillage, conquer and, perhaps even found a great empire.

II

More than a thousand years before the Mongols, the Scythians, a fierce tribe that lived north of Persia and of the Black Sea, had been a constant menace to the great Persian Empire. Aside from the Greeks, they seemed to be the only people the really gave the Persians much difficulty in warfare. Five hundred years later, the Huns, driven out by the Han empire of China, had attacked the barbarian tribes of eastern Europe, causing many of them, in turn, to attack the declining Roman Empire. Later, under their great leader Attila, they had terrorized the empire themselves. The Avars and the Magyars, the ancestors of the modern Hungarians, terrorized early Medieval Europe. Around 1000 AD, a group called the Turks destroyed the Islamic Empire and set up one of their own. When they became Muslims themselves, their persecution of Christian pilgrims was one of the causes of the crusades. Though the Mongols had defeated them, they would later form another empire, called the Ottoman Empire which would eventually conquer all of the Byzantine empire, large parts of the Latin West and even besiege Vienna several times! Though the Mongol Empire was not the first, or even the last, great empire founded by steppe nomads, it was probably the greatest. When its founder, Genghis Kahn, died, he had created the largest empire ever created in the lifetime of one man! When Marco Polo reached China, Genghis' grandson, Kublai Kahn, was in charge. Under Kublai, the empire reached its high point. When he died, it gradually began to break up into various pieces.

Vocabulary

1. *originally:*
2. *nomadic:*
3. *inhabited:*
4. *menace:*
5. *besiege:*
6. heartland:

Key Word Outline

I

1
2
3
4
5
6
7

8 ______________________________

9 ______________________________

10 ______________________________

11 ______________________________

12 ______________________________

II ______________________________

1 ______________________________

2 ______________________________

3 ______________________________

4 ______________________________

5 ______________________________

6 ______________________________

7 ______________________________

8 ______________________________

9 ______________________________

10 ______________________________

11 ______________________________

12 ______________________________

13 ______________________________

Project 2, Page 4

Answers

Vocabulary

1. *originally:* in the beginning
2. *nomadic:* with no permanent home
3. *inhabited:* populated
4. *menace:* threat
5. *besiege:* surround and attack a heavily fortified place
6. *heartland:* area that occupies the center of a continent

Key Word Outline

I.The Nomads and the Heartland
1.Marco Polo, found, Mongols
2.Not, first, impact
3.Invasions, important, themes
4.Why ?
5.First, natural, warriors
6.Lived, horseback, hunt
7.Difficult, part, life
8.Settled, didn't, advantage
9.Second, inhabited, "heartland"
10.Notice, center, "steppes"
11.Civilizations, located, rim
12.Nomads, leader, conquer

II.The Nomads' Impact on History
1.Scythians, menace, Persia
2.Only, gave, difficulty
3.Later, Huns, driven
4.Terrorized, empire, themselves
5.Ancestors, Hungarians, Medieval
6.1000 AD, Turks, empire
7.Persecution, causes, Crusades
8.Ottomans, conquer, besiege
9.Mongol, greatest
10.Genghis Kahn, created, lifetime
11.Marco Polo, Kublai, in charge
12.Reached, high, point
13.Died, break up

Marco Polo
Test

Write a paragraph describing the life of Marco Polo. Include as many details as possible.

MARCO POLO
Test, Page 2

Review

1. What was the Magna Carta?

2. What were the five reasons that people went on the Crusades?

3. Describe the hierarchy in the feudal system.

4. What split occurred because of the East-West Schism?

5. List in chronological order all the events studied to date.

   Next to each one list the appropriate date.

THE HUNDRED YEARS WAR, THE BLACK DEATH, AND JOAN OF ARC

Worksheet

1. Who started the Hundred Years War? When did it begin and end?

2. What caused the Hundred Years War to begin?

3. Who won the Hundred Years War?

4. What was the Black Death? Approximately how many people died?

5. Who was Joan of Arc and what did she claim?

6. What disguise did she use to lead the French in their conquest of Orleans?

7. How did Joan of Arc die?

The Hundred Years War, The Black Death, and Joan of Arc

Project

Edward the Black Prince

For a number of years England carried on a war with Scotland which ended with the battle of Bannockburn. This war would not have lasted so long if the French had not been afraid that England would become stronger than they, and therefore had done a great deal to help Scotland. This did not make the English feel very friendly toward the French. Moreover, Edward III, King of England, claimed the French crown, because of his relationship to the late King of France. The result was a struggle which lasted more than a century, and which is, therefore, called the Hundred Years' War. It was in the early part if this war that the famous battles of Crecy and Poitiers were fought which showed the English yeomen, that is, common people, that they could defend themselves with their bows and arrows, and need not depend upon the knights for protection. At the battle of Crecy, King Edward shared the command with his son, called the Black Prince from the color of his armor. In the course of the battle, a messenger came galloping up to the king and told him that his son was in great danger. "If the Frenchmen increase, your son will have too much to do," he said. The king asked, "Is my son dead, unhorsed, or so badly wounded that he cannot support himself?" "No, sir," answered the messenger, "but he is in so hot an engagement that he has great need of your help. "The king must have longed to go to his son, but he replied firmly, "Tell those who sent you not to send again for me so long as my son has life; and say I command them to let the boy win his spurs; for I am determined, if it please God, that all the glory and honor of the day shall be given to him and to those into whose care I have entrusted him." The brave prince did win his spurs, that is, performed deeds which proved him worthy of knighthood; and when the battle was over the king kissed him and said, "You are worthy to be a sovereign."

After this battle, the English pressed on to besiege Calais. One whole year the French refused to yield, and they would not give up the town until they were starving. Edward was so angry at the long resistance that he told the people of Calais there was only one way in which they could look for any mercy from him. If six of their principal men would come to him in their shirts, bareheaded, barefooted, and with ropes about their necks, he would be merciful to the others.

The richest man in the town offered himself first, and five others followed. "Take them away and hang them," commanded King Edward; but his wife Philippa fell upon her knees before him and said, "Since I crossed the sea with great danger to see you, I have never asked you one favor. Now I most humbly ask for the sake of the Son of the Blessed Mary, and for your love to me that you be merciful to these six men." The king replied, "Ah, lady, I wish you had been anywhere else than here, but I cannot refuse you. Do as you please with them." The queen feasted them, and gave them clothes and sent them back safely to their homes. This story was told by Queen Philippa's secretary, a man named Froissart.

Froissart tells another story about the courtesy and modesty of the Black Prince after the French king had been taken prisoner at the battle of Poitiers. Here it is just as the old chronicler told it: "The Prince of Wales gave a supper in his pavilion to the king of France and to the greater part of the princes and barons who were prisoners. The prince seated the king of France and his son, the Lord Philip, at an elevated and well covered table. With them were Sir James de Bourbon, the Lord John d'Artois, the earls of Tancarville, of Estampes, of Dammartin, of Graville, and the lord of Partenay. The other knights and squires were placed at different tables. The prince himself served the king's table as well as the others with every mark of humility, and would not sit down at it, in spite of all his entreaties for him so to do, saying that he was not worthy of such an honor nor did it appertain to him to seat himself at the table of so great a king, or of so valiant a man as he had shown himself by his actions that day. He added, also, with a noble air, 'Dear sir, do not make a poor meal because the Almighty God has not gratified your wishes in the event of this day; for be assured that my lord and father will show every honor and friendship in his power, and will arrange your ransom so reasonably that you will henceforth always remain friends. In my opinion, you have cause to be glad that the success of this battle did not turn out asyou desired; for you have this day acquired such high renown for prowess that you have surpassed all the best knights on your side. I do not, dear sir, say this to flatter you, for all those of our side who have seen and observed the actions of each party have unanimously allowed this to be your due, and decree you the prize and garland for it.' At the end of this speech there were murmurs of praise heard from every one. And the French said the prince had spoken nobly and truly; and that he would be one of the most gallant princes in Christendom if God should grant him life to pursue his career of glory."

The Black Prince never came to the throne, for he died one year before his father. If he had lived, his courage and gentleness and kindly tact might have prevented some of the troubles that England had to meet later.

The Black Death

The emancipation of the peasantry was hastened, strangely enough, as a result of perhaps the most terrible calamity that has ever affected mankind. About the middle of the fourteenth century a pestilence of Asiatic origin, now known to have been the bubonic plague, reached the West. The Black Death, so called because among its symptoms were dark patches all over the body, moved steadily across Europe. It caused inflammatory boils and tumors of the glands. The black spots on the skin were actually putrid decompositions of the skin. The way for its ravages had been prepared by the unhealthy conditions of ventilation and drainage in the towns and villages.

The precise days of its breakouts in individual towns are not known, but they were not simultaneous. In Florence, the disease appeared early in April of 1347. In Cesena it was the first of June, and many other places got it throughout that whole year. After it had passed through all of France and Germany, it made no further ravages and did not break out until August of 1348 in England. There it advanced so gradually that it did not reach London for three months. The northern kingdoms were not affected until 1349. Sweden was attacked in November as was Poland. In Russia, the plague did not appear until 1351, three years after it had broken out in Avignon, and two years after Constantinople was infected.

The pestilence in England, as in other countries, caused a great scarcity of labor. For want of hands to bring in the harvest, crops rotted on the ground. Sheep and cattle, with no one to care for them, strayed through the deserted fields. The free peasants who survived demanded and received higher wages. Even the serfs, whose labor was sorely needed, found themselves in a better position. This lead to their emancipation and the end of serfdom.

Joan of Arc

The Hundred Year's War dragged on, and at length the French became so discouraged that they agreed that when their king should die they would accept an English ruler. At the death of their sovereign, the king of England was a little boy. His guardians tried to enforce his claims, and they invaded France. They succeeded in getting possession of northern France, but they could not press any farther into the country unless they could capture the city of Orleans. They besieged it; it grew weaker and weaker, and all saw that it must soon fall into their hands.

The French were good soldiers, but they needed a leader. They were fighting for the rights of the young Prince Charles, but it did not seem to enter his mind that there was

anything for him to do except to wear the crown after they had captured it for him. At length word came to him that a young peasant girl named Joan of Arc insisted upon seeing him. She declared that she had seen visions of angels and had heard voices bidding her raise the siege of Orleans and conduct him to Rheims to be crowned.

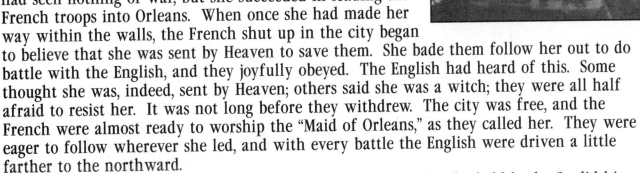

She was brought before the prince, but he had dressed himself more plainly than his courtiers to see if she would recognize him. She looked about her a moments, then knelt before him. "I am not the king," said Charles. "Noble prince, you and no one else, are the king," Joan responded; and she told him of the voices that she had heard. Now, there was an old saying in France that someday the country would be saved by a maiden, and both king and courtiers became interested. They gave her some light armor, all white and shining, and set her upon a great white charger with a sword in her hand. Her banner was a standard of pure white, and on it was a picture of two angels bearing lilies and one of God holding up the world. The French were wild with enthusiasm. They fell down before her, and those who could come near enough to touch her armor or even her horse's hoofs thought themselves fortunate. Joan was only seventeen, and she had seen nothing of war, but she succeeded in leading the French troops into Orleans. When once she had made her way within the walls, the French shut up in the city began to believe that she was sent by Heaven to save them. She bade them follow her out to do battle with the English, and they joyfully obeyed. The English had heard of this. Some thought she was, indeed, sent by Heaven; others said she was a witch; they were all half afraid to resist her. It was not long before they withdrew. The city was free, and the French were almost ready to worship the "Maid of Orleans," as they called her. They were eager to follow wherever she led, and with every battle the English were driven a little farther to the northward.

Joan now urged Charles to go to Rheims to be crowned, but he held back. So did his brave old generals. "It is folly," they said, "to try to make our way through a country where the English are still in power. Let us first drive them from Normandy and from Paris. Let the coronation wait until we have possession of our capital." Still Joan begged Charles to go, and at length he yielded. There was much fighting on the way, but the French were victorious, and Joan led her king to Rheims. He was crowned in the cathedral, and she stood near him, the white war banner in her hand.

The Hundred Years War, The Black Death, and Joan of Arc

Project, Page 5

Then Joan prayed to be allowed to go home, but Charles would not think of giving her up. His people had come to believe that they would win a victory wherever she led; they even fancied that they saw fire flashing around her standard. "I work no miracles," she declared. "Do not kiss my clothes or armor. I am nothing but the instrument that God uses." She continued to lead the army, but at length she was captured and fell into the hands of the English. They fired cannons and sang the Te Deum in the churches and rejoiced as if they had conquered the whole kingdom of France.

Joan was kept in prison for a year, loaded with irons and chained to a pillar. She was tried for witchcraft and was condemned and sentenced to be burned. Charles, to whom she had given a kingdom, made no effort to save her. A stake was set up in the market place of Rouen. To this she was bound, and sticks were heaped up around it. "Let me die with the cross in my hands," she pleaded; but no one paid any attention to her request, until at length an English soldier tied two sticks together in the form of a cross and gave it to her. She kissed it and laid it upon her heart. Then a brave and kindly monk ventured to bring her the altar cross from a church near at hand. The flames rose around her. Those who stood near heard her say, "Jesus! Jesus!" and soon her sufferings ended. Her ashes were thrown into the Seine, but today on the spot where she died a noble statue stands in her honor.

After reading the three stories, write a children's book about England and France during the years of 1337 - 1453. Be sure to include information on The Hundred Years War, The Black Death and Joan of Arc. Make sure you have illustrations and explanations.

The Hundred Years War, The Black Death, and Joan of Arc

Project, Page 6

Use the template below for your book.

The Hundred Years War, The Black Death, and Joan of Arc

Project 2

During tournament times and when knights went into battle, many carried banners to display their coat of arms or other ideas that they wanted to convey. It is said that Joan of Arc went into battle with a banner of pure white, and on it a picture of two angels bearing lilies and the other one of God holding up the world.

Enlarge the pattern shown and either cut out of paper of white fabric (old sheets work very well). Then allow your students to design their own banner to illustrate something about themselves. Remember, a knight's coat of arms told people who he was when his face was covered with armor. Attach the completed banner to a dowel or a stick.

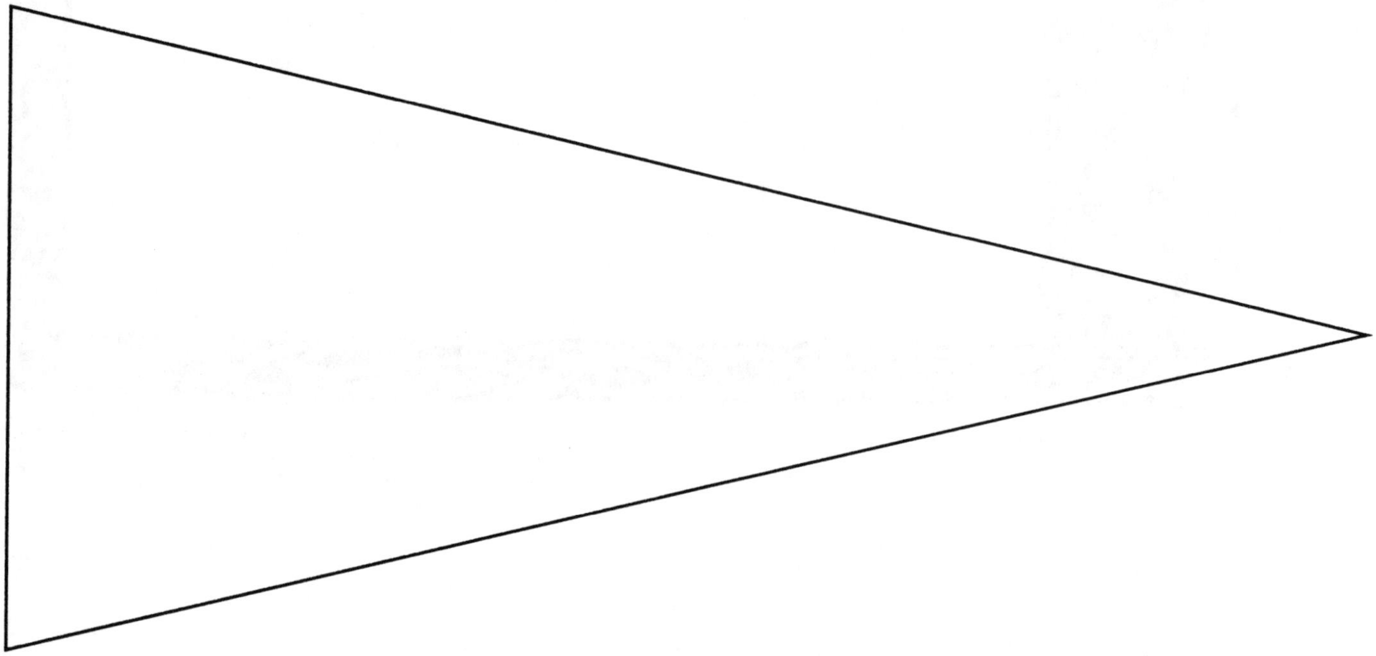

The Hundred Years War, The Black Death, and Joan of Arc

Test

1. How did the Hundred Year War begin and in what year?

____

____

2. Where and when was the final battle fought? Who won the war?

____

____

3. Describe the Black Death? Approximately how many people died from it?

____

____

4. Where was Joan of Arc born? What was her upbringing?

____

____

5. What did Joan of Arc claim to have seen?

____

____

6. What was the name of the king whose coronation she ensured?

____

____

7. How did she dress when she went into battle?

____

____

8. How did Joan of Arc die?

____

____

The Hundred Years War, The Black Death, and Joan of Arc

Test, Page 2

1. Who was St. Francis of Assisi? What did he preach?

____

____

____

2. What three things did Charlemagne wish to establish in his Empire?

____

____

____

3. Who was the founder of Islam?

____

____

____

4. What four things must Muslims do during their lifetime?

____

____

____

5. List in chronological order all the events studied to date.

   Next to each write the appropriate date.

____

____

____

____

____

____

THE GREAT PAPAL SCHISM
Worksheet

1. What were the dates for the Great Papal Schism?

____

____

2. Who succeeded in bringing the papacy back from France to Rome after seventy years?

____

____

3. Why did the cardinals reject the election of Urban VI?

____

____

4. Why did Urban VI move to Avigon? What did this cause?

____

____

5. Who was elected by the Council of Constance to be the first pope in forty years to rule the entire Latin Church ending the schism?

____

____

6. The council also established the pope as a ________________ ruler with __________________ authority, rather than an absolute ________________.

7. As the difficulties of the schism faded into the past, what happened to papal authority?

____

____

____

____

The Great Papal Schism
Project

Vocabulary Excercise

Using a Dictionary define the following terms.

1. papacy:
2. cardinal (in reference to the church):
3. compromise:
4. claimant:
5. pope:
6. monarch:
7. schism:

THE GREAT PAPAL SCHISM
Project 2

Reading

The following reading is intended for teachers only because it may be a bit difficult for most grammar school students to comprehend. However, if you are using the reading with older students (say 6th grade and up) you should consider having them read it, too.

The Papal Power

INTRODUCTION

Some of the influences that led to the supremacy of the Roman bishop in Europe have already been described. We have seen that the pope in the course of time became not only a spiritual ruler, but a secular prince, and that he claimed supremacy over kings and emperors. His supremacy in religious matters was early admitted in western Europe. It now remains to see how far he succeeded in gaining temporal power. Italy, it will be remembered, was, in theory at least, a part of the Holy Roman Empire of the German Nation. The relations of the pope to the emperor became a matter of great importance, and during a large portion of the Middle Ages there was a struggle for supremacy between the two. The imperial party held that the emperor, as representing the highest civil authority in the world, was superior to the pope, while the papal party held that the pope, as the vicar of God on earth, was above all earthly rulers.

THE CHOICE OF POPES

Down to nearly the middle of the twelfth century there had been much confusion in regard to the system of papal elections. Kings and nobles had often interfered in the choice of popes and caused men to be chosen merely because they were likely to favor their interests. On many occasions the German emperors had acted as if the Holy See were an office at their own disposal, and the result had been the degradation of the papacy and its subjection to the emperor.

REFORM OF CHURCH DISCIPLINE

A young monk named Hildebrand (afterward Gregory VII), who had been educated at the Abbey of Cluny in France, came to Rome on the occasion of a papal election in 1044, and saw the abuses of the system. He thought that the only way to secure peace and honesty in papal elections was to transfer the choice of the pope to the clergy. In 1048 he came to Rome and soon rose to the rank of Cardinal. For many years, although he was not pope himself, he really controlled the policy of the papacy, and worked steadily to make the Church pure within and independent of all earthly power. To accomplish these things, he thought it necessary to change the method of electing popes, to take action against the vices of the clergy, and to make ecclesiastics more completely subject to the Holy See. He did his best to uproot the evil known as simony, which consists in the buying and selling of appointments to office in the Church, for this practice tends to make the clergy the mere tools of the civil ruler. Another matter on which he insisted was the celibacy of priests, for he held their marriage to be in violation of the laws of the Church, He succeeded in advancing these reforms, and the effect of his efforts greatly increased the power of the Church.

Reform of Papal Elections

In the matter of the election of popes he was equally successful. On the death of Pope Victor II, Hildebrand saw a chance for introducing his proposed reform, for the emperor on the German throne, Henry IV, was then a mere child. The new pope was chosen by the Roman clergy and people, and quite independently of the choice of the emperor. In 1059 the new method of papal elections was formally decreed, and thenceforth the choice of the popes was made by a small assembly of the high dignitaries of the Roman Catholic Church called the Sacred College of Cardinals.

Gregory VII

Hildebrand was elected pope in 1073 under the title of Gregory VII, and though chosen unanimously, accepted the office unwillingly, for he knew what difficulties awaited him. In the first year of his pontificate he issued decrees against the marriage of priests and the purchase of the Church offices. This caused a great storm among the clergy, but in the end the law of celibacy prevailed. He tried also to carry out the other reform which he had at heart, namely the removal of the clergy from subjection to the state. To do this it was necessary to wrest powers from the emperor powers which both he and his predecessors had constantly exercised.

Investiture

The question was whether the civil ruler could grant Church offices at will. The bestowal upon a candidate of the symbols of office was called *investiture*, and the struggle between the emperor and the pope is sometimes known as the War of Investitures. It had become the custom for the feudal lords to bestow on the bishops and abbots the symbols of their office without distinguishing between their secular and their ecclesiastical rights. Thus the feudal lord appeared to be the source of spiritual power. The emperor claimed this as a right and had frequently practiced it.

Contest between Gregory and Henry IV

In 1075 Gregory issued a decree forbidding any one to receive a Church office from a lay power. To this the emperor refused to submit, and, after bringing to a close a war which he was waging with the Saxons, he went on selling Church offices as usual. Gregory summoned him to Rome, but the papal ambassadors were driven from the emperor's courts with insults. At Rome a plot was formed against the pope, and he was seized and imprisoned by one of the Roman nobles, but an uprising of the people caused his release. Henry called a council which declared the pope deposed, but the pope retorted by excommunicating Henry. The latter was hampered by troubles with his German subjects, many of whom were glad to take sides with the enemy.

The Great Papal Schism

Project 2, Page 3

Canossa (1077)

Henry was soon deserted by his followers, and arrangements were made for summoning a diet, or formal assembly, to consider the question of his deposition. The pope was invited to preside at the diet, which was to meet in Germany. Henry was now afraid of losing his throne, and he tried to obtain an interview with the pope before the latter started for Germany. The pope did not wish this, but Henry went into Italy and intercepted him at Canossa (1077), where he implored forgiveness and promised to yield to all the pope's demands. Before Gregory granted this request, he required the emperor to undergo a painful and humiliating penance, standing for three days, it is said, barefoot in the snow. At last he was admitted to the castle at which the pope was staying, and forgiveness was granted on conditions that he present himself for trial at a later time and that he respect the rights of the Church.

Henry had now gained what he wished, and proceeded to break all his promises. He was successful in his war with the nobles of Germany and defeated the forces of the pope. Finally, invading Italy, he gained access to Rome, and Gregory was driven into exile.

Henry V

Gregory's great rival, Henry IV, outlived him twenty-one years. The latter part of his life was full of misfortunes and embittered by the revolt of his son. The new emperor, Henry V, was a more dangerous enemy of the papacy even than his father. He claimed all the rights that the latter had exercised, and, entering Rome, obliged the pope to crown him emperor and acknowledge the imperial right of investiture. As soon as Henry left Italy, however, the pope renounced his promise, and the struggle continued ten years longer. Finally, after nearly half a century had passed since the quarrel between Henry IV and Gregory, a settlement was reached by the Concordat of Worms in 1122. This was of the nature of a compromise, for while it was seen that the empire was too weak to enforce its claims to supremacy, it appeared still too strong to be made completely subordinate to the popes.

Death and Character of Gregory VII

Gregory died at Salerno in 1085, saying, as he approached his end, the oft-quoted words: "I have loved justice and hated iniquity; therefore I die in exile." Apparently he had failed to realize his great aims, but in reality he had done more to increase the power of the papacy than any pope that had preceded him, for he had mapped out the policy which his successors on the papal throne carried to success, and this policy raised the papal power for a time above all the civil rulers of Europe. It was his theory that the papal power in spiritual matters was the highest in the world, and that emperors and kings could be compelled to obedience by spiritual weapons. He thought that the great evil of his time was the dependence of the clergy upon the civil ruler, which obedience was maintained by the emperor's exercise of the right of investiture, for the emperor gave not only the symbols of secular power, but of spiritual. The clergy under this system were vassals of the crown; Gregory wished them to be under the sole power of the Church. As to his personal character, no one, not even his enemies, denied his sincerity and unselfishness. He was, moreover, the greatest man of his time, and his work left its stamp upon the Church for centuries.

THE GREAT PAPAL SCHISM
Project 2, Page 4

CONCORDAT OF WORMS.

The Concordat of Worms was an attempt to settle the matter without humbling either party. By it the emperor agreed to give up the right of bestowing the symbols of Church authority and to acknowledge the free election of the clergy by the clergy. The pope, on the other hand, agreed that the emperor or his representative should be present at the elections of clergy, provided that bribery or intimidation was not employed. The emperor also was to bestow crown properties as before. Thus neither party gained all that it had been striving for, and neither had the right to bestow both spiritual and secular authority. These rights were divided between the two, the pope bestowing the signs of spiritual authority and the king bestowing the signs of temporal.

Nevertheless the Concordat of Worms was really a triumph for the Church. The long struggle had shown clearly the great power of the popes, especially in its effect of weakening the loyalty of the feudal vassals of the king. As the great crown vassals became stronger, the power of the emperors was lessened. Moreover, the popes, being the natural allies of all enemies of the emperors, took sides with the cities which, although legally the vassals of the emperor, were fast increasing in power and asserting the right to govern themselves.

Another effect of the weakness of the emperor and his hostility to the papacy was to make the popes and not the emperors the promoters of the crusades, an office which would naturally have fallen to the lot of the emperor in his capacity of defender of the faith. The popes received the credit for the crusades, and acquired, as a result of them, a far greater influence in Europe.

FREDERICK I (BARBAROSSA) AND THE PAPACY

Frederick Barbarossa, one of the ablest of all the German emperors, was a far more powerful enemy than the popes had yet encountered. He came to the throne with a fixed resolve to extend the powers of his empire, and one of the first difficulties that he attacked was the growing independence of the Italian cities. They had united with the Church vassals and had gained such a measure of local self-government as to threaten the imperial power over them. He treated them as his fiefs and demanded the usual feudal services. The cities refused these demands and Milan, being the chief offender, was the first to suffer punishment. A large part of the city was destroyed; a portion of the walls were pulled down and the inhabitants were forced to a humiliating surrender.

This, however, did not break the spirit of these cities, and the so-called Lombard League was formed under the leadership of Milan. Then followed a sharp conflict between the emperor and the league. But in spite of his energy and ability he made no headway against it, and finally in the battle of Legnano (1176) was completely defeated. One of the chief reasons for his failure was the disloyalty of the German princes.

THE GREAT PAPAL SCHISM

Project 2, Page 5

TREATY OF VENICE

In 1177, he made with the pope the famous Treaty of Venice, whose terms were greatly to the disadvantage of the emperor, for the pope no less than the cities had profited by the victory at Legnano. In the Treaty of Venice, Frederick virtually acknowledged that the imperial power was secondary to the papal.

The terms made with the cities were very important. According to the feudal laws, the allegiance of the matter was due to the emperor as their overlord. But he was obliged to yield his lawful claim and grant the cities the right of self-government. These concessions were made by the Treaty of Constance in 1183.

DECAY OF THE IMPERIAL POWER

These events mark another stage in the great papal and imperial conflicts The Concordat of Worms in 1122 was, as we have seen, a compromise in which the advantage was on the side of the Church. The renewal of the conflict by the emperors in the hope of regaining what had been lost resulted in a still greater triumph for the Holy See in the treaties of Venice and Constance. A great blow was dealt to the power of the empire. The cities were independent, the Church was hostile, and the nobles were defiant. Although Frederick and his successors struggled bravely to maintain the power of their house, the foundation of the empire was shattered, and after the death of Frederick II, in 1250, the imperial throne became the prize of any one who was strong enough to seize it.

INNOCENT III (1198-1216)

The reign of Innocent III marks the highest point which the papal power ever attained. He followed in the footsteps of Gregory VII, aiming constantly at the supremacy of the Church over the State.

The success with which he carried out this policy is illustrated by his contests with Philip Augustus of France and John of England. Before Innocent came to the throne, Philip Augustus had divorced his wife and illegally married Agnes of Meran. The divorce had been approved by the highest ecclesiastical authorities in France, but the ex-queen appealed to Innocent III, who saw an opportunity to test the question of papal supremacy and determined to force Philip Augustus to put away his new wife. The king paid no attention to the pope's demand, for he trusted to the loyalty of his people and felt himself strong enough to resist.

The pope thereupon inflicted the severest punishment that the Church had in its power. He laid the kingdom under an interdict. This meant that all the offices of the Church were suspended, with the exception of the most necessary sacraments. The Church doors were closed, the dead were buried in unconsecrated ground, and the people were deprived of the consolation of religion. To a pious people this was unendurable, and the pressure on the king to comply with the pope's demand became too strong to be resisted. Philip Augustus finally yielded and sent away Agnes of Meran, who died soon afterwards. Since Philip Augustus was one of the strongest as well as the most headstrong monarch in Europe, this triumph was a remarkable proof of the pope's power.

THE GREAT PAPAL SCHISM
Project 2, Page 6

CONTEST WITH KING JOHN

In the quarrel with John of England the issue was not a matter of personal morality, but of Church authority. There was a dispute about the election to the Archbishopric of Canterbury, the most important Church office in England. The monks of Canterbury chose one candidate and the king another, and then both parties appealed to the pope. Innocent rejected both candidates and proposed one of his own, Stephen Langton, a man in every way suitable for the office. John refused to submit, and the pope used against him the same means that had been employed to coerce Philip Augustus. He laid England under an interdict, and, though its effect was not so immediate as in France, it finally brought John to terms. Not only was John obliged to accept the pope's candidate, but he went so far as to surrender the kingdom of England to the pope and receive it back as the pope's vassal, paying in token of vassalage a sum of money each year.

SUPPRESSION OF HERESY

Innocent was equally vigorous in suppressing heresy, and in doing so he employed the same means as were used against the infidels. A crusade against the Albigenses, an heretical sect in southern France, was undertaken and carried out with success, but was marked by revolting cruelties.

The popes continued to wield a vast power for many years after the death Innocent was equally vigorous in suppressing heresy, and in doing so he employed the same means as were used against the infidels. A crusade against the Albigenses, an heretical sect in southern France, was undertaken and carried out with success, but was marked by revolting cruelties.

DECLINE OF THE PAPAL POWER

The popes continued to wield a vast power for many years after the death of Innocent III. They were strengthened by two new orders of monks which were founded early in the thirteenth century and named after their founders, St. Dominic and St. Francis. These Dominican and Franciscan monks returned to a more rigid discipline and a more complete exclusion from worldly things, and having no ambitions or hopes outside of the Church, they directed all their efforts to advancing its interests, and were staunch supporters of the pope.

But toward the close of the thirteenth century, the papal authority began to show signs of weakness, and as the reign of Innocent III illustrates the power of the popes, their waning influence can also be illustrated by an example. Boniface VIII, who ruled from 1294 to 1303, became involved in a quarrel with Philip IV of France over the question of taxing the clergy. Philip claimed that right, and when Boniface ordered him to desist, saying that he was subject in spiritual things to the Holy See, Philip returned a defiant answer. Although Boniface issued decree after decree against him, placed him under the ban and declared him deposed from the throne, the king gained his point, for the people were on his side. In the Assembly of the States-General, it was declared that France was not subject to the pope in temporal matters. For many years after this the papacy was wholly subject to French influence, and in 1309 the Holy See was removed from Rome to

Avignon, in France, where it remained for nearly seventy years (1309-1378), a period known in Church history as the Babylonian Captivity of the Church. As a natural result of this, the respect for the papacy declined.

THE GREAT SCHISM (1378-1417)

The removal of the papal seat to Avignon gave offense to the Italian members of the Sacred College, and they chose a pope who promised to take up his residence at Rome. The French cardinals, preferring Avignon as the seat of the pope, chose an antipope of their own. There was thus a division or schism in the Church, and there were for many years two lines of popes. This of course weakened the influence of the papacy, for people did not know who was the rightful pope.

COUNCIL OF PISA

These years were a dark period in the history of the Church, and the evils of the time led to efforts for reform, notably the movements of John Wycliffe and John Huss. Finally, as the only way of settling the matter, a council of the Church was called to decide who was the just claimant to the papal throne. This council, which assembled at Pisa in 1409, recognized neither of the popes, and set up a third one, but as both the deposed popes insisted on maintaining their rule, the decision of the council only made matters worse, for there were now three popes instead of two.

COUNCIL OF CONSTANCE

But the Council of Constance was more successful. After deposing the three popes, it chose Martin V, in 1417, and he was generally acknowledged. This brought the Great Schism to an end, but the effect of it was none the less important. The papacy thenceforth had no chance of gaining that supremacy over the civil power which was aimed at by Gregory VII and his immediate successors.

CONCLUSION

As a result of the long struggle between the papacy and the civil powers, it may be said that the attempt to make the Church supreme in temporal matters had failed. As the Middle Ages drew toward their close, the feeling of nationality became stronger and the power of the kings increased. Both these facts tended to lessen the authority of the popes when they interfered in secular affairs. On the other hand, their spiritual supremacy remained. Here and there it was questioned, and reform movements were started, but throughout the fifteenth century the Holy See continued to be the highest authority in spiritual matters. It was not until the following century that any of the states of Europe ventured to separate from the Roman Catholic Church.

The Great Papal Schism
Project 3

Timeline

Use the following summary of information concerning the Great Papal Schism to create a classroom line graph depicting the rise and fall of papal power from 1073 - 1417. You should keep the chart on display for the next card.

The pope was a spiritual ruler and a prince. He claimed supremacy over kings and emporers. in effect the pope desired to be above all kings and overlords in the feudal system.

Pope Gregory VII (Pope from 1073 - 1085)
Investiture was the custom of a fuedal lord giving a man the office of bishop or abbot, thus the fuedal lord appeared to have spiritual power. Late in life, Pope Gregory VII was driven into exile by Emporer Henry IV after a long battle over the right of investiture.

Treaty of Venice (1177)
Emperer Frederick Barbarossa acknowledges imperial power is secondary to papal power.

Pope Innocent III (Pope from 1198 - 1216)
Pope Innocent III represents the high point of papal power. He had disagreements with King Philip Augustus of France and with King John of England. He forced the kings to back down through issuing interdicts against the countries. An interdict meant that throughout the country churches were closed, all offices of the church were suspended, except for the most necessary duties, and the dead were buried in unconsecrated ground. In short, the people could not practice their religion.

Pope Boniface VIII (Pope from 1294 - 1378)
Boniface represents the decline of papal power. He quarrelled with King Philip IV of France over the king's right to tax the clergy. Despite attempts at interdiction, Philip would not yield. This time the French people were supportive of their king. For many years the French controlled the papacy and the Pope's court, the Holy See, was moved to Avignon, France.

Great Schism (1378 - 1417)
The Pope in Avignon is supported by the French and the Pope in Rome is supported by the Italians.

Council of Pisa (1409)
In a botched attempt to end the schism, the Council of Pisa sets up a third Pope.

Council of Constance (1417)
Deposed all three ruling popes and set up Martin V. He was accepted by most, and thus the Great Papal Schism ended.

The Great Papal Schism

Test

1. What are the dates of the Great Papal Schism?

2. Where did the papacy originally reside? Where did it go after the schism?

3. What great success did Gregory XI have?

4. Describe Urban VI.

5. How did the Latin Church end up with two leaders rather than one?

6. What was the Council of Constance?

7. How did the Council of Constance change the role of the pope?

THE GREAT PAPAL SCHISM
Test, Page 2

1. Write a paragraph about what you believe the most interesting event you have studied to date. It must be at least seven sentences. Be sure to include dates, places and names of the important people involved.

2. List in chronological order all the events studied to date.
   Next to each place the appropriate date.

John Wycliffe and John Huss

Worksheet

John Wycliffe (left) and John Huss

1. What are the approximate dates for John Wycliffe and John Huss?

   ____

   ____

   ____

2. While the English and __________ were fighting the Hundred Years War, seeds for the ________________ were being sown in England.

3. Who was John Wycliffe?

   ____

   ____

4. What did Wycliffe believe regarding Scripture?

   ____

   ____

5. Who did Wycliffe openly criticize?

   ____

   ____

6. To what did Wycliffe believe the Church should return?

   ____

   ____

   ____

7. What did Wycliffe call the Pope?

   ____

   ____

JOHN WYCLIFFE AND JOHN HUSS

Worksheet, Page 2

8. What were followers of Wycliffe called?

____

____

9. Wycliffe produced a(n) ____________ translation of the Bible.

10. Who was John Huss? What person influenced his beliefs?

____

____

____

11. Huss preached in __________ and won most of the country to his beliefs while the ____________ ____________ raged on in Rome and ____________.

12. Why did Huss appeal to the Council of Constance in 1414?

____

____

13. What eventually happened to John Huss?

____

____

____

14. Huss followers developed into what modern day denomination?

____

____

____

JOHN WYCLIFFE AND JOHN HUSS

Project

Biographies Excercise

Using the resources listed on your card, especially *The Church in History,* fill in the information below.

John Wycliffe

John Huss

Birth year:		
Place of birth:		
Profession:		
View of condition of Church:		
View of condition of clergy:		
View of Scripture:		
Name of followers:		
Type of death:		

John Wycliffe and John Huss

Test

1. Who was John Wycliffe?

2. What does "sola Scriptura" mean?

3. What did Wycliffe believe about the Church and its leaders?

4. Who were the Lollards?

5. What translation of the Bible did Wycliffe produce?

6. To where did Wycliffe's teachings spread that John Huss heard them?

7. What was Huss' occupation?

8. Why did Huss appeal to the Council of Constance in 1414?

9. How did Huss die?

10. What Church did the followers of Huss form?

John Wycliffe and John Huss
Test, Page 2

Review

1. What is the book by Augustine entitled *Confessions* about?

2. Describe the barbarians.

3. Why did St. Jerome find it necessary to translate the Bible into Latin?

4. Who was St. Benedict?

5. In chronological order list all the events studied to date.

   Next to each place the appropriate dates.

FALL OF CONSTANTINOPLE TO MOHAMMED II
Worksheet

1. What was the date of the Fall of Constantinople to Mohammed II?

2. What two empires vied for control of the Byzantine empire in the late Middle Ages?

3. In 1453 the Turks, under the leadership of ________________, made a final assault on ________________.

4. What weapons did the Turks use to attack the city?

5. Compare the number of soldiers used by Constantine XI to that of Mohammed II.

6. What happened to the city of Constantinople?

7. What happened to the Church of Santa Sophia?

8. What had happened to the Old Roman Empire?

Fall of Constantinople to Mohammed II
Project

Chronology

THE FALL OF CONSTANTINOPLE

Turkey had been part of the Eastern Empire even after the fall of Rome in 476, but it had come to be so little Roman and so completely Greek that it is spoken of as the Greek, or Byzantine Empire. It was destined, however, to belong to neither Romans nor Greeks, for the Mohammedans were pressing hard upon its boundaries. They had won Asia Minor and the lands lying directly south of the Danube. Gradually they got Greece, north of the Isthmus, into their power, and in 1453 Mohammed II led the Ottoman Turks, who were of the same race as Attila and his Huns, against the capital of the Eastern Empire, the great rich city of Constantinople.

Gunpowder had been invented before this time, but the cannons were small. When the great Turkish gun fired its heavy stone balls, men and women rushed into the streets, beating their breasts and crying aloud, "God have mercy upon us!" Day after day the besiegers continued the attack. They used arrows, catapults for throwing stones, and a few rifles. They wheeled a two-story tower covered with buffalo hides near enough to the city so that archers in the second story could shoot at the defenders on the walls. But the Greeks threw their famous Greek fire upon it and it burned to ashes. Both parties dug mines. Sometimes these were blown up, sometimes the workers in them were suffocated by smoke or gas.

Finally the Turks dug a narrow canal five miles long from the Sea of Marmora to the harbor of Constantinople. They paved it with beams, well greased, and one morning the Greeks found thirty Turkish ships lying almost under their walls, for the buffaloes of the Turks had dragged them to the shore during the night, Then the people of the city were in despair and begged their emperor to escape and flee for his life, but he refused. "I am resolved to die here with you," he declared.

When it was seen that the city must fall, thousands of the citizens crowded into the vast church of St. Sophia, for there was an old prophecy that some day the Turks would force their way into the city, but that when they had reached St. Sophia an angel would appear with a celestial sword, and that at sight of it the Turks would flee. The emperor knelt long in prayer, received the Holy Communion, and then begged the priests and all the members of his court to forgive him if he had ever wronged them. The sobs and wails of the people echoed in the great building.

The Turks made their way without hindrance into the city. They did not stop at the church; and no angel brought a miraculous weapon to drive them back. The emperor fell, sword in hand, fighting to the last for his empire and the Christian faith. The Turkish

Fall of Constantinople to Mohammed II
Project, Page 2

commander gave over the city to his soldiers, and they stole everything worth stealing, wonderful treasures of gold, silver, bronze, and jewels. Thousands of citizens were roughly bound together and dragged off to the boats to be sold as slaves. The cross was torn down from beautiful St. Sophia, and the crescent, the emblem of Mohammedanism, was put in its place.

The emperor's body, however, was buried by the Turks with all honors. A lamp was lighted at his grave. It is still kept burning, and at the charge of the Turkish government. This was commanded by the Turkish ruler as a mark of respect and regard for Constantine Palaeologos, the last Christian emperor in the Empire of the East.

At the coming of the Turks, many of the Greeks had seized their most valued treasures and fled. The scholars carried away with them the rare old manuscripts of the early Greek writers. More went to Italy than anywhere else, and the Italian scholars gave them a hearty welcome. There had been learned Greeks in Italy long before this time, and the Italian scholars had been interested in the Greek literature, but now such a wealth of it was poured into the country that the Italians were aroused and delighted. They read the manuscripts eagerly; they sent copies to their friends, and gradually a knowledge of the literature of the Greeks and a love for it spread throughout Europe.

Fall of Constantinople to Mohammed II

Project, Page 3

After reading about "The Fall of Constantinople," number the following events in Chronological order.

___The people of Constantinople beg their emperor to flee for his life.

___The Turkish fired heavy stone balls into Constantinople.

___The cross was torn down from St. Sophia and the emblem of Mohammedanism put in its place.

___The Greeks found thirty Turkish ships lying almost under their walls.

___The Mohammedans had won Asia Minor and the lands lying directly south of the Danube and part of Greece.

___Citizens crowded into the Church of St. Sophia believing an angel would appear with a celestial sword and cause the Turks to flee.

___The Greeks threw fire on the Turk's tower and burned it to ashes.

___The Turks bury the emperor with honors.

___The Turkish wheeled a two story tower covered with buffalo hides near the city to fight.

___Thousands of citizens are dragged to boats to be sold as slaves.

___The Turks dug a narrow canal five miles long from the sea of Marmora to the harbor of Constantinople.

___Turks made their way into Constantinople and the Emperor fell , fighting to the end.

Fall of Constantinople to Mohammed II
Project, Page 4

Answers

7. The people of Constantinople beg their emperor to flee for his life.
2. The Turkish fired heavy stone balls into Constantinople.
11. The cross was torn down from St. Sophia and the emblem of Mohammedanism put in its place.
6. The Greeks found thirty Turkish ships lying almost under their walls.
1. The Mohammedans had won Asia Minor and the lands lying directly south of the Danube and part of Greece.
8. Citizens crowed into the Church of St. Sophia believing an angel would appear with a celestial sword and cause the Turks to flee.
4. The Greeks threw fire on the Turk's tower and burned it to ashes.
12. The Turks bury the emperor with honors.
3. The Turks wheeled a two story tower covered with buffalo hides near the city to fight.
10. Thousands of citizens are dragged to boats to be sold as slaves.
5. The Turks dug a narrow canal five miles long from the sea if Marmora to the harbor of Constantinople.
9. Turks made their way into Constantinople and the Emperor fell, fighting to the end.

FALL OF CONSTANTINOPLE TO MOHAMMED II

Project 2

Map Excercise

Use a map to color the Mohammedan Territory in 1453. Make a salt relief map of the canal from the Sea of Marmora. Use popsicle sticks to represent the beams. Make small models of the Turkish ships and of buffaloes to drag the ships to Constantinople.

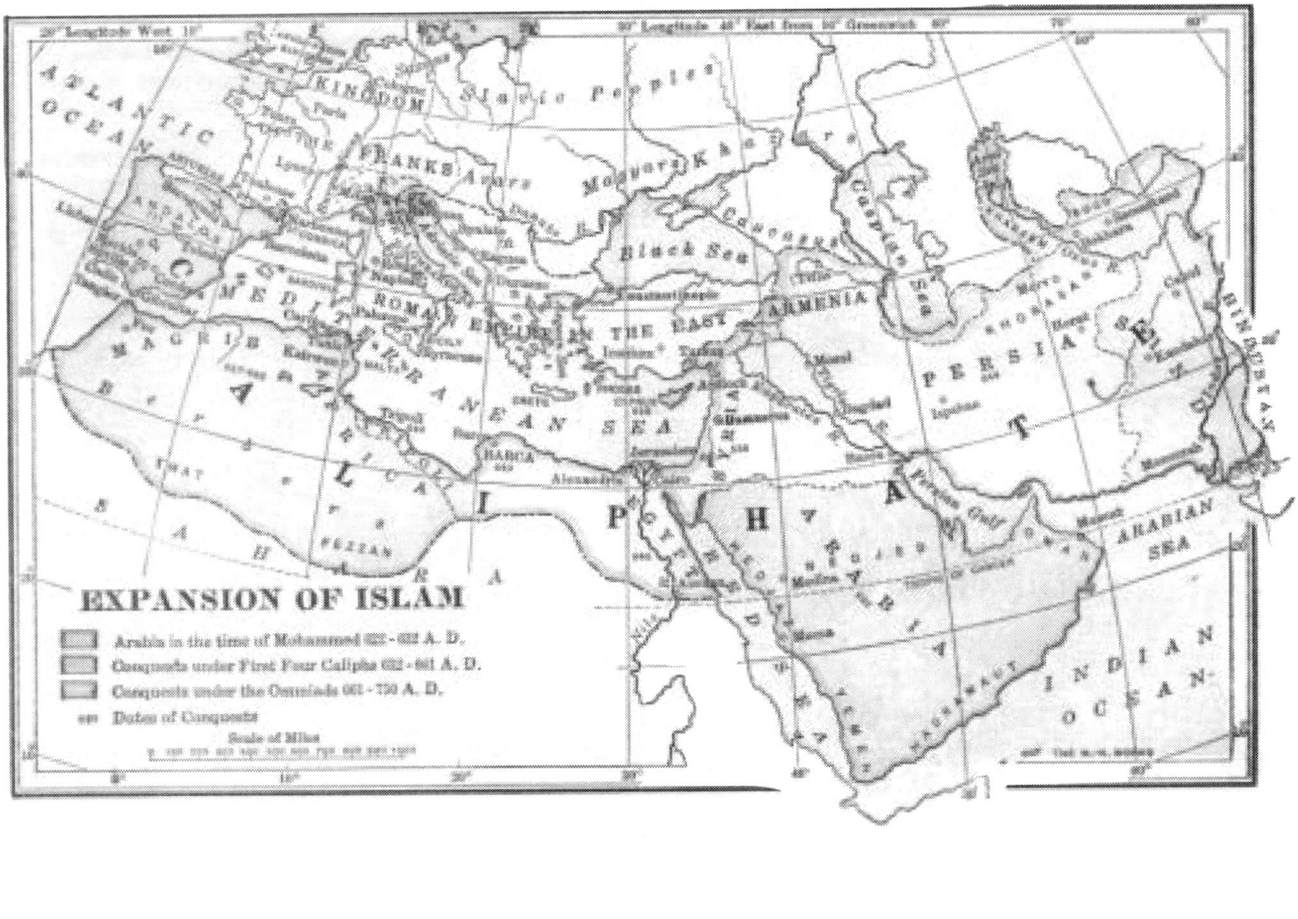

Fall of Constantinople to Mohammed II
Test

1. What was the date of the fall of Constantinople to Mohammed II?

2. What two empires vied for control of the Byzantine empire in the late Middle Ages?

3. Write a paragraph describing what happened in the battle between the two empires above when trying to fight over Constantinople.

4. What eventually happened to the Church of Santa Sophia?

5. What happened to the Old Roman Empire?

Fall of Constantinople to Mohammed II

Test, Page 2

Review

1. What was the Vulgate?

2. What made Charlemagne a great ruler?

3. Who was the founder of Islam?

4. Who were the Vikings?

5. In chronological order list all the events studied to date.

   Next to each place the approximate date.

Gutenberg Prints the Bible

Worksheet

1. In what year did Gutenberg print the Bible?

2. What was John Gutenberg taught as a child that was unusual?

3. What were manuscripts? Why did Gutenberg read these instead of books?

4. Describe block printing.

5. Describe the type of printing that Gutenberg developed.

6. What was the first book Gutenberg printed? Describe the book.

GUTENBERG PRINTS THE BIBLE
Project

Reading

JOHN GUTENBERG

The fall of Constantinople had brought the Greek scholars with their manuscripts to Italy, but it would have been a long while before even the most learned men of Western Europe could have read the writings if a German named John Gutenberg had not been working away for many years, trying to invent a better process of making books than the slow, tiresome method of copying them by hand, letter by letter. When Gutenberg was a boy, this was the way in which all books were made. Moreover, they were generally written on parchment, and this added to the expense. The result was that a book was a costly article, and few people could afford to own one. After Gutenberg became a young man, a way of making books was invented which people thought was a most wonderful improvement. For each page the printer took a block of fine-grained wood, drew upon it whatever picture he was to print, then cut the wood away, leaving the outlines of the picture. By inking this and pressing it upon the paper he could print a page. Only one side of the paper was used, and so every pair of leaves had to be pasted together. At first only pictures were printed, but after a while some lettering was also done. Such books were called block books. Many were printed in this way whose pictures illustrated Bible history. These were known as poor men's Bibles.

Although the block books were much less expensive than the books written by hand, still they were by no means cheap. It was long, slow work to cut a block for each page; and after as many books had been printed as were needed, the blocks were of no further use. Gutenberg wondered whether there was not some better way to print a book. He pondered and dreamed over the matter and made experiments. At last the idea which he sought came to him, an idea so simple that it seems strange no one had thought of it sooner. It was only to cut each

GUTENBERG PRINTS THE BIBLE

Project, Page 2

letter on a separate piece of wood, form the letters into words bind them together the shape and size of a page, print as many copies as were desired, then separate the letters and use them in other books till they were worn out. Here was the great invention; but it was a long way from this beginning to a well-printed book.

Now people began to wonder what Gutenberg could be working at so secretly. In those days everything that was mysterious was explained as witchcraft, so the inventor, in order to avoid any such charge, made himself a workshop in a deserted monastery outside of the town. He had yet to learn how to make his types of metal, how to fasten them together firmly in forms, how to put on just enough ink, and how to make a press.

At length he carried through a great undertaking He printed a Latin Bible. This was completed in 1455, and was the first Bible ever printed. But Gutenberg was in trouble. He had not had the money needed to carry on this work without help, and he had been obliged to take a partner by the name of John Faust. Faust was disappointed in not making as much money as he had expected. The Bible had taken longer to complete and had cost more than Gutenberg had planned, and at length Faust brought a suit to recover what he had loaned. The judge decided in his favor, and everything that the inventor owned went to him. Gutenberg was left to begin again. Nevertheless he went on bravely with his printing, trying all the time to print better and better. By and by the Elector Adolphus of Nassau gave him a pension. This is all that is known of the last few years of his life. He died in 1468, but the art of printing lived. Printing presses could hardly be, set up fast enough, for every country wanted them. England, France, Holland, Germany had presses within a few years after the death of Gutenberg. The Jews carried one to Constantinople, and a century later even Russia had one.

So it was that the knowledge of printing flashed over Europe. Of course those old Greek manuscripts were printed and sent from country to country. A Venetian printer named Aldo Manuzio issued especially accurate and well-made copies, which became known as the Aldine editions. The crusades had aroused people and made them ready and eager to learn. Now they found in the ancient writings of the Greeks and Romans nobler poems, more dignified histories, and more brilliant orations than they had known before. By this "New Learning," as it was called, men were stimulated to think. They felt as if they were brighter and keener than they used to be, as if they were not their old slow, dull selves, but were becoming quick and clear-minded. They felt so much as if they had just been born into a new, fresh world that the name Renaissance, or new birth, has been given to this period.

Gutenberg Prints the Bible

Project 2

Potato Prints

After reading the information on Gutenberg, try *your* hand at block printing. We will be using potatoes in order to make the block letters.

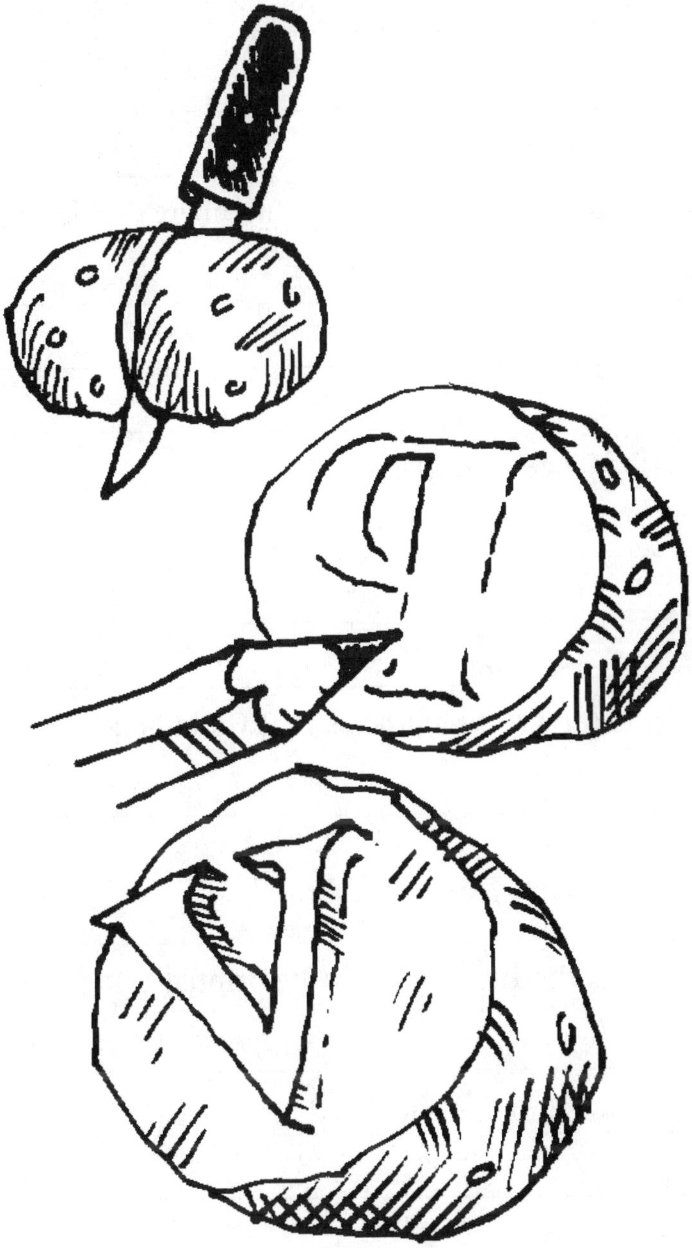

Supplies

2 potatoes per person

white construction paper

tempera paint

knife

Instructions

Cut the potatoes in half. With a pencil draw on the potato the letter or shape that you want to cut out. Cut out the shape with the knife. It is best to carve small pieces away at a time. Dip the potato into paint and press onto the construction paper.

GUTENBERG PRINTS THE BIBLE

Test

1. In what year did Gutenberg print the Bible?

___

___

2. What were hand-written books called?

___

___

3. What was unusual about John Gutenberg's childhood education?

___

___

___

4. Describe block printing.

___

___

___

5. Describe the printing process that Gutenberg invented.

___

___

___

6. What was the first book that he printed using the above invention?

___

___

___

Gutenberg Prints the Bible

Test, Page 2

Review

1. What four ideas did the Council of Chalcedon affirm?

2. What vows did the Benedictine monks take?

3. Who was St. Francis?

4. What was the Magna Carta?

5. In chronological order list the cards studied to date.

   Next to each place the approximate date.

The Renaissance
Worksheet

1. What are the dates of the Renaissance?

2. What was the Renaissance?

3. What blasphemous idea did some have during this period?

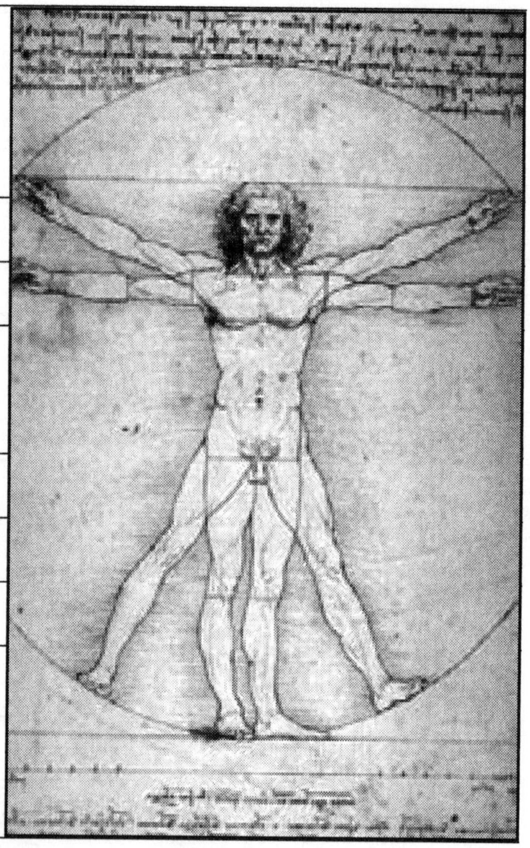

4. Where did the Renaissance begin?

5. Who was the main sponsor of the arts during this time?

6. What is humanism?

The Renaissance
Worksheet

7. The revived interest in ____________ affected the arts, science, architecture, and sculpture.
8. Describe paintings and statues during this time.

____

____

____

____

9. What discipline sometimes found itself in conflict with the church?

____

____

____

10. What does "Renaissance Man" mean?

____

____

____

____

____

The Renaissance

Project

Research Project

Choose one or more of the following ideas for your students to pursue.

1. Discuss the rise of humanism, the increase of knowledge, and the rapid spread of information via the printing press. What are the benefits and disadvantages of the new learning?
2. Research as a class, or in groups, the four great artistic innovations during the Renaissance: oil on canvas, perspective, use of light and shadow to create depth, and the pyramid configuration.
3. Assign each student a Renaissance artist or architect to explore and present. The presentation should include any innovations, specialties, and well known works. Each child should attempt a copy of one of the master's work.

Suggested list:

da Vinci	Botticelli
Donatello	Michelangelo
Brunelleschi	Durer
Buonarroti	Raphael
Titian	Palladio
van Eyck	Bruegel

The Renaissance

Project 2

Study in Perspective

Perspective is the visual communication of relationships between objects spatial in a two-dimensional medium. In Egyptian art, size and spatial relationship was ignored because they wanted to show a hierarchy of importance. Therefore they would make the Pharaoh the largest figure and others would be shown smaller and smaller, regardless of actual size. During the Middle Ages the artwork created was stylized and flat. For some, the reason for this was theological, they did not want to illustrate anything God had created in a realistic manner. But for most, the artwork was flat because of ignorance. The Renaissance ushered in a new way of drawing—by using linear perspective.

The illustration above is by Albrecht Durer and is called *Draughtsman Making a Perspective Drawing of a Woman.* In the picture we see a grid has been set up and the artist has drawn an identical grid on his paper. By keeping his head in a fixed position, he can use the grid to draw in perspective. He would follow the lines and curves of the model and where they hit the grid he also would reproduce the same lines on his sheet of grid paper. This helps the artist draw a foreshortened view of the model—parts that are closer are bigger than parts that are farther away. You can see roughly how this works by looking out a window and observing where the edges of buildings and cars "hit" the grid of the window panes.

Explore the idea of perspective. Draw the same subject, once with and once without perspective. An excellent resource for is the book *The Renaissance: The Invention of Perspective.*

The Renaissance
Test

1. What are the dates of the Renaissance?

2. What was the Renaissance?

3. Where did the Renaissance begin?

4. Who was the main sponsor of the arts during this time?

5. What is humanism?

6. What discipline sometimes found itself in conflict with the church?

The Renaissance

Test, Page 2

Review

1. In what language was the Vulgate written?

2. Name three barbarian tribes.

3. Who won the Hundred Years War?

4. What was the first book Gutenberg printed?

5. In chronological order list the events studied to date.

   Next to each place the approximate date.

THE INQUISITION
Worksheet

1. What is the date given for the Inquisition?

2. Who were the rulers of Spain when the Spanish Inquisition was begun?

3. What is an inquisition?

4. Who was persecuted? By whom?

5. Describe some of the effects of the Spanish Inquisition.

THE INQUISITION
Project

Writing Excercise

This persecution of all non-Catholics was a dreadful time for Spain. Under the courts of Inquisition, many Jews, Muslims, and others were expelled from Ferdinand and Isabella's kingdom. Many who would not accept the Catholic church's teaching were tortured and killed. This is not an atrocity that is isolated to the Middle Ages or to the Roman Catholic Church. Using your card and resources, write a paragraph that defines what the Inquisition attempted to accomplish.

THE INQUISITION

Test

1. Who were the rulers of Spain when the Spanish Inquisition was begun?

2. What is an inquisition?

3. Who was persecuted? By whom?

4. What were some of the effects of the Spanish Inquisition?

Review

1. Who was Joan of Arc?

2. What book by Marco Polo enticed men to seek a quicker route to China?

The Inquisition
Test, Page 2

3. What dates are given for Otto I?

4. Who did William the Conqueror conquer?

5. Write out the history song that covers the Middle Ages.

Martin Luther Begins the Reformation
Worksheet

1. In what year did Martin Luther begin the Reformation?

2. How did the Reformation begin?

3. Who was Martin Luther?

4. What was the *95 Theses?* In what language was it written?

5. What is *sola fide?*

6. What is *sola Scriptura?*

7. What did (does) the Roman Catholic Church believe about faith and works?

8. In 1520 what did Rome threaten to do to Luther if he did not recant his position?

Martin Luther Begins the Reformation

Worksheet, Page 2

9. What did Luther do at the Diet of Worms?

10. What did Luther's courage cause?

Martin Luther Begins the Reformation
Project

Newspaper Article

Pretend you are the first reporter in Wittenberg! Write a newspaper article about Luther nailing his 95 Theses to rhe castle door. Remember it was not that long ago that the printing press was invented and people are just beginning to have access to the written word on a somewhat mass produced basis.

Wittenberg
Today

MARTIN LUTHER BEGINS THE REFORMATION
Project 2

Vocabulary Excercise

Use a dictionary to define each of the followings words and then use each word in a paragraph summarizing Luther's trouble with the Roman Church.

theses:

indulgences:

reformation:

recant:

excommunicate:

Martin Luther Begins the Reformation

Project 3

Read and discuss the importance of the 95 Theses.

Disputation of Doctor Martin Luther on the Power and Efficacy of Indulgences (aka "95 THESES")

OCTOBER 31, 1517

Out of love for the truth and the desire to bring it to light, the following propositions will be discussed at Wittenberg, under the presidency of the Reverend Father Martin Luther, Master of Arts and of Sacred Theology, and Lecturer in Ordinary on the same at that place.

Wherefore he requests that those who are unable to be present and debate orally with us, may do so by letter.

In the Name our Lord Jesus Christ. Amen.

1. Our Lord and Master Jesus Christ, when He said Poenitentiam agite, willed that the whole life of believers should be repentance.

2. This word cannot be understood to mean sacramental penance, i.e., confession and satisfaction, which is administered by the priests.

3. Yet it means not inward repentance only; nay, there is no inward repentance which does not outwardly work divers mortifications of the flesh.

4. The penalty [of sin], therefore, continues so long as hatred of self continues; for this is the true inward repentance, and continues until our entrance into the kingdom of heaven.

5. The pope does not intend to remit, and cannot remit any penalties other than those which he has imposed either by his own authority or by that of the Canons.

6. The pope cannot remit any guilt, except by declaring that it has been remitted by God and by assenting to God's remission; though, to be sure, he may grant remission in cases reserved to his judgment. If his right to grant remission in such cases were despised, the guilt would remain entirely unforgiven.

7. God remits guilt to no one whom He does not, at the same time, humble in all things and bring into subjection to His vicar, the priest.

8. The penitential canons are imposed only on the living, and, according to them, nothing should be imposed on the dying.

9. Therefore the Holy Spirit in the pope is kind to us, because in his decrees he always makes exception of the article of death and of necessity.

10. Ignorant and wicked are the doings of those priests who, in the case of the dying, reserve canonical penances for purgatory.

11. This changing of the canonical penalty to the penalty of purgatory is quite evidently one of the tares that were sown while the bishops slept.

Martin Luther Begins the Reformation

Project 3, Page 2

12. In former times the canonical penalties were imposed not after, but before absolution, as tests of true contrition.

13. The dying are freed by death from all penalties; they are already dead to canonical rules, and have a right to be released from them.

14. The imperfect health [of soul], that is to say, the imperfect love, of the dying brings with it, of necessity, great fear; and the smaller the love, the greater is the fear.

15. This fear and horror is sufficient of itself alone (to say nothing of other things) to constitute the penalty of purgatory, since it is very near to the horror of despair.

16. Hell, purgatory, and heaven seem to differ as do despair, almost-despair, and the assurance of safety.

17. With souls in purgatory it seems necessary that horror should grow less and love increase.

18. It seems unproved, either by reason or Scripture, that they are outside the state of merit, that is to say, of increasing love.

19. Again, it seems unproved that they, or at least that all of them, are certain or assured of their own blessedness, though we may be quite certain of it.

20. Therefore by "full remission of all penalties" the pope means not actually "of all," but only of those imposed by himself.

21. Therefore those preachers of indulgences are in error, who say that by the pope's indulgences a man is freed from every penalty, and saved;

22. Whereas he remits to souls in purgatory no penalty which, according to the canons, they would have had to pay in this life.

23. If it is at all possible to grant to any one the remission of all penalties whatsoever, it is certain that this remission can be granted only to the most perfect, that is, to the very fewest.

24. It must needs be, therefore, that the greater part of the people are deceived by that indiscriminate and highsounding promise of release from penalty.

25. The power which the pope has, in a general way, over purgatory, is just like the power which any bishop or curate has, in a special way, within his own diocese or parish.

26. The pope does well when he grants remission to souls [in purgatory], not by the power of the keys (which he does not possess), but by way of intercession.

27. They preach man who say that so soon as the penny jingles into the money-box, the soul flies out [of purgatory].

28. It is certain that when the penny jingles into the money-box, gain and avarice can be increased, but the result of the intercession of the Church is in the power of God alone.

29. Who knows whether all the souls in purgatory wish to be bought out of it, as in the legend of Sts. Severinus and Paschal.

Martin Luther Begins the Reformation

Project 3, Page 3

30. No one is sure that his own contrition is sincere; much less that he has attained full remission.

31. Rare as is the man that is truly penitent, so rare is also the man who truly buys indulgences, i.e., such men are most rare.

32. They will be condemned eternally, together with their teachers, who believe themselves sure of their salvation because they have letters of pardon.

33. Men must be on their guard against those who say that the pope's pardons are that inestimable gift of God by which man is reconciled to Him.

34. For these "graces of pardon" concern only the penalties of sacramental satisfaction, and these are appointed by man.

35. They preach no Christian doctrine who teach that contrition is not necessary in those who intend to buy souls out of purgatory or to buy confessionalia.

36. Every truly repentant Christian has a right to full remission of penalty and guilt, even without letters of pardon.

37. Every true Christian, whether living or dead, has part in all the blessings of Christ and the Church; and this is granted him by God, even without letters of pardon.

38. Nevertheless, the remission and participation [in the blessings of the Church] which are granted by the pope are in no way to be despised, for they are, as I have said, the declaration of divine remission.

39. It is most difficult, even for the very keenest theologians, at one and the same time to commend to the people the abundance of pardons and [the need of] true contrition.

40. True contrition seeks and loves penalties, but liberal pardons only relax penalties and cause them to be hated, or at least, furnish an occasion [for hating them].

41. Apostolic pardons are to be preached with caution, lest the people may falsely think them preferable to other good works of love.

42. Christians are to be taught that the pope does not intend the buying of pardons to be compared in any way to works of mercy.

43. Christians are to be taught that he who gives to the poor or lends to the needy does a better work than buying pardons;

44. Because love grows by works of love, and man becomes better; but by pardons man does not grow better, only more free from penalty.

45. Christians are to be taught that he who sees a man in need, and passes him by, and gives [his money] for pardons, purchases not the indulgences of the pope, but the indignation of God.

46. Christians are to be taught that unless they have more than they need, they are bound to keep back what is necessary for their own families, and by no means to squander it on pardons.

MARTIN LUTHER BEGINS THE REFORMATION

Project 3, Page 4

47. Christians are to be taught that the buying of pardons is a matter of free will, and not of commandment.

48. Christians are to be taught that the pope, in granting pardons, needs, and therefore desires, their devout prayer for him more than the money they bring.

49. Christians are to be taught that the pope's pardons are useful, if they do not put their trust in them; but altogether harmful, if through them they lose their fear of God.

50. Christians are to be taught that if the pope knew the exactions of the pardon-preachers, he would rather that St. Peter's church should go to ashes, than that it should be built up with the skin, flesh and bones of his sheep.

51. Christians are to be taught that it would be the pope's wish, as it is his duty, to give of his own money to very many of those from whom certain hawkers of pardons cajole money, even though the church of St. Peter might have to be sold.

52. The assurance of salvation by letters of pardon is vain, even though the commissary, nay, even though the pope himself, were to stake his soul upon it.

53. They are enemies of Christ and of the pope, who bid the Word of God be altogether silent in some Churches, in order that pardons may be preached in others.

54. Injury is done the Word of God when, in the same sermon, an equal or a longer time is spent on pardons than on this Word.

55. It must be the intention of the pope that if pardons, which are a very small thing, are celebrated with one bell, with single processions and ceremonies, then the Gospel, which is the very greatest thing, should be preached with a hundred bells, a hundred processions, a hundred ceremonies.

56. The "treasures of the Church," out of which the pope grants indulgences, are not sufficiently named or known among the people of Christ.

57. That they are not temporal treasures is certainly evident, for many of the vendors do not pour out such treasures so easily, but only gather them.

58. Nor are they the merits of Christ and the Saints, for even without the pope, these always work grace for the inner man, and the cross, death, and hell for the outward man.

59. St. Lawrence said that the treasures of the Church were the Church's poor, but he spoke according to the usage of the word in his own time.

60. Without rashness we say that the keys of the Church, given by Christ's merit, are that treasure;

61. For it is clear that for the remission of penalties and of reserved cases, the power of the pope is of itself sufficient.

62. The true treasure of the Church is the Most Holy Gospel of the glory and the grace of God.

63. But this treasure is naturally most odious, for it makes the first to be last.

64. On the other hand, the treasure of indulgences is naturally most acceptable, for it makes the last to be first.

65. Therefore the treasures of the Gospel are nets with which they formerly were wont to fish for men of riches.

66. The treasures of the indulgences are nets with which they now fish for the riches of men.

67. The indulgences which the preachers cry as the "greatest graces" are known to be truly such, in so far as they promote gain.

68. Yet they are in truth the very smallest graces compared with the grace of God and the piety of the Cross.

69. Bishops and curates are bound to admit the commissaries of apostolic pardons, with all reverence.

70. But still more are they bound to strain all their eyes and attend with all their ears, lest these men preach their own dreams instead of the commission of the pope.

71. He who speaks against the truth of apostolic pardons, let him be anathema and accursed!

72. But he who guards against the lust and license of the pardon-preachers, let him be blessed!

73. The pope justly thunders against those who, by any art, contrive the injury of the traffic in pardons.

74. But much more does he intend to thunder against those who use the pretext of pardons to contrive the injury of holy love and truth.

75. To think the papal pardons so great that they could absolve a man even if he had committed an impossible sin and violated the Mother of God—this is madness.

76. We say, on the contrary, that the papal pardons are not able to remove the very least of venial sins, so far as its guilt is concerned.

77. It is said that even St. Peter, if he were now Pope, could not bestow greater graces; this is blasphemy against St. Peter and against the pope.

78. We say, on the contrary, that even the present pope, and any pope at all, has greater graces at his disposal; to wit, the Gospel, powers, gifts of healing, etc., as it is written in 1 Corinthians xii.

79. To say that the cross, emblazoned with the papal arms, which is set up [by the preachers of indulgences], is of equal worth with the Cross of Christ, is blasphemy.

80. The bishops, curates and theologians who allow such talk to be spread among the people, will have an account to render.

81. This unbridled preaching of pardons makes it no easy matter, even for learned men, to rescue the reverence due to the pope from slander, or even from the shrewd questionings of the laity.

82. To wit: —"Why does not the pope empty purgatory, for the sake of holy love and of the dire need of the souls that are there, if he redeems an infinite number of souls for the

sake of miserable money with which to build a Church? The former reasons would be most just; the latter is most trivial."

83. Again: —"Why are mortuary and anniversary masses for the dead continued, and why does he not return or permit the withdrawal of the endowments founded on their behalf, since it is wrong to pray for the redeemed?"

84. Again: —"What is this new piety of God and the pope, that for money they allow a man who is impious and their enemy to buy out of purgatory the pious soul of a friend of God, and do not rather, because of that pious and beloved soul's own need, free it for pure love's sake?"

85. Again: —"Why are the penitential canons long since in actual fact and through disuse abrogated and dead, now satisfied by the granting of indulgences, as though they were still alive and in force?"

86. Again: —"Why does not the pope, whose wealth is today greater than the riches of the richest, build just this one church of St. Peter with his own money, rather than with the money of poor believers?"

87. Again: —"What is it that the pope remits, and what participation does he grant to those who, by perfect contrition, have a right to full remission and participation?"

88. Again: —"What greater blessing could come to the Church than if the pope were to do a hundred times a day what he now does once, and bestow on every believer these remissions and participations?"

89. "Since the pope, by his pardons, seeks the salvation of souls rather than money, why does he suspend the indulgences and pardons granted heretofore, since these have equal efficacy?"

90. To repress these arguments and scruples of the laity by force alone, and not to resolve them by giving reasons, is to expose the Church and the pope to the ridicule of their enemies, and to make Christians unhappy.

91. If, therefore, pardons were preached according to the spirit and mind of the pope, all these doubts would be readily resolved; nay, they would not exist.

92. Away, then, with all those prophets who say to the people of Christ, "Peace, peace," and there is no peace!

93. Blessed be all those prophets who say to the people of Christ, "Cross, cross," and there is no cross!

94. Christians are to be exhorted that they be diligent in following Christ, their Head, through penalties, deaths, and hell;

95. And thus be confident of entering into heaven rather through many tribulations, than through the assurance of peace.

MARTIN LUTHER BEGINS THE REFORMATION

Project 4—Literature Unit

Thunderstorm in Church

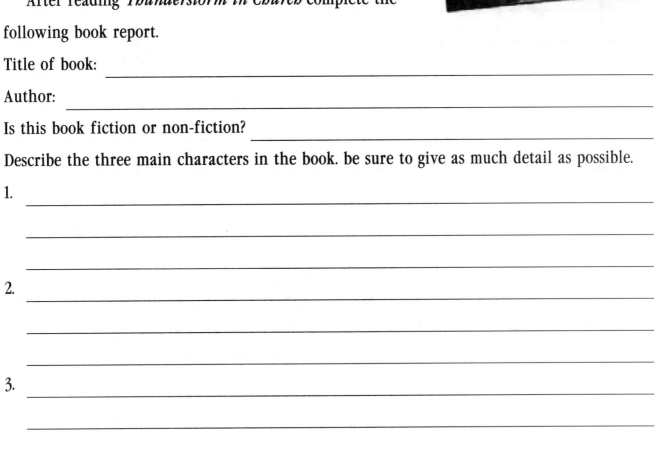

Thunderstorm in Church is about Hans Luther, Martin Luther's young son. He is constantly overshadowed by his famous father. As you read this book told from Hans' eyes you will learn to know Martin Luther, not only as the great reformer-preacher, but also as a father with a sense of humor and as a friend.

After reading *Thunderstorm in Church* complete the following book report.

Title of book: ______________________________

Author: ______________________________

Is this book fiction or non-fiction? ______________________________

Describe the three main characters in the book. be sure to give as much detail as possible.

1. ______________________________

____

____

2. ______________________________

____

____

3. ______________________________

____

____

Martin Luther Begins the Reformation

Project 4, Page 2—Literature Unit

Thunderstorm in Church

What time in history does this story take place? ______________________

Write a two paragraph summary of the book.

Martin Luther Begins the Reformation

Project 5

Martin Luther, Indulgences and the Reformation

I

The first step in Martin Luther becoming a great reformer was his realization of his own sin. It is easy to think that you can be saved by works if you don't appreciate just how serious your sin really is. Martin had no illusions about that. In fact, he would spend hours in the confessional booth confessing his sin. The other monks thought he was crazy, but he was only being honest. When he discovered the passages in Galations which spoke of salvation by grace, not works, it changed everything for him. He had always known, deep down, that none of his works was ever good enough to make up for his sin, but now he had found a way to be saved that didn't depend on him. Only God had the power to forgive sins like this.

II

That's why the men who sold indulgences made him so mad. There was no where in the Bible that said that God would forgive sins for merely giving the Church money. What's more, the Church based its argument for the effectiveness of indulgences based on the idea that the "good works" of the saints created a "pool" of grace that the Church could dispense as it pleased. Martin knew that no one, not even the "saintliest of saints" could possibly have done enough good works to exceed the seriousness of even his or her own sins, much less create a "pool" of grace.

III

One of the most famous sellers of indulgences was Johann Tetzel. There is a story about him that points out some of the problems with indulgences. It actually may not have really happened, but just the possibility of it occurring proves the point. It is said that a group of men once asked Tetzel if they could buy indulgences for future sins. When Tetzel said yes, they all bought one. When Tetzel left town with the money, however, they robbed him of everything. To Tetzel's protests and threats of judgement, they merely responded that they had already bought an indulgence to cover their sin.

Martin Luther Begins the Reformation
Project 5, Page 2

Vocabulary

1. *realization:* ______________________________

2. *illusions:* ______________________________

3. *confessional booth:* ______________________________

4. *indulgences:* ______________________________

5. *argument:* ______________________________

6. *pool:* ______________________________

7. *dispense:* ______________________________

8. *salvation:* ______________________________

9. *grace:* ______________________________

Key Word Outline

I ____________________

1 ____________________

2 ____________________

3 ____________________

4 ____________________

5 ____________________

6 ____________________

7 ____________________

8 ____________________

II ____________________

1 ____________________

2 ____________________

3 ____________________

4 ____________________

III ____________________

1 ____________________

2 ____________________

3 ____________________

4 ____________________

5 ____________________

6 ____________________

MARTIN LUTHER BEGINS THE REFORMATION

Project 5, Page 2

Answers

Vocabulary

1. *realization:* a sudden arrival at new understanding
2. *illusions:* things that seem true but aren't
3. *confessional booth:* a place where Roman Catholics are required to confess their sins to a priest in order to be forgiven them
4. *indulgences:* certificates that show a person has paid the Church a specific sum to obtain pardon for sin
5. *argument:* a reasoned statement justifying a belief of doctrine
6. *pool:* place where things are collectively stored for future use
7. *dispense:* to give out
8. *salvation:* deliverance from the power and penalty of sin
9. *grace:* unmerited, freely given love and favor from God

Key Word Outline

I Sin, Salvation and the Reformation
1. First, step, realization
2. Appreciate, serious, sin
3. Martin, no, illusions
4. Hours, confessing
5. Monks, thought, crazy
6. Discovered, Galatians, changed
7. Found, way, saved
8. Only, God, power

II Good Works and Indulgences
1. Indulgences, made, mad
2. No, forgive, money
3. Based, pool, grace
4. No one, done enough

III Tetzel's Poetic Justice
1. Story, Tetzel, problems
2. May, not, occurred
3. Group, asked, future
4. Tetzel, said, yes
5. Left, robbed, everything
6. Responded, bought, indulgences

Martin Luther Begins the Reformation

Test

1. Who was Martin Luther?

____

____

2. In what year did Martin Luther begin the Reformation?

____

____

3. Where did Luther post the 95 Theses?

____

____

4. What was the 95 Theses? In what language was it written?

____

____

5. What two teachings of Wycliffe and Huss did Luther follow?

____

____

____

6. What position of the Catholic Church did Luther oppose?

____

____

____

7. In 1520, Rome threatened to ________________ Luther if he did not recant his positions. He refused to recant and was ________________.

Martin Luther Begins the Reformation

Test, Page 2

8. What did Luther do at the Diet of Worms?

9. What did Luther's courage cause?

Review

1. In what language was the Vulgate written?

2. Name three barbarian tribes.

3. Who was St. Benedict?

4. Who was the founder of Islam?

5. In chronological order list the events studied to date.

   Next to each place the approximate date.

ULRICH ZWINGLI AND THE ANABAPTISTS
Worksheet

1. Ulrich Zwingli is associated with the ___________ Reformation.
2. When did Zwingli become pastor of the church of Zurich?

____

____

3. Did Zwingli know about Luther when he came up with his ideas about the Roman Catholic Church?

____

____

4. About what did Zwingli and Luther disagree?

____

____

5. How did Zwingli die?

____

____

6. What distinctives did Menno Simons and his group believe?

____

____

____

____

____

____

ULRICH ZWINGLI AND THE ANABAPTISTS
Project

Using the resources on the card write a paragraph about the differences between Luther and Zwingli.

Ulrich Zwingli and the Anabaptists

Test

1. Ulrich Zwingli was part of the ________________ Reformation.
2. True or false: Luther got his convictions from Zwingli about the need for reformation in the Catholic Church. Why is the answer true or false?

    ____

    ____

    ____

3. Why did a civil war break out in the Swiss Confederation?

    ____

    ____

    ____

4. How did Zwingli die?

    ____

    ____

    ____

5. Who was the founder of the Mennonites? What did they believe?

    ____

    ____

    ____

Review

1. List two things John Wycliff believed about the Church.

    ____

    ____

ULRICH ZWINGLI AND THE ANABAPTISTS
Test, Page 2

2. What did the Great Papal Schism establish?

3. What is Thomas Aquinas' greatest work?

4. How many Crusades were there?

5. In chronological list order all the events studied to date.

   Next to each place the approximate date.

Act of Supremacy
Worksheet

1. What is the date given for the Act of Supremacy?

____

____

____

2. Why did King Henry want to divorce Catherine of Aragon?

____

____

____

3. What led up to Parliament's proclamation that the king was the head of the Church of England?

____

____

____

4. Who became the highest spiritual authorities in England after the Act of Supremacy?

____

____

____

____

5. Whose reign shaped the Anglican Church?

____

____

____

____

____

ACT OF SUPREMACY
Project

Movie

View the film, *A Man For All Seasons*

Catherine, Henry VIII's wife, has been unable to produce an heir to the throne. Henry (Robert Shaw), having fallen in love with Anne Buleyne, asks the Pope to grant him a divorce. The King is backed by everyone except the highly regarded Sir Thomas More (Paul Scofield). When Cardinal Wolsey (Orsen Welles), Chancellor of England, names More his successor, it becomes increasingly important for Henry to get More's support. But More cannot be swayed. Henry demands the clergy to renounce the Pope and name him the head of the Church of England. Cromwell (Leo McKern), leader of the divorce campaign, frames More, forcing him to resign as Chancellor. Eventually More is brought to trial, found guilty of treason, and beheaded.

ACT OF SUPREMACY

Test

1. What is the date given for the Act of Supremacy?

____

____

2. Why was Henry VIII troubled by his marriage to Catherine of Aragon?

____

____

3. The Pope refused to grant Henry VIII's request for a ______________ from Catherine of Aragon.

4. What led up to Parliament's proclamation that the king was the head of the Church of England?

____

____

____

5. Who became the highest spiritual authorities in England after the Act of Supremacy?

____

____

6. Whose reign shaped the Anglican Church?

____

____

Review

1. What are the best known books by St. Augustine of Hippo?

____

____

Act of Supremacy

Test, Page 2

2. What are the three vows made by monks?

3. Who was Alfred the Great?

4. List the structure of society under the feudal system.

5. In chronological order list all the events studied to date.

   Next to each place the approximate date.

John Calvin and the Institutes

Worksheet

1. What is the date given for John Calvin and the Institutes?

2. What was John Calvin's motto?

3. What was the *Institutes of the Christian Religion* about?

4. To whom was the Institutes dedicated?

5. From his understanding of Scripture, what form of church government did Calvin develop?

6. What did Calvin do in Geneva?

John Calvin and the Institutes
Project

Reading and Discussion

Below is an excerpt from Calvin's Institutes. He is explaining what it is to God and in knowing Him how one's life will change. After reading the passage, discuss the following questions:

What does Calvin think is needed before one can know God?

Describe Calvin's "two-fold" knowledge of God.

What does Calvin believe that men owe to God? What does understanding this allow?

To what do the "punishment of the impious" and reward of life eternal to the righteous equally pertain?

What is pure and real religion?

From the *Institutes of the Christian Religion* –

CHAPTER II

What It Is to Know God, and to What Purpose the Knowledge of Him Tends

1. Piety is requisite for the knowledge of God

Now, the knowledge of God, as I understand it, is that by which we not only conceive that there is a God but also grasp what befits us and is proper to his glory, in fine, what is to our advantage to know of him. Indeed, we shall not say that, properly speaking, God is known where there is no religion or piety. Here I do not yet touch upon the sort of knowledge with which men, in themselves lost and accursed, apprehend God the Redeemer in Christ the Mediator; but I speak only of the primal and simple knowledge to which the very order of nature would have led us if Adam had remained upright. In this ruin of mankind no one now experiences God either as Father or as Author of salvation, or favorable in any way, until Christ the Mediator comes forward to reconcile him to us. Nevertheless, it is one thing to feel that God as our Maker supports us by his power, governs us by his providence, nourishes us by his goodness, and attends us with all sorts of blessings—and another thing to embrace the grace of reconciliation offered to us in Christ. First, as much in the fashioning of the universe as general teaching of Scripture the Lord shows himself to be simply the Creator. Then in the face of Christ [cf. 11 Cor. 4:6] he shows himself the Redeemer. Of the resulting two-fold knowledge of God we shall now discuss the first aspect; the second will be dealt with in its proper place .

Moreover, although our mind cannot apprehend God without rendering some honor to him, it will not suffice simply to hold that there is One whom all ought to honor and adore, unless we are also persuaded that he is the fountain of every good, and that we must seek nothing elsewhere than in him. This I take to mean that not only does he sustain this universe (as he once founded it) by his boundless might, regulate it by his wisdom, preserve it by his goodness, and especially rule mankind by his righteousness and judgment, bear with it in his mercy, watch over it by his protection; but also that no drop will be found either of wisdom and light, or of righteousness or power or rectitude, or of genuine truth, which does not flow from him, and of which he is not the cause. Thus we may learn to await and seek all these things from him, and thankfully to ascribe them, once received, to him For this sense of the powers of God is for us a fit teacher of piety, from which religion is born. I call "piety" that reverence joined with love of God which the knowledge of his benefits induces. For until men recognize that they owe everything to God, that they are nourished by his fatherly care, that he is the Author of their every good, that they should seek nothing beyond him they will never yield him willing service. Nay, unless they establish their complete happiness in him, they will never give themselves truly and sincerely to him.

2. Knowledge of God involves trust and reverence

What is God? Men who pose this question are merely toying with idle speculations. It is more important for us to know of what sort he is and what is consistent with his nature. What good is it to profess with Epicurus some sort of God who has cast aside the care of the world only to amuse himself in idleness? What help is it, in short, to know a God with whom we have nothing to do? Rather, our knowledge should serve first to teach us fear and reverence; secondly, with it as our guide and teacher, we should learn to seek every good from him, and, having received it, to credit it to his account, for how can the thought of God penetrate your mind without your realizing immediately that, since you are his handiwork, you have been made over and bound to his command by right of creation, that you owe your life to him?—that whatever you undertake, whatever you do, ought to be ascribed to him? If this be so, it now assuredly follows that your life is wickedly corrupt unless it be disposed to his service, seeing, that his will ought for us to be the law by which we live. Again, you cannot behold him clearly unless you acknowledge him to be the fountainhead and source of every good. From this too would arise the desire to cleave to him and trust in him, but for the fact that man's depravity seduces his mind from rightly seeking him.

For, to begin with, the pious mind does not dream up for itself any god it pleases, but contemplates the one and only true God. And it does not attach to him whatever it pleases, but is content to hold him to be as he manifests himself; furthermore, the mind always exercises the utmost diligence and care not to wander astray, or rashly and boldly to go beyond his will. It thus recognizes God because it knows that he governs all things; and trusts that he is its guide and protector, therefore giving itself over completely to trust in him. Because it understands him to be the Author of every good, if anything oppresses, if anything is lacking, immediately it betakes itself to his protection, waiting for help from him. Because it is persuaded that he is good and merciful, it reposes in him with perfect trust, and doubts not that in his loving-kindness a remedy will be provided for all its ills. Because it acknowledges him as Lord and Father, the pious mind also deems it meet and right to observe his authority in all things, reverence his majesty, take care to advance his glory, and obey his commandments. Because it sees him to be a righteous judge, armed with severity to punish wickedness, it ever holds his judgment seat before its gaze, and through fear of him restrains itself from provoking his anger, and yet it is not so terrified by the awareness of his judgment as to wish to withdraw, even if some way of escape were open. But it embraces him no less as punisher of the wicked than as benefactor of the pious. For the pious mind realizes that the punishment of the impious and wicked and the reward of life eternal for the righteous equally pertain to God's glory. Besides, this mind restrains itself from sinning, not out of dread of punishment alone; but, because it loves and reveres God as Father, it worships and adores him as Lord. Even if there were no hell, it would still shudder at offending him alone.

Here indeed is pure and real religion: faith so joined with an earnest fear of God that this fear also embraces willing reverence, and carries with it such legitimate worship as is prescribed in the law. And we ought to note this fact even more diligently: all men have a vague general veneration for God, but very few really reverence him; and wherever there is great ostentation in ceremonies, sincerity of heart is rare indeed.

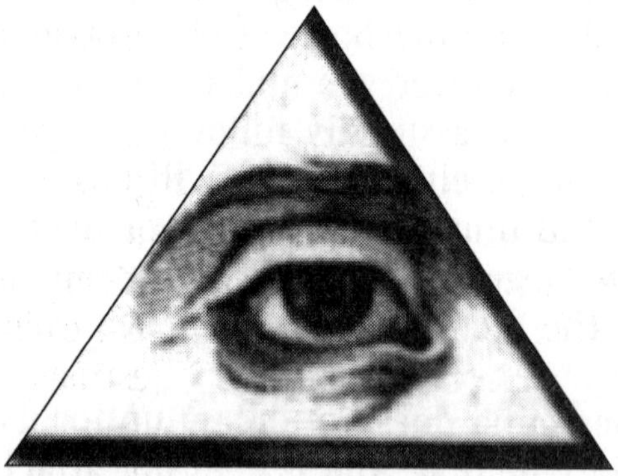

JOHN CALVIN AND THE INSTITUTES

Project 2–Literature Unit

This Was John Calvin Study Guide

Suggested Eight Day Plan

Day One	Read the Preface and back cover information about the author.
Day Two	Read 6 Chapters
Day Three	Read 6 Chapters
Day Four	Read 6 chapters
Day Five	Read 5 chapters
Day Six	Read 6 chapters
Day Seven	Read 6 chapters
Day Eight	Review student folders for assessment.

Each day read 3 or 4 chapters in class and assign others for homework. A chapter takes about 5 minutes to read. The chapter questions can be used as a transitional activity each morning to check on the student's completion and understanding of homework. Each student should maintain a folder with vocabulary and question responses for review and assessment. Upon completion of the book, students should have copies of the comprehension questions, written complete answers, a glossary of words, a chart of Geneva's councils, a map of France, Switzerland, and Germany, a daily planner page for John Calvin, and a drawing representing the entrance to Geneva Academy. For the vocabulary, use 13 pages of notebook paper folded in half top to bottom. On each half (front only) write one letter of the alphabet. Each word from the chapter questions should be defined before the day's reading. This will allow the student to have a glossary of words from *This Was John Calvin.* Copy student maps and have students use colored pencils to trace Calvin's travels.

Before starting *This Was John Calvin*, decorate the entrance to your classroom with pillars made from painted carpet tubes. Make 3 banners for the texts to hang outside your door or over your chalkboard. The texts are: The fear of the Lord is the beginning of wisdom; Christ has become to us the wisdom of God; and The wisdom which comes from above is pure, peaceful, and full of mercy. Place a large map of France, Switzerland, and Germany on the wall and use yarn to mark Calvin's travels.

Discuss the genre of biography and how it differs from historical fiction. Which is *This Was John Calvin*? How does Mrs. Van Halsema advance the story? Note that she uses written material for her quotations by John Calvin, not fictional dialogue.

John Calvin and the Institutes

Project 2, Page 2—Literature Unit

Comprehension questions for This Was John Calvin

All answers should be complete sentences. Whenever possible use supporting quotes from the book, listing the page number in parentheses (p.#). Record your definitions in a glossary made by folding 13 notebook pages in half top to bottom. On the top and middle of each page, front side only, write a letter of the alphabet. All words beginning with that letter should be listed and defined below the letter heading.

Background and Preface

Who is the author?
When was the book written?
What is one of the author's desires in telling Calvin's story?

Chapter One

Describe John Calvin's father.
How could Gerard Calvin's position as church attorney have influenced Calvin?
Describe Calvin's mother.
When and where was John Calvin born?

Chapter Two

Define *benefice, tonsure*
How did John Calvin become a chaplain?
Where did John study in 1523?

Chapter Three

Define *indulgence, purgatory, heresy*
What money making scheme did Leo X use to build St. Peter's in Rome?
What world shaping event began in 1517?
Who was Jacques Lefevre?
How did Lefevre influence William Farel?
What was a driving force in the Reformation?
Describe the political and religious situation in France when John Calvin arrived in Paris.

Chapter Four

Where did Calvin study theology?
For what was his college famous?
What subjects did Calvin study?

Chapter Five

Define *faggot, uncouth, provoked*
Describe some of the martyrs mentioned in this chapter.
What brought about Gerard Calvin's decision for John to study law, not religion?

Chapter Six

Define *canon*
Describe life in Orleans.
How did Calvin discipline his mind?
When did Calvin leave the study of law?
Describe humanism.
What did Calvin study at the College Fortet?

Chapter Seven

What was Calvin's first book?
Was it successful?
Why did Calvin return to Orleans?
Why did he return to Noyon?

John Calvin and the Institutes
Project 2, Page 3–Literature Unit

Chapter Eight
What did Nicolas Cop speak about on All Saints' Day?
Who was rumored to have helped write Cop's speech?
What was the result of the speech for Cop? For Calvin?
Read Romans 9:1-19 to understand the reference to Paul and the Damascus Road. How did Calvin's sudden conversion change his life?

Chapter Nine
What influence did Margaret, Queen of Navarre, have for Calvin and other Reformers?
What decision did Calvin make regarding the reforming of the Roman church from within?

Chapter Ten
Define *trinity, conversion, placard*
Who was hunting Calvin?
What work kept Calvin busy?
Who was Servetus?
What was Calvin's first book after conversion?
What happened following the Affair of the Placards?
Who was the King of France during the Affair of the Placards?
Who were some of the influential men in Calvin's life?
When and to where did Calvin flee? Then on to?

Chapter 11
Define *triune, divine, scourge, tumult, connivance*
What is the purpose of the *Institutes of the Christian Religion*?
To whom did Calvin dedicate the *Institutes?*
Did that man read the book?
How many editions were there?
What happened with each edition?
What languages were the four editions in?

Chapter 12
Define *mitre, prelate, macebearer, pious*
Why did King Francis allow the Protestants six months in France without persecution?
Why couldn't Calvin travel straight from Paris to Strasbourg?
What did Calvin hope to do in Strasbourg?
What city did he stop in for lodging?

Chapter 13
Describe the government of the Swiss cantons.
Who was preaching the Reformation in the middle north?
What decision was being made by the cantons?
What was William Farel's calling?
Describe William Farel.
Which canton did Farel represent?
If some people in a town were converted, what was the official procedure?
What happened if the townspeople voted to become Protestants?

Chapter 14
Define *apothecary, ultimatum, disputation*
Describe Geneva.
For what were the people of Geneva struggling?
How was Farel received in Geneva?
What plan did Farel come up with for reaching the people of Geneva?
Was the plan successful?
What was on the verge of happening between the Catholics and Protestants?
Who stopped it?

John Calvin and the Institutes
Project 2, Page 4–Literature Unit

What happened to Canon Wernli a few weeks later?
What were the results?
Which side won the disputation?
What was the response of the Duke of Savoy? The canton of Fribourg? The canton of Bern?
What did Geneva decide?

Chapter 15
Define *edict*
Against whom was Geneva fortifying the city?
How is God's providence evident in the poisoning of Viret?
With the edict of August 27, 1535, what happened?
Who helped the city of Geneva and why?
To what did the people agree on May 21, 1536?

Chapter 16
Define *torrent, timid, bled, poultices, gaudy*
How did Farel convince Calvin to stay in Geneva?
Why did Farel want Calvin in Geneva?
What were the different groups who worked against the Reformation?
How was Calvin perfectly fitted for the work of changing Geneva?
What was Calvin's title in Geneva?
What challenges did Calvin face concerning the people's lifestyles?

Chapter 17
Define *theses, syndic*
What was the disagreement concerning the presence of Christ's body in the Holy Supper?
What was the result of Calvin's response to the Catholic position?
How did Calvin set about building up the church of Geneva?
Do you think people can be forced to live in a way in which they do not believe?
Who were the Libertines?
Use the paragraph on pages 84-85 to lay out the governing councils of Geneva. Include how each of the councils were elected or chosen?

Chapter 18
Define *devoutly, excommunication, catechism, contempt*
The preachers proposed four reforms for the church of Geneva, what were they?
Which reforms caused great controversy?
Why did the desired reform in the Lord's Supper and the power of excommunication cause so much uproar?
Did the people of Geneva respect the law?

Chapter 19
In Calvin's time what did the Anabaptists preach and believe?
List the problems with Caroli's beliefs.
What happened to Calvin's friend du Tillet?
How did Calvin respond?
What was happening politically in Geneva around February 1538?
What did the canton of Bern request from the councils of Geneva?
When Geneva's Council of Two Hundred agreed with the requests from Bern, what was the response of Corault, Calvin, and Farel?
How did the people of Geneva behave toward Calvin and Farel while Corault was imprisoned?
Why did the Council of Two Hundred force Calvin, Corault, and Farel out of Geneva?

John Calvin and the Institutes
Project 2, Page 5—Literature Unit

Chapter 20

After Farel and Calvin reconsidered their positions at Zurich, what did the councils of Geneva decide?

Where did Farel go to minister?

Where did Calvin go to minister?

Read Acts 11:19-26 and Genesis 13:13 to understand the references. Write a few sentences comparing Antioch to Sodom.

How was Calvin received in Strasbourg?

Chapter 21

Define *chastised, trifling, paroxysm, solace, besetting, inured*

Why did Calvin believe he had been chastised?

Describe Martin Bucer.

Describe Calvin's life in Strasbourg.

List Calvin's writings while at Strasbourg.

What trouble was Calvin having in Strasbourg?

What physical problems did Calvin continue to have?

What happened with Caroli?

Chapter 22

Define *chaste, fastidious, audacity, demented, predicament, tiff, wont, tertian fever*

What did Calvin desire in a wife?

How many times did Calvin nearly marry?

Who did he finally marry?

Describe Calvin's wife.

Chapter 23

Define *dissent*

Why was Emperor Charles of Spain pushing for a union between the Protestants and the Roman church?

What were the conferences called?

With whom did Calvin form a life-long friendship at the Diets?

Who was Philip Melancthon?

What nickname did Melancthon give Calvin?

About what did Luther and Calvin disagree concerning the Lord's Supper?

Despite their disagreements, how was the relationship between Luther and Calvin?

Chapter 24

Define *stifle, entreaty, stooge, ambiguous, transubstantiation, wistfully, vehemently, incomparable, tempestuous*

What did the letter to Calvin request?

Was Calvin surprised at Geneva's request? Were you?

What happened to the Genevan church in Calvin's absence?

At first, what did Calvin think about returning to Geneva?

What did Calvin mean when he said, "I offer my heart a slain victim for a sacrifice to the Lord. I yield my soul chained and bound unto obedience to God."?

What decision did Calvin finally make concerning Geneva?

Chapter 25

How did Calvin change since his first stay in Geneva?

How did Geneva change?

What did Calvin propose immediately?

Chapter 26

Define *ecclesiastical, ordinances, font, abstain, persistent*

What were the Ecclesiastical Ordinances of the Church of Geneva?

What are the four offices of the church?

How many days a week were there church services?

Why should a man be told to abstain from the Lord's Supper?

JOHN CALVIN AND THE INSTITUTES
Project 2, Page 6—Literature Unit

Which churches have as their foundation the Ordinances?
What is unique about the offices of elder and deacon?
How long did it take to put the Ordinances fully into practice?

CHAPTER 27
How did some people of Geneva, including Calvin, believe the plague was being spread?
How many children did Calvin have? How many survived?
Write out a weekly plan for John Calvin, including his writing time.

CHAPTER 28
Define *hart, prostrate*
When did Martin Luther die, and under what circumstances?
What work had Luther done for the Reformation?
What was Calvin's work for the Reformation?
What great sadness entered Calvin's world in March, 1549?

CHAPTER 29
Define *benediction, fleet*
Describe John Calvin's character in a paragraph.

CHAPTER 30
Define *incognito, puns, intrigues*
Was Calvin greedy for money?
What other churches did Calvin show concern for besides Geneva?
What happened to the French Protestants during the 42 years of the reign of Francis I and Henry II?
What did the Zurich Consensus of 1549 and the Helvetic Confession of 1566 mean?

CHAPTER 31
Define *consistory, lenient, tribunal, insolent*
What is the doctrine of election? Look up this doctrine in Calvin's Institutes or The Westminster Confession of Faith (Of God's Decree). Read Romans 9, Romans 11:6, Ephesians 2:8, 1 Peter 1:2, Romans 8:30, and 2 Peter 1:10 and write a three or four sentence summary of the doctrine of election.
Why did Calvin keep Castellio from becoming a pastor?
What happened with Pierre Ameaux?
Why did the Libertines hate John Calvin?

CHAPTER 32
Define *smolder, lewd, incessant, malicious, pleurisy, hemorrhoids, influenza, vixen*
For what reasons were citizens brought before the Little Council?
Why was Jacques Gruet executed?

CHAPTER 33
Define *astrology, blaspheme, pestilence, effigy, incorrigible*
Who was the Spanish heretic?
What heresy concerning the Trinity did Servetus hold?
What was the response of the Supreme council of the Spanish Inquisition toward Servetus' heresy?
How did Servetus hide?
How did Servetus escape the French prison?
Who sided with Servetus in Geneva?
What law condemned Servetus?

CHAPTER 34
Who had the power to sentence Servetus?
What happened concerning the Lord's Supper with Berthelier?
What did Servetus think the outcome of his trial would be?
How was Servetus sentenced to die?

Why did Calvin ask that he die by the sword instead?
By whom was Servetus actually condemned?

Chapter 35
Define *fracas*
On whom did the Libertines turn for their final attack?
List several of the health and safety laws Calvin influenced the councils to pass.
How many books did Calvin write?
What changes in church music did Calvin encourage?
Describe The Geneva Academy.
On a separate sheet of paper, draw an arched roof porch with pillars and write out the three texts from The Geneva Academy building on it.
What influence did Geneva Academy have on Europe and the world?

Chapter 36
Define *wry, gouty, notary*
How did Calvin spend his final years, despite great illness?

John Calvin and the Institutes

Test

1. What was John Calvin's motto?

2. What was the *Institutes of the Christian Religion* about?

3. To whom was the Institutes dedicated?

4. From his understanding of Scripture, what form of church government did Calvin develop?

5. What did Calvin do in Geneva?

Review

1. What is the Magna Carta?

John Calvin and the Institutes
Test, Page 2

2. Write a summary of Joan of Arc's life. Include when and where she lived and any unusual facts about her life.

3. What was the Renaissance an attempt to recover?

4. In what architectural style are the cathedrals of Europe designed?

5. List the events you have studied in order. Include the dates for each event.

COUNCIL OF TRENT
Worksheet

1. What is the date given for the Council of Trent?

2. What was the Council of Trent?

3. Who called it together?

4. What were three outcomes of the Council of Trent?

5. What was the effect of the Council's rejection of justification by faith alone and the use of scripture alone?

6. What did the Council of Trent define?

Council of Trent
Project

Using the resources, write a paragraph discussing whether the Council of Trent erred in its view. Use biblical support to discuss sola fida, sola scriptura, and sola gratia.

Council of Trent
Test

1. What is the date given for the Council of Trent?

2. What was the Council of Trent?

3. Who called it together?

4. What were three outcomes of the Council of Trent?

5. What was the effect of the Council's rejection of justification by faith alone and the use of scripture alone?

6. What did the Council of Trent define?

7. Why did the Council of Trent seal the Roman Catholic's church apostacy?

COUNCIL OF TRENT

Test, Page 2

Review

1. What was the Council of Chalcedon?

2. What people did Charlemagne rule?

3. In what book did Marco Polo describe China?

4. In which language did John Huss preach?

5. In chronological order list the events you have studied. Include the date for each event.

John Knox, Scottish Reformer
Worksheet

1. What is the date given for John Knox, Scottish Reformer?

2. Where was John Knox born?

3. When was Knox made a prisoner of the French?

4. What became of him during his life as a prisoner?

5. After his release what became of Knox? Why was this important?

6. After leaving England to where did Knox go?

7. What teachings did he learn from after leaving England?

JOHN KNOX, SCOTTISH REFORMER
Worksheet, Page 2

8. What was the "Common Band"?

9. Why did Knox go back to Scotland?

10. Describe Knox' preaching style.

John Knox, Scottish Reformer
Project

Web Excercise

After reading *The Church in History* pgs. 216 - 219 draw a picture on the next page of five important events Knox made to society.

JOHN KNOX, SCOTTISH REFORMER
Project, Page 2

John Knox, Scottish Reformer
Project 2

The Thirty-Nine Articles
THE ARTICLES OF RELIGION

Agreed upon by the Archbishops, Bishops, and the whole clergy of the Provinces of Canterbury and York, London, 1562

Article I
Of Faith in the Holy Trinity

There is but one living and true God, everlasting, without body, parts, or passions; of infinite power, wisdom, and goodness; the Maker, and Preserver of all things both visible and invisible. And in unity of this Godhead there be three Persons, of one substance, power, and eternity; the Father, the Son, and the Holy Ghost.

Article II
Of the Word or Son of God, which was made very Man

The Son, which is the Word of the Father, begotten from everlasting of the Father, the very and eternal God, and of one substance with the Father, took Man's nature in the womb of the blessed Virgin, of her substance: so that two whole and perfect Natures, that is to say, the Godhead and Manhood, were joined together in one Person, never to be divided, whereof is one Christ, very God, and very Man; who truly suffered, was crucified, dead, and buried, to reconcile His Father to us, and to be a sacrifice, not only for original guilt, but also for all actual sins of men.

Article III
Of the going down of Christ into Hell

As Christ died for us, and was buried, so also is it to be believed, that he went down into Hell.

Article IV
Of the Resurrection of Christ

Christ did truly rise again from death, and took again his body, with flesh, bones, and all things appertaining to the perfection of Man's nature; wherewith he ascended into Heaven, and there sitteth, until he return to judge all Men at the last day.

Article V
Of the Holy Ghost

The Holy Ghost, proceeding from the Father and the Son, is of one substance, majesty, and glory, with the Father and the Son, very and eternal God.

Article VI
Of the Sufficiency of the holy Scriptures for salvation

Holy Scripture containeth all things necessary to salvation: so that whatsoever is not read therein, nor may be proved thereby, is not to be required of any man, that it should be believed as an article of the Faith, or be thought requisite or necessary to salvation. In the name of the holy Scripture, we do understand those Canonical books of the Old and New Testament, of whose authority was never any doubt in the Church.

Of the Names and Number of the Canonical Books—

Genesis
Exodus
Leviticus
Numbers
Deuteronomy
Joshua
Judges
Ruth
The First Book of Samuel
The Second Book of Samuel

The First Book of Kings
The Second Book of Kings
The First Book of Chronicles
The Second Book of Chronicles
The First Book of Esdras
The Second Book of Esdras
The Book of Esther
The Book of Job
The Psalms
The Proverbs
Ecclesiastes or Preacher
Cantica, or Songs of Solomon
Four Prophets the greater
Twelve Prophets the less

And the other Books (as Hierome saith) the Church doth read for example of life and instruction of manners; but yet doth it not apply them to establish any doctrine; such are these following—

The Third Book of Esdras
The Fourth Book of Esdras
The Book of Tobias
The Book of Judith
The rest of the Book of Esther
The Book of Wisdom
Jesus, the Son of Sirach
Baruch the Prophet
The Song of the Three Children
The Story of Susanna
Of Bel and the Dragon
The Prayer of Manasses
The First Book of Maccabees
The Second Book of Maccabees

All the Books of the New Testament, as they are commonly received, we do receive, and account them Canonical.

Article VII

Of the Old Testament

The Old Testament is not contrary to the New: for both in the Old and New Testament everlasting life is offered to Mankind by Christ, who is the only Mediator between God and Man, being both God and Man. Wherefore there are not to be heard, which feign that the old Fathers did look only for transitory promises. Although the Law given from God by Moses, as touching Ceremonies and Rites, do not bind Christian men, nor the Civil precepts thereof ought of necessity to be received in any commonwealth; yet, notwithstanding, no Christian man whatsoever is free from the obedience of the Commandments which are called Moral.

Article VIII

Of the Three Creeds

The Three Creeds, Nicene Creed, Athanasius's Creed, and that which is commonly called the Apostles' Creed, ought thoroughly to be received and believed: for they may be proved by most certain warrants of holy Scripture.

Article IX

Of Original or Birth-Sin

Original Sin standeth not in the following of Adam, (as the Pelagians do vainly talk), but it is the fault and corruption of the Nature of every man, that naturally is ingendered of the offspring of Adam; whereby man is very far gone from original righteousness, and is of his own nature inclined to evil, so that the flesh lusteth always contrary to the spirit; and therefore in every person born into this world, it deserveth God's wrath and damnation. And this infection of nature doth remain, ye, in them that are regenerated; whereby the lust of the flesh, called in Greek, phronema sarkos, which some do expound the wisdom, some sensuality, some the affection, some the desire, of the flesh, is not subject to the

Law of God. And although there is no condemnation for them that believe and are baptized, yet the Apostle doth confess, that concupiscence and lust hath of itself the nature of sin.

ARTICLE X

Of Free-Will

The condition of Man after the fall of Adam is such, that he cannot turn and prepare himself, by his own natural strength and good works, to faith, and calling upon God: Wherefore we have no power to do good works pleasant and acceptable to God, without the grace of God by Christ preventing us, that we may have a good will, and working with us, when we have that good will.

ARTICLE XI

Of the Justification of Man

We are accounted righteous before God, only for the merit of our Lord and Saviour Jesus Christ by Faith, and not for our own works or deservings: Wherefore, that we are justified by Faith only is a most wholesome Doctrine, and very full of comfort, as more largely is expressed in the Homily of Justification.

ARTICLE XII

Of Good Works

Albeit that Good Works, which are the fruits of Faith, and follow after Justification, cannot put away our sins, and endure the severity of God's Judgement; yet are they pleasing and acceptable to God in Christ, and do spring out necessarily of a true and lively Faith; insomuch that by them a lively Faith may be as evidently known as a tree discerned by the fruit.

ARTICLE XIII

Of Works before Justification

Works done before the grace of Christ, and the Inspiration of his Spirit, are not pleasant to God, forasmuch as they spring not of faith in Jesus Christ, neither do they make men meet to receive grace, or (as the School-authors say) deserve grace of congruity: yea, rather, for that they are not done as God hath willed and commanded them to be done, we doubt not but they have the nature of sin.

ARTICLE XIV

Of Works of Supererogation

Voluntary Works besides, over, and above, God's Commandments, which they call Works of Supererogation, cannot be taught without arrogancy and impiety: for by them men do declare, that they do not only render unto God as much as they are bound to do, but that they do more for his sake, than of bounden duty is required: whereas Christ saith plainly, When ye have done all that are commanded to you, say, We are unprofitable servants.

ARTICLE XV

Of Christ alone without Sin

Christ in the truth of our nature was made like unto us in all things, sin only except, from which he was clearly void, both in his flesh, and in his spirit. He came to be the Lamb without spot, who, by sacrifice of himself once made, should take away the sins of the world, and sin, as Saint John saith, was not in him. But all we the rest, although baptized, and born again in Christ, yet offend in many things; and if we say we have no sin, we deceive ourselves, and the truth is not in us.

Article XVI
Of Sin after Baptism
Not every deadly sin willingly commited after Baptism is sin against the Holy Ghost, and unpardonable. Wherefore the grant of repentance is not to be denied to such as fall into sin after Baptism. After we have received the Holy Ghost, we may depart from grace given, and fall into sin, and by the grace of God we may arise again, and amend our lives. And therefore they are to be condemned, which say, thay can no more sin as long as they live here, or deny the place of forgiveness to such as truly repent.

Article XVII
Of Predestination and Election
Predestination to Life is the everlasting purpose of God, whereby (before the foundations of the world were laid) he hath constantly decreed by his counsel secret to us, to deliver from curse and damnation those whom he hath chosen in Christ out of mankind, and to bring them by Christ to everlasting salvation, as vessels made to honour. Wherefore, they which be endued with so excellent a benefit of God be called according to God's purpose by his Spirit working in due season: they through Grace obey the calling: they be justified freely: they be made sons of God by adoption: they be made like the image of his only-begotten Son Jesus Christ: they walk religiously in good works, and at length, by God's mercy, they attain to everlasting felicity.

As the godly consideration of Predestination, and our Election in Christ, is full of sweet, pleasant, and unspeakable comfort to godly persons, and such as feel in themselves the working of the Spirit of Christ, mortifying the works of the flesh, and their earthly members, and drawing up their mind to high and heavenly things, as well because it doth greatly establish and confirm their faith of eternal Salvation to be enjoyed through Christ, as because it doth fervently kindle their love towards God: So, for curious and carnal persons, lacking the Spirit of Christ, to have continually before their eyes the sentence of God's Predestination, is a most dangerous downfall, whereby the Devil doth thrust them either into desperation, or into wretchlessness of most unclean living, no less perilous than desperation.

Furthermore, we must receive God's promises in such wise, as they be generally set forth to us in holy Scripture: and, in our doings, that Will of God is to be followed which we have expressly declared unto us in the Word of God.

Article XVIII
Of obtaining eternal Salvation only by the Name of Christ
They also are to be had accursed that presume to say, That every man shall be saved by the Law or Sect which he professeth, so that he be diligent to frame his life according to that Law, and the light of Nature. For holy Scripture doth set out unto us only the Name of Jesus Christ, whereby men must be saved.

Article XIX
Of the Church
The visible Church of Christ is a congregation of faithful men, in the which the pure Word of God is preached, and the Sacraments be duly ministered according to Christ's ordinance in all those things that of necessity are requisite to the same.

As the Church of Jerusalem, Alexandria, and Antioch have erred: so also the Church of Rome hath erred, not only in their living and manner of Ceremonies, but also in matters of Faith.

Article XX
Of the Authority of the Church

The Church hath power to decree Rites or Ceremonies, and authority in Controversies of Faith: And yet it is not lawful for the Church to ordain anything contrary to God's Word written, neither may it so expound one place of Scripture, that it be repugnant to another. Wherefore, although the Church be a witness and a keeper of holy Writ, yet, as it ought not to decree any thing against the same, so besides the same ought it not to enforce any thing to be believed for necessity of Salvation.

Article XXI
Of the Authority of General Councils

General Councils may not be gathered together without the commandment and will of Princes. And when they be gathered together, (forasmuch as they be an assembly of men, whereof all be not governed with the Spirit and Word of God,) they may err, and sometimes have erred, even in things pertaining unto God. Wherefore things ordained by them as necessary to salvation have neither strength nor authority, unless it may be declared that they be taken out of holy Scripture.

Article XXII
Of Purgatory

The Romish Doctrine concerning Purgatory, Pardons, Worshipping, and Adoration as well of Images as of Reliques, and also invocation of Saints, is a fond thing vainly invented, and grounded upon no warranty of Scripture, but rather repugnant to the Word of God.

Article XXIII
Of Ministering in the Congregation

It is not lawful for any man to take upon him the office of publick preaching, or ministering the Sacraments in the Congregation, before he be lawfully called, and sent to execute the same. And those we ought to judge lawfully called and sent, which be chosen and called to this work by men who have publick authority given unto them in the Congregation, to call and send Ministers into the Lord's vineyard.

Article XXIV
Of speaking in the Congregation in such a tongue as the people understandeth

It is a thing plainly repugnant to the Word of God, and the custom of the Primitive Church, to have publick Prayer in the Church, or to minister the Sacraments in a tongue not understanded of the people.

Article XXV
Of the Sacraments

Sacraments ordained of Christ be not only badges or tokens of Christian men's profession, but rather they be certain sure witnesses, and effectual signs of grace, and God's good will towards us, by the which he doth work invisibly in us, and doth not only quicken, but also strengthen and confirm our Faith in him.

There are two Sacraments ordained of Christ our Lord in the Gospel, that is to say, Baptism, and the Supper of the Lord.

Those five commonly called Sacraments, that is to say, Confirmation, Penance,

Orders, Matrimony, and extreme Unction, are not to be counted for Sacraments of the Gospel, being such as have grown partly of the corrupt following of the Apostles, partly are states of life allowed in the Scriptures; but yet have not like nature of Sacraments with Baptism, and the Lord's Supper, for that they have not any visible sign or ceremony ordained of God.

The Sacraments were not ordained of Christ to be gazed upon, or to be carried about, but that we should duly use them. And in such only as worthily receive the same have they a wholesome effect or operation: but they that receive them unworthily purchase to themselves damnation, as Saint Paul saith.

Article XXVI

Of the Unworthiness of the Ministers, which hinders not the effect of the Sacrament

Although in the visible Church the evil be ever mingled with the good, and sometimes the evil have chief authority in the Ministration of the Word and Sacraments, yet forasmuch as they do not the same in their own name, but in Christ's, and do minister by his commission and authority, we may use their Ministry, both in hearing the Word of God, and in the receiving of the Sacraments. Neither is the effect of Christ's ordinance taken away by their wickedness, nor the grace of God's gifts diminished from such as by faith and rightly do receive the Sacraments ministered unto them; which be effectual, because of Christ's institution and promise, although they be ministered by evil men.

Nevertheless it appertaineth to the discipline of the Church, that inquiry be made of evil Ministers, and that they be accused by those that have knowledge of their offences; and finally being found guilty, by just judgement be deposed.

Article XXVII

Of Baptism

Baptism is not only a sign of profession, and mark of difference, whereby Christian men are discerned from others that be not christened, but is also a sign of Regeneration or new Birth, whereby, as by an instrument, they that receive Baptism rightly are grafted into the Church; the promises of the forgiveness of sin, and of our adoption to be the sons of God by the Holy Ghost, are visibly signed and sealed; Faith is confirmed, and Grace increased by virtue of prayer unto God. The Baptism of young Children is in any wise to be retained in the Church, as most agreeable with the institution of Christ.

Article XXVIII

Of the Lord's Supper

The Supper of the Lord is not only a sign of the love that Christians ought to have among themselves one to another; but rather it is a Sacrament of our Redemption by Christ's death: insomuch that to such as rightly, worthily, and with faith, receive the same, the Bread which we break is a partaking of the Body of Christ; and likewise the Cup of Blessing is a partaking of the Blood of Christ.

Transubstantiation (or the change of the substance of Bread and Wine) in the Supper of the Lord, cannot be proved by holy Writ; but is repugnant to the plain words of Scripture, overthroweth the nature of a Sacrament, and hath given occasion to many superstitions.

The Body of Christ is given, taken, and eaten, in the Supper, only after an heavenly and spiritual manner. And the mean whereby the Body of Christ is received and eaten in the Supper is Faith.

The Sacrament of the Lord's Supper was not by Christ's ordinance reserved, carried about, lifted up, or worshipped.

Article XXIX

Of the Wicked which do not eat the Body of Christ in the use of the Lord's Supper

The Wicked, and such as be void of a lively faith, although they do carnally and visibly press with their teeth (as Saint Augustine saith) the Sacrament of the Body and Blood of Christ, yet in no wise are they partakers of Christ: but rather, to their condemnation, do eat and drink the sign or Sacrament of so great a thing.

Article XXX

Of both kinds

The Cup of the Lord is not to be denied to the Lay-people; for both the parts of the Lord's Sacrament, by Christ's ordinance and commandment, ought to be ministered to all Christian men alike.

Article XXXI

Of the one Oblation of Christ finished upon the Cross

The Offering of Christ once made is that perfect redemption, propitiation, and satisfaction, for all the sins of the whole world, both original and actual; and there is none other satisfaction for sin, but that alone. Wherefore the sacrifices of Masses, in the which it was commonly said, that the Priest did offer Christ for the quick and the dead, to have remission of pain or guilt, were blasphemous fables, and dangerous deceits.

Article XXXII

Of the Marriage of Priests

Bishops, Priests, and Deacons, are not commanded by God's Law, either to vow the estate of single life, or to abstain from marriage: therefore it is lawful for them, as for all other Christian men, to marry at their own discretion, as they shall judge the same to serve better to godliness.

Article XXXIII

Of Excommunicated Persons, how they are to be avoided

That person which by open denunciation of the Church is rightly cut off from the unity of the Church, and excommunicated, ought to be taken of the whole multitude of the faithful, as an Heathen and Publican, until he be openly reconciled by penance, and received into the Church by a Judge that hath authority thereunto.

Article XXXIV

Of the Traditions of the Church

It is not necessary that Traditions and Ceremonies be in all places one, and utterly like; for at all times they have been divers, and may be changed according to the diversities of countries, times, and men's manners, so that nothing be ordained against God's Word. Whosoever through his private judgement, willingly and purposely, doth openly break the traditions and ceremonies of the Church, which be not repugnant to the Word of God, and be ordained and approved by common authority, ought to be rebuked openly, (that others may fear to do the like,) as he that offendeth against the common order of the Church, and hurteth the authority of the Magistrate, and woundeth the consciences of the weak brethren.

Every particular or national Church hath authority to ordain, change, and abolish, ceremonies or rites of the Church ordained only by man's authority, so that all things be done to edifying.

Article XXXV
Of Homilies
The second Book of Homilies, the several titles whereof we have joined under this Article, doth contain a godly and wholesome Doctrine, and necessary for these times, as doth the former Book of Homilies, which were set forth in the time of Edward the Sixth; and therefore we judge them to be read in Churches by the Ministers, diligently and distinctly, that they may be understanded of the people.

Of the Names of the Homilies

1. Of the right Use of the Church.
2. Against peril of Idolatry.
3. Of the repairing and keeping clean of Churches.
4. Of good Works: first of Fasting.
5. Against Gluttony and Drunkenness.
6. Against Excess of Apparel.
7. Of Prayer.
8. Of the Place and Time of Prayer.
9. That Common Prayers and Sacraments ought to be ministered in a known tongue.
10. Of the reverent estimation of God's Word.
11. Of Alms-doing.
12. Of the Nativity of Christ.
13. Of the Passion of Christ.
14. Of the Resurrection of Christ.
15. Of the worthy receiving of the Sacrament of the Body and Blood of Christ.
16. Of the Gifts of the Holy Ghost.
17. For the Rogation-days.
18. Of the State of Matrimony.
19. Of Repentance.
20. Against Idleness.
21. Against Rebellion.

Article XXXVI
Of Consecration of Bishops and Ministers
The Book of Consecration of Archbishops and Bishops, and Ordering of Priests and Deacons, lately set forth in the time of Edward the Sixth, and confirmed at the same time by authority of Parliament, doth contain all things necessary to such Consecration and Ordering: neither hath it any thing, that of itself is superstitious or ungodly. And therefore whosoever are consecrated or ordered according to the Rites of that Book, since the second year of the forenamed King Edward unto this time, or hereafter shall be consecrated or ordered according to the same Rites; we decree all such to be rightly, orderly, and lawfully consecrated or ordered.

Article XXXVII
Of the Civil Magistrates
The Queen's Majesty hath the chief power in this Realm of England, and other her Dominions, unto whom the chief Government of all Estates of this Realm, whether they be Ecclesiastical or Civil, in all causes doth appertain, and is not, nor ought to be, subject to any foreign Jurisdiction.

Where we attibute to the Queen's Majesty the chief government, by which Titles we understand the minds of some slanderous folks to be offended; we give not to our Princes the ministering either of God's Word, or of the Sacraments, the which thing the Injunctions also lately set forth by Elizabeth our Queen doth most plainly testify; but only that prerogative, which we see to have been given always to all godly Princes in holy Scriptures by God himself; that is, that they should rule all estates and degrees committed to their charge by God, whether they be Ecclesiastical or Temporal, and restrain with the civil sword the stubborn and evildoers.

The Bishop of Rome hath no jurisdiction in this Realm of England.

The Laws of the Realm may punish Christian men with death, for heinous and grievous offences.

It is lawful for Christian men, at the commandment of the Magistrate, to wear weapons, and serve in the wars.

ARTICLE XXXVIII

Of Christian men's Goods, which are not common

The Riches and Goods of Christians are not common, as touching the right, title, and possession of the same, as certain Anabaptists do falsely boast.

Notwithstanding, every man ought, of such things as he possesseth, liberally to give alms to the poor, according to his ability.

ARTICLE XXXIX

Of a Christian man's Oath

As we confess that vain and rash Swearing is forbidden Christian men by our Lord Jesus Christ, and James his Apostle, so we judge, that Christian Religion doth not prohibit, but that a man may swear when the Magistrate requireth, in a cause of faith and charity, so it be done according to the Prophet's teaching, in justice, judgement, and truth.

John Knox, Scottish Reformer
Test

1. What is the date given for John Knox, Scottish Reformer?

2. Where was John Knox born?

3. When was Knox made a prisoner of the French?

4. What became of him during his life as a prisoner?

5. After his release what became of Knox? Why was this important?

6. After leaving England to where did Knox go?

7. What teachings did he learn from after leaving England?

8. What was the "Common Band"?

9. Why did Knox go back to Scotland?

10. Describe Knox' preaching style.

Review

1. Write a paragraph about the most interesting event you have studied this year. Include all pertinent details.

2. In chronological order list the events you have studied. Include the date for each event.

Cumulative Review

Test

Card:

Date:

Two Facts:

Card:

Date:

Two Facts:

Card:

Date:

Two Facts:

Card:

Date:

Two Facts:

READING PROJECTS
Instructions

Teacher's Instructions for Integrating History and Writing

1. Vocab: Before giving the assignment the teacher should look at the vocabulary and make a judgement as to whether or not the students will be likely to know most of them. If the answer is yes, skip to step #2 and have them look up the vocabulary afterward. If not, have them look up the vocab words first.

2. Reading/Note-taking: have the students read the passage while taking notes using the "key-word method." In brief, this means ***no more than 3*** words from each sentence that will help the student remember what is said in it. Appropriate answers can, of course vary, but sample answers are given in the answer key. Two general rules can help these notes to be meaningful:
   a. Distilling the grammatical core—words that are part of the grammatical core of the sentence, particularly subjects, action verbs, direct objects, predicate nouns and adjectives.
   b. Note that *linking verbs* are not listed above. Though they are just as much a part of the grammatical core, they are easy to assume (i.e., instead of writing "Alexander was brutal," it is more effective to write, "Alexander brutal").

3. Title: have the students try to come up with a title for each paragraph. This forces them to try to look at each paragraph and try to understand its main point. Sample titles are given on the answer key.

4. Summary paragraph: Have the students turn the page and try to reconstruct, in brief, the essence of the original on a separate sheet of paper using only their notes.

5. Improved paragraph: have the students spruce up their paragraphs using a list of "modifiers", "power words" or grammatical constructions that can help the students to make their writing more interesting. (Andrew Pudewa's "Excellence in Writing" method is a good example of how to do this in practice.)

Middle Ages, Reformation and Renaissance

Project—Study Guide for Beowulf

By Christi McCullars and Kerry Carr
Using the translation by Frederick Rabsamen

Supplies

Black Duo-Tang® folder (without brads) for each student
Copies of pages to create notebook for each student. Colored paper makes an appealing notebook, but dark colors make it difficult to read the penciled in answers.
Poster board for classroom sized chart (day six).
Map of Northern Europe
Gluesticks
Scissors
Sharp paring knife

General Instructions For Using the Study Guide and Notebook

Each day's activities are broken into several sections. Read all the information and decide ahead of time what you will discuss. Words in bold are defined in the glossary. Review should be a regular part of each day. Some teachers prefer to have students retell (act out, draw, or journal) the story of the most recent day's reading. Comprehension questions have been included for each day. These questions make great review and daily quiz material.

Notebooks are best assembled by older children or by an adult. There are several suggestions to decorate the cover of the student notebook. One of the best is to enlarge and color laser copy the cover of the book translated by Frederick Rabsamen. It makes a fantastic cover! Another, less expensive, option would be to allow each student to design their own cover on separate paper and glue them in place. After Day Eight, students will have a plaster mask of Grendel or Grendel's mother to photograph for the cover.

Background Information

Day One

Beowulf is not a story about the Middle Ages. It is a story actually told during the Middle Ages. Why should you study Beowulf? Beowulf is the best surviving example of Old English poetry. It represents a transition from the ancient world to the Middle Ages. It was probably written between 700 and 1000 A. D. but the exact date is unknown. The poet is also unknown. He was obviously very good at his job, though. Mr. Rabsamen is the translator of choice because he tried to maintain key features of Old English poetry. Why do we need a translator if the poem is in Old English? Use the Old English versus Modern English flap to illustrate the point. Vocabulary to introduce and record: meadhall, thane, exile, corpse, mere, fiend, hoard, moor, shirker, kin, pyre, mailcoat, wyrd, wergild and gore. There are many new words that could be defined, however, it is probably advantageous to limit the Vocabulary booklet to those words which are essential to understanding the plot. Discuss the "compounds" that abound such as thane-sorrow, bone-house, etc. Mr. Rabsamen was careful to maintain the flavor of the compounds even where the translation could not be literal. Include some of the compounds in the Vocabulary booklet as you go.

Day Two

Explain that Beowulf is a poem. Ask students to recite a familiar poem. Most will say one with a rhyming pattern. Use several lines of the text to show that the poem does not rhyme. Define alliteration and point out examples in several lines. For older children you may want to discuss the assonance of Old English poetry. Stress how the lines are divided into half-lines and that the alliteration ties the lines together. Discuss wergild and include it in the Vocabulary booklet. Instruct students to listen carefully for a reference to wergild today. Read lines 1-194 of the text together. Pause occasionally and allow the students to relate what is happening in the story. You may have to do most of the reading until the students understand how to pause and to watch for periods in the half-lines. Spend a few minutes letting students find the most alliterative alliterations that they can. Have them record several in the notebook. Then instruct them to make up several alliterative phrases or sentences. They may record them in the notebook at this point. (You may wish to check them.)

Comprehension

Who is the king when Grendel starts killing?
What did Hrothgar call the hall he built?
What was the poet's explanation of why Grendel killed?
Retell the story of Cain and Abel. (Genesis 4:1-16)
Why does the poet say Grendel had no plans for payment (lines 155-158)?
What was Hrothgar's response to the murderous Grendel?

Day Three

Remind students that Beowulf is a poem. Give students a definition of style to record in their notebooks. (Style is the choice and arrangement of words.) In what style is Beowulf written? Younger students can just answer that Beowulf is a poem with a lot of alliteration. Older students may be required to recognize it as heroic-elegiac or extended narrative recounting the triumphs of a hero. Read to line 498. Mark any references to God in the appropriate booklet.

Comprehension

Who came to rescue Heorot?
Reenact what happens when Beowulf lands on the shore.
How does Hrothgar respond to Beowulf's arrival?
How does Beowulf propose to fight Grendel?
What do the Geats and the Danes do after the greetings are exchanged?

Day Four

Tell students about the author. The author is unknown, even his name. We can assume that he was a trained poet and probably a Christian. During this time period, Christianity co-existed with pagan worship. Early missionaries sent by Pope Gregory were instructed to introduce Christianity slowly, not to destroy all the pagan beliefs at once. Read to line 863. Have students write a summary paragraph about the author in their notebooks.

Comprehension

What was Unferth's challenge to Beowulf?
What was Beowulf's version of the story with Breca?
Who is Hrothgar's queen?
What was Beowulf's boast about his grip?
Describe the fight between Beowulf and Grendel.
What was done with Grendel's arm?

Project, Page 3—Study Guide for Beowulf

Day Five

Read to line 1062. Assign students to write a paragraph with three main points about Grendel. Check for accuracy and then allow students to record the paragraph in the Grendel booklet. Each student should draw a picture of Grendel to glue into their notebooks.

Comprehension

What is Unferth's response to Beowulf's victory?
What gifts did Hrothgar give Beowulf for his victory?
Did Beowulf deserve these gifts?
To whom does the poet attribute the defeat of Grendel in the final lines of the section?

Day Six

Read to line 1382. Summarize the characters of Beowulf and Hrothgar. Use the relationship between Beowulf and Hrothgar to develop an understanding of feudalism. Make a classroom sized chart depicting what Hrothgar gave to his vassals (defense from outside invaders, land, treasures for deeds) and what the vassals owe to the lord (loyalty, readiness to fight for the lord). Discuss how Beowulf fit into each of the roles of nobleman, warrior, vassal, and lord.

Comprehension

How does Wealhtheow treat Beowulf?
Has Beowulf proven to be a worthy, gentle hero as Wealhtheow charges him to be?
Describe Grendel's mother.
Who was Aeschere?
Where did the monsters live?
What does Hrothgar promise Beowulf if he avenges Aeschere's murder?

Day Seven

Read to line 1651. Students should write a paragraph to describe Grendel's mother. When their paragraphs are complete, students should work on the Character booklets. You should confirm that the References to God booklet and the Vocabulary booklet are up to date.

Comprehension

Does Beowulf wish to fight or mourn?
What is the scene when the warriors arrive at the mere?
What gesture does Unferth make toward Beowulf?
What does Beowulf do before entering the water?
Describe the battle with Grendel's mother.
How did Beowulf finally win?
When the blood welled up what was the Danes' response? What was the Geats' response?
What happened to the sword blade used to kill Grendel's mother?
What prize did the Geats carry back to Heorot?

Day Eight

In lines 1840-1865, the poet uses foreshadowing. Discuss foreshadowing and have the students try to identify it in the passage. Read to line 1931. Complete the Character booklets, except Wiglaf. Make a classroom list of references to Beowulf, such as Ecgtheow's son, champion, chieftain, and Hygelac's thane. Students can make a list of how they might be known to others.

Comprehension

What was on the sword handle that Beowulf gave to Hrothgar?
What advice does Hrothgar offer to Beowulf?

What do the Geats desire to do first thing in the morning?
How does Beowulf show his loyalty to Hrothgar? Is he continuing his role as vassal?
What does Hrothgar say about Beowulf?
Describe Hrothgar's parting with Beowulf.
Did Hrothgar prove to be a good lord to Beowulf?

Day Nine

Read to line 2199. Define setting. (Setting is when and where the action takes place.) Have students summarize the setting of the first two sections. Using a map of Northern Europe, locate Denmark. The Geats probably lived on the coast of southern Sweden. You may wish to discuss living by the sea and what impact that would have on the lifestyle of the Danes and the Geats. The setting of Beowulf is somewhat questionable but sometime between 500-600 AD is probable. Using plaster of Paris in a mold (a box with sand in it) or papier-mâché make masks of either Grendel or his mother. The sand will give the mask an interesting texture. If you lay items such as cut up wig hair and marbles in the sand before pouring the plaster, you will have an unusual ogre mask to represent the monsters.

Comprehension

How do Hygelac and Hygd receive Beowulf?
What does Beowulf do with some of the gifts from Hrothgar?
How was Beowulf thought of as a youth?
What reward does Hygelac give Beowulf?

Day Ten

Define flashback and instruct students to listen for the flashback in this section. Read to line 2509. Have students research dragons in order to evaluate the myth versus the reality. What creatures do they seem like? Emphasize that all over the earth legends exist about dragons. If you would like to research it deeply, some interesting books are ***Dragons Truth, Myth and Legend*** by David Passes; ***The Great Dinosaur Mystery and the Bible*** by Paul Taylor, and ***Dinosaurs: Those Terrible Lizards*** by Duane Gish. The Bible also has a description of an unusual animal in Job 41:18-21. Students should write a summary paragraph on dragons.

Comprehension

What caused the dragon to begin destroying the land of the Geats?
How does Beowulf become king?
How did Beowulf gain the sword with which he intends to fight the gold hoard?

Day Eleven

Read to line 2845. Assign the paragraph on and picture of the Gold Hoard.

Comprehension

Who joins Beowulf in the battle?
What do the other hall thanes do?
Draw a picture of what Wiglaf saw in the gold hoard's cave.
What did Beowulf hope would be done with the gold hoard's treasure?

Day Twelve

Complete the poem. Allow time to finish any incomplete sections. Assign student to "interview" one of the main characters like a modern newscaster. Each student or group of students should ask 5-8 pertinent questions of the character. Conclude with a classroom presentation of the interviews. You may wish to video tape the interviews.

Project, Page 5—Study Guide for Beowulf

Comprehension

What does the messenger say will happen when news of Beowulf's death reaches the other peoples of Europe?

The messenger suggests that the treasure should melt with Beowulf on the pyre. Did Beowulf want the treasure to be burned or buried with him?

What did the Geats do with the dragon?

Was Beowulf a beloved king?

Day Thirteen

Review the poem and notebooks in preparation for testing. Complete the booklet on the Importance of Beowulf.

Glossary

alliteration (e-lît´e-râ´shen) noun
The repetition of the same consonant sounds or of different vowel sounds at the beginning of words or in stressed syllables, as in "on scrolls of silver snowy sentences" (Hart Crane). [From AD- + Latin *littera,* letter.]

assonance (âs´e-nens) noun
1. Resemblance of sound, especially of the vowel sounds in words, as in: "that dolphin-torn, that gong-tormented sea" (William Butler Yeats).
2. The repetition of identical or similar vowel sounds, especially in stressed syllables, with changes in the intervening consonants, as in the phrase tilting at windmills. [French, from Latin *assonâre,* to respond to : ad-, *ad-* + *sonâre,* to sound.]

corpse (kôrps) noun
A dead body, especially the dead body of a human being. [Middle English corps, from Latin *corpus.*]

elegiac (èl´e-jï´ek, î-lê´jê-âk´) adjective
1. Of, relating to, or involving elegy or mourning or expressing sorrow for that which is irrecoverably past: an elegiac lament for youthful ideals.
Of or composed in elegaic couplets. [Late Latin *elegìacus,* from Greek *elegeiakos,* from *elegeia,* elegy.]

exile (èg´zïl´, èk´sïl´) noun
1. a. Enforced removal from one's native country. b. Self-imposed absence from one's country. 2. The condition or a period of living away from one's native country.
3. One who lives away from one's native country, whether because of expulsion or voluntary absence.

Feudalism (fyood´l-îz´em) noun
A political and economic system of Europe from the 9th to about the 15th century, based on the holding of all land in fief or fee and the resulting relation of lord to vassal and characterized by homage, legal and military service of tenants, and forfeiture.

fiend (fênd) noun
1. a. An evil spirit; a demon. b. The Devil; Satan. c. A diabolically evil or wicked person.

flashback (flâsh´bàk´) noun
1. a. A literary or cinematic device in which an earlier event is inserted into the normal chronological order of a narrative. b. The episode or scene depicted by means of this device.

foreshadow (fôr-shâd´o, for-) verb, transitive
To present an indication or a suggestion of beforehand.

gore (gôr) noun
Blood, especially coagulated blood from a wound. [Middle English, filth, from Old English *gor.*]

Middle Ages, Reformation and Renaissance

Project, Page 6—Study Guide for Beowulf

hoard (hôrd, hord) noun
A hidden fund or supply stored for future use; a cache.
kin (kĭn) noun
(used with a pl. verb). One's relatives; family; kinfolk.
mail (mâl) noun
Flexible armor composed of small overlapping metal rings, loops of chain, or scales.
meadhall (med hal) noun
A large hall where the lord's thanes ate and slept.
mere (mir)
An expanse of standing water; lake; pool
moor (moor) noun
A broad area of open land, often high but poorly drained, with patches of heath and peat bogs. [Middle English *mor,* from Old English *mor.*]
pyre (pĭr) noun
A heap of combustibles for burning a corpse as a funeral rite. [Latin *pyra,* from Greek *pura,* from *pur,* fire.]
setting
When and where the action of a story takes place.
shirker noun
One who avoids his duty.
thane (thân) noun
a. A freeman granted land by the king in return for military service in Anglo-Saxon England. b. man ranking above an ordinary freeman and below a nobleman in Anglo-Saxon England. [Middle English, from Old English *thegn.*]
vassals (văs´el) noun
1. A person who held land from a feudal lord and received protection in return for homage and allegiance. 2.A subordinate or dependent. [Middle English, from Old French, from Vulgar Latin *vassallus,* from *vassus,* of Celtic origin.]
wergild (wûr´gĕld´) also wergeld noun
In Anglo-Saxon and Germanic law, a price set upon a person's life on the basis of rank and paid as compensation by the family of a slayer to the kindred or lord of a slain person to free the culprit of further punishment or obligation and to prevent a blood feud. [Middle English *wargeld,* from Old English *wergeld: wer,* man + *geld,* payment.]
wyrd
Fate

Middle Ages, Reformation and Renaissance

Project, Page 7—Study Guide for Beowulf

Assembly Instructions

Fold lines are indicated by dotted lines; cutting lines are indicated by broken lines. A glue-stick is recommended for pasting. Crisp folds produce the best results. A sharp paring knife is more exact than scissors for cutting along creased fold lines. BEFORE PASTING, make all folds and cuts and place on folder for best alignment. You may wish to attach additional lined paper to one or more of the booklets.

Folder

Open the Duo-Tang® folder flat and refold each side to the center, creating a french door fold. As you open the folder you will see the quarter sections created by the new fold lines which will be your guides for arranging the booklets.

What is Style?

With title in bottom right hand corner, fold in half from top to bottom, with lines inside, and then in half from side to side with the title on the front and the word "back" on the back. Cut along dotted lines through all thicknesses. Place on open folder at the upper left hand corner.

What is Alliteration?

With the title at the lower right hand corner, fold in half from side to side with the title "What is Alliteration?" showing. Then fold in half from top to bottom, the title still showing. Cut through all thicknesses. Slide knife along the left fold to *cut only the upper corner* so that the page may be lifted to expose "Examples from Beowulf." Place below "Style" on folder. When you assemble the folder you may wish to glue inside *blank* pages together.

"Who Was the Author?" and "What is the Setting?"

Make cuts on unfolded page, then fold each piece in half from top to bottom with lines inside. "Author" is to be placed on the bottom of the first fold column and "Setting" in the middle of the second fold column.

"Who are the Main Characters?"

With the name "Hygelac" at the lower right hand corner, fold in half from side to side with the name still showing. Fold the page roughly in thirds with "Wealhtheow" folding down to reveal the title frame on top. Being careful to avoid the names, cut along the fold between the title and Wealtheow *only to the cross fold.* Open page out, and then follow instructions for removing the marked section. When you assemble the folder you may wish to glue the *blank* pages together. Place at the top of the second fold column.

Middle Ages, Reformation and Renaissance

Project, Page 8—Study Guide for Beowulf

"Old English vs. New English"
Keeping the title showing, fold in half from top to bottom, then in half from side to side. Cut away marked section. Place at bottom of second fold column.

"The Importance of Beowulf"
Fold in half from side to side and cut along the fold. Make folds with lines inside and trim margins at cutting lines. Place at top of third column in folder.

"References to God"
Fold in half from top to bottom and side to side. Make cuts through all thicknesses. This will fully unfold for listing references inside as well. Place directly below "Importance."

"Dragons"
Fold in half from top to bottom and make cut through both layers. Place in folder to complete third column.

"Vocabulary"
Make fold along fold line having title inside. Make cuts through both layers and refold so title shows. Trim bottom edge on cut line through both thicknesses.

"Monsters"
Cut the page along the cutting line and fold each half on the fold lines. They will fit inside one another exposing the title and the names of the three monsters.

Staple through all thicknesses near the fold at the top and glue to the remaining space in the fourth fold column.

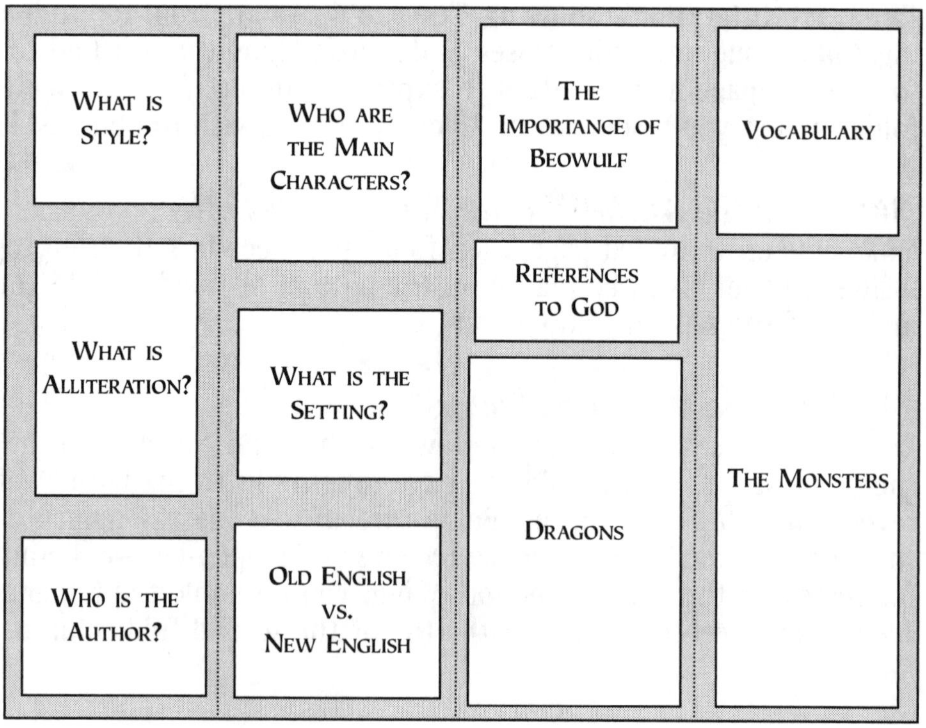

Project, Page 9—Study Guide for Beowulf

In What style is Beowulf written?

Define:

back

What is Style?

Make cuts after folds.

Amazing Alliterations

What is Alliteration?

back

EXAMPLES FROM BEOWULF

Project, Page 12—Study Guide for Beowulf

WHO IS THE AUTHOR?

WHAT IS THE SETTING?

Middle Ages, Reformation and Renaissance

Project, Page 13—Study Guide for Beowulf

Who Are the Main Characters?

back

Wealhtheow

Unferth

Hygelac

BEOWULF

HROTHGAR

Cut along top fold and side fold,
then remove this section

WIGLAFW

Hweat! we Gar-Dena in
gear-dagum beod
cyninga byrm gefrunon,
hu ba aebelingas ellen
fremedon.

Cut along top fold and side fold,
then remove this section

back

Old English vs. New English

Cut after folding.

Middle Ages, Reformation and Renaissance

Project, Page 17—Study Guide for Beowulf

Yes! We have heard of years long vanished
how Spear-Danes struck sang victory-songs
raised from a wasteland walls of glory

Cut along this fold

back

THE IMPORTANCE OF BEOWULF

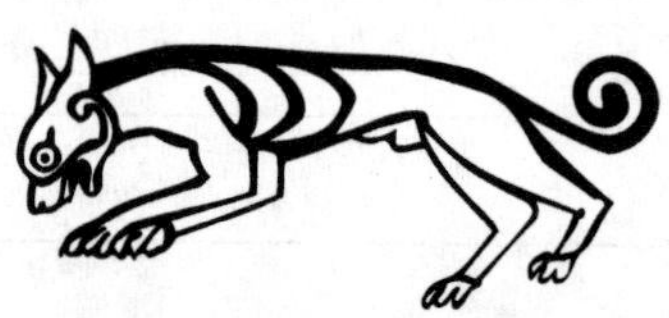

Project, Page 19—Study Guide for Beowulf

Project, Page 20—Study Guide for Beowulf

back

References to God

Make cuts after folding

Project, Page 21—Study Guide for Beowulf

Middle Ages, Reformation and Renaissance

Project—
Study Guide for Beowulf

back

Dragons

back

VOCABULARY

back

THE MONSTERS

GRENDEL

Gold Hoard

Grendel's Mother

Project, Page 28–Study Guide for Beowulf

Middle Ages, Reformation and Renaissance

Project—The Door in the Wall

A Play

Scene One

(Ringing church bells. Robin lying in the bed.)

Robin:"Ever since I can remember I have been expected to be a knight. Sons of noble families are always sent away from their mother and father to learn to be courteous, gentle and strong of heart. It makes me sad to think of the day my father said farewell and left for the Scottish wars. My mother also said farewell the day after my tenth birthday. She told me she would be going to serve the Queen and Dame Ellen would care for me until John-the-Fletcher arrived to take me to Sir Peter de Lindsay." (Footstep sounds in the background)

Robin:"I cannot move. Something is wrong with my legs. They fail me. What will I do?" (Enter Dame Ellen)

Dame Ellen: "Turn over, do, there's a good lad. Wilt not have this good porridge all with honey spreads. Sweet lad twill give thee strength and mend those ailing limbs. Come my pretty—." (Robin flings his arm toward the bowl sending the porridge flying.)

Dame Ellen: "Wicked boy! No more will I serve thee. Scarce able to stand have I been this day, yet have I been faithful. But I am a free woman and can go my way. Just wait and see when no more victuals are brought to thee! Ungrateful wretch!"(Ellen breaks out weeping and leaves the stage.)

Robin:"She will come back as she has done before and bring something I like if she wants me to eat it. I wander where Dame Ellen could be? So much time has gone by and she is no where to be seen."

(Enter Brother Luke.)

Brother Luke: "Good eve, my son. I am Brother Luke, a wandering friar, newly come to St. Mark's. I have brought thee food, and cause tis Friday fish." (Robin smiles up at Brother Luke.)

Brother Luke: "A poor widow, who twice a week is fed from our hospice, told me of thy need. She said that Dame Ellen, who lately served thee, has this very day been taken of the plague. She it was who told us that all thy servants, too, are fled, because of the plague and some are dead of it. Dame Ellen told thee not; pitying thee. Now, be a good lad and take thy supper." (Robin eats his food.)

Robin: "Thank you for the food." (Brother Luke rubs Robin's legs.)

Brother Luke: "It is well known that thy noble father hath of his goodness given money to St. Mark's. So to St. Mark's I'll take thee, and will care for thee in mine own quarters, because all other beds and places are already taken by those in the parish who have great need. Even the corridors are filled and the cloisters lined with pallets."

Robin:"But I cannot walk. See you my two legs are as useless as if they were logs of wood. How shall I go there? My father is with the King at the Scottish wars, and with him are all his men at arms. My lady mother has been commanded to attend upon Her Majesty the Queen. It is supposed by them that I am now a page in the household of Sir Peter de Lindsay at his castle in the north. John-the-Fletcher was to have come for me in March, before the Feast of St. Gregory. Instead, a messenger came on that day to say that he had been set upon by thieves and lay wounded in the hospice at Reading. He came to fetch me, but found me thus, unable to walk or ride. He brought a surgeon who said I had not the plague but some other malady. He told Ellen to feed me well and that he would return. He came not again nor did John-the Fletcher."

Brother Luke: "Alas, because of the plague all the physicians are working night and day. Either he himself has been so busy caring for others he has not been able to return. As for John-the-Fletcher, he may have gone out the city gate and not been allowed to reenter. Fear not for the manner of our going to St. Mark's. Tethered in the courtyard is a jennet ready saddled with blankets whereon thou'lt ride softly. Walking beside thee, I shall support thee, and so we shall go to St. Mark's. Dost remember the long wall that is about the garden of thy father's house?

Robin: "Yes of course. Why?"

Brother Luke: "Dost thou remember, too, the wall about the Tower or any other wall? Have thy not all a door somewhere?"

Robin: "Yes"

Brother Luke: "Always remember that thou hast only to follow the wall far enough and there will be a door in it.

Robin: "I promise I will remember." (Say under your breath "Even though I am not sure what it means.")

(Brother Luke opens a chest and pulls out clothes for Robin. He then helps him to dress.)

Bother Luke: "The evening damp creeps up from the Thames. Good English wool will keep thee warm."' (Brother Luke puts Robin on his back and departs. He then places him on the horse. Walk the horse and Robin off the stage.)

Robin: Will I go back home soon? Will a message be sent to my father? Or to my mother?"

Scene Two

Narrator: May came in with a burst of bloom in hedge and field. There was hawthorn both pink and white, and primroses and buttercups carpeted the fields with yellow. In every garden wallflowers blossomed in bright color and filled the air with perfume.

For days Robin was cared for as if he were a little child. Brother Luke brought him food, kept him washed, and changed his clothes, but he was too much occupied with other things to stay with Robin for a very long time. The bells clamored as loudly as ever, but now the sound was associated with the regular procession of monks going to devotions. Robin grew to like it.

He began to sleep well on the hard cot and to feel at home in the little cell. He could see nothing but the sky through the small wind hole, for it was high in the stone wall and only in the morning allowed a ray of sunshine to come in. Against another wall stood a prayer stool and desk combined, with a smaller one beside it. On the wall hung a little cupboard which held Brother Luke's few personal belongings and his breviary.

Robin couldn't see into the corridor, and at first couldn't identify all the sounds he heard. He liked the "s-s-shing" sound of feet on stone, as the monks passed to and fro. Sometimes, when they passed in procession, chanting, he joined in the singing, for most of the plain songs were known to him. Sometimes there were long silences, when he heard nothing but the mewing of the cat Millicent, or the squeaking of a mouse she had caught.

There were hundreds of people within the hospice, but they were separated by thick walls and long passages. The outer court was far away at the other side of the monastery. There, visiting pilgrims, knights at arms, merchants, and minstrels gathered, each waiting the attention of the Prior. Because there were few inns, the monasteries were open for the entertainment of wayfarers, rich and poor alike. Besides that portion reserved for travelers there was an almonry overflowing with the poor of London, seeking food and clothing. St. Mark's was a busy place. But most of the activity was far from Robin. He was much alone, and time seemed long.

We now take you to St. Mark's where you will see Robin begin his new life. (Robin is lying on his cot and Brother Luke is in attendance.)

Brother Luke: "It is time now to try thee sitting up." (Brother Luke rubs Robin's legs while speaking.) "If thy hands are busy, time will pass more quickly. Dost like to whittle?"

Robin:"Of course. Who does not? But I have naught to whittle."

Brother Luke: "I shall find thee a piece of soft pine and will lend thee my knife. Tis sharp and of good steel. This bench will fit against thy back to support thee. (Brother Luke sets the oaken bench at Robin's back.)

Robin:"Can I make a boat? Can I make it now?"

Brother Luke: 'Just wait. I will return in a moment. Be patient my boy." (Brother Luke exits and returns momentarily.) "Robin here is a fine knife and a piece of pine. It will be good to whittle."

Robin:"Perhaps I can make it into a sailing boat like the fishermen bring to Berlin's gate, or a barge such as the King uses. Perhaps when it is done I will be able to walk, and can go to the Thames to sail it."

Brother Luke: "Perhaps. I will return in a moment with nourishment for you my young lad." (Brother Luke exits.)

Robin:"I scarce know if this is the correct way to make a boat. It is begging to have a point at one end as if it is a prow." (Brother Luke returns with soup.)

Brother Luke: "Here is some good soup. Tis made of mutton in which bay and marigold have been seethed. Brother Michael grows these fragrant herbs in the garden. Bay is tasty and gives good appetite; marigold is said to be of value against poor sight and angry words. It is said twill draw evil humors out of the head, and the flowers make fair garlands for maidens because of their golden color."

Robin:"What care I for garlands for maidens or fragrant herbs. Soppy food I despise. But, eat I must and so I will. Brother Luke will you teach me to write? We were taught singing at the Brother's School, but I know not writing. Will you teach me then?"

Brother Luke: "Yes, my son, truly I will when there are not so many people to care for. Let us stop to say a prayer for thy strengthening."

Robin: "Keep your filthy hands off me!

(Shouting) Lout!"

Brother Luke: "Now say there thy prayers and in thy mind know thou art on thy knees. Forget not to be thankful for all thou hast. Remember thy lady mother and Sir John, thy father who is at the wars, and pray for us all. '(Brother Luke departs.)

Robin: "But what have I to be thankful for? Our Father which art in heaven ...."
(Lights out with Robin praying.)

Scene 3

Narrator: As the days grew warmer, the plague abated somewhat. Fewer people came to the hospital and those who had not died became well and went home. Robin continued to grow stronger . He spent much of his time whittling. Brother Luke continued to care for Robin. Let us look into more of Robin's life at St. Mark's.

Robin: "Today in the garden I felt that soon I should walk. I must get well before my father returns from the wars."

Brother Luke: "Whether thou'lt walk soon I know not. This I know. We must teach thy hands to be skillful in many ways and we must teach thy mind to get about whether thy legs will carry thee or no. I will teach thee to read. For reading is another door in the wall dost understand, my son?"

Robin: "Yes I see now what you mean by the door in the wall."

Brother Luke: "We shall read together. Then there is somewhat of the earth and stars that Brother Halbert can tell thee: how they go in their seasons so that in summer when we rise for the midnight office Orion is here. Yet in winter, at the same hour, he is over there." (Brother Luke points in different directions as he is saying this.)

Robin: "Will you teach me to write like you promised? I wish to send a letter to my father."

Brother Luke: "We shall begin today. We shall divide the day into teaching thy hands and thy mind, then weariness shall not give thee excuse for discouragement. Rest while I am gone and I shall bring quill and parchment to pen a letter for thee. It so happens that a hundred men at arms and a hundred foot soldiers have sworn to serve loyally their King and the city of London and are leaving for the Scottish border tomorrow. With them goes a minstrel well known to us, one John-go-in-the-wynd. He will gladly carry thy letter and put it in thy father's hands."

Narrator: The letter was soon written describing what had happened to Robin over the last few months. It was given to John-go-in-the-wynd to deliver to Robin's father. Robin wondered how his father would feel to have a son who could not fulfill his knightly duties?

Brother Luke even taught Robin to swim. Soon he was able to dive beneath the water and play tricks on Brother Luke. He began to think about Geoffrey-Atte-water and his crutches. Brother Luke reminded him that even his crutches could be a door in a wall. Before long Robin was able to use his crutches.

One day messenger appeared with a letter from Robin's father. He was so excited as he was now able to read it himself. It began:

Middle Ages, Reformation and Renaissance

Project, Page 5—The Door in the Wall

Robinson of John de Bureford, from his father, Greeting, It grieves me, my son, more than I can tell you to know that you are ill. I thank Heaven it is not the Plague you have had, for that enemy has slain more men than battle, besides the women and children it has taken toll of. It shocked me to learn that you had been left to the care of strangers. Your mother would hardly bear it if I should tell her, but I will not. She is with the Queen, who is in delicate health. I dare not say where, lest this letter fall into unfriendly hands.

She supposes that you are far away from London, in Shropshire. It is well. Let her continue to think so, for in truth you soon will be, God willing and your health permitting, for I have requested the prior to arrange your journey with all speed. You will travel in care of Brother Luke and John-go-in-the-Wynd.

I had a message from Sir Peter only the day before your letter reached me asking what had happened to you, for John-the-Fletcher never returned. Some evil befell surely, for he was an honorable servant. Sir Peter was wounded while bringing up forces to my aid, so sorely wounded that he has been taken to a castle nearby where he will stay until he is able to be taken home.

The Scots are being slowly pushed back and we are gaining ground, since receiving the added help from London and the nearby towns. The King hopes for a peace by the Sacrament of Christmas, but the Scots are a stubborn race.

I trust that you are improving in health, my son, and in God's grace.

So Farewell,

Preparations for Robin's departure began immediately. Brother Luke and Brother Matthew between them devised sort of chair-saddle in which Robin could ride.

So they set out Robin, Brother Luke and John-go-in the wynd, They have over a hundred English miles to go so they must go steadily.

Let us look down the road at them on their journey.

Scene Four

John-go-in-the-wynd: "We've come a goodly way since early morning. But we must not linger or we shall not reach the White Swan by nightfall. I have it from Sir Peter the Hayne that it lies a good days journey out of London. It is well to be safe housed after dark, for cutpurses and roisterers do roam the country hereabout."

Robin: "If my father were with us, we should have no fear of anyone."

Brother Luke: "We shall have faith in the Father of us all."

John-go-in-the wynd: (John plays the harp while walking.) "We have been traveling most of the day. Now we have reached a fork and I do not know whichaway to go."

Brother Luke: "My memory serves me ill. I know not which way to go. Let us say the office here at the cross before we go on. Then we shall go to the right. But it may be that we shall not find the White Swan and shall have to sleep in a hedgerow."

John-go-in-the-wynd: "We must have taken the wrong fork. I see no inn and night is nigh. Ahead lies a dark forest and see tis

Project, Page 6—The Door in the Wall

raining now. Shall we seek shelter here by the road?"

Brother Luke: "It is an ill thing for young Robin to sleep out in the damp, but if such be our fortune, then we must make the best of it."

Robin: "Shall we sleep on the ground? What a lark! I have never yet in my life slept out of doors, though I may as well have been out of doors when the east wind blew through the wind hole."

John-go-in-the-wynd: "We might go on to the forest and be more sheltered from wind and rain but that wild beasts do roam about and highwaymen lurk in the edge of it and leap at passersby. I am for staying here."

Brother Luke: "Tis naught for me to sleep in Mother Nature's arms. Many a night have I been grateful for the comfort of solid ground. And mayhap we can cover young Robin to keep him dry." (Luke and Robin walk to the side of the stage.)

John-go-in-the-wynd: "Why, here tis. The very thing! An ancient tree trunk fallen from age and hollowed with dry rot. It hath stood enough years to make it both wide and deep. We shall not be ill-found after all. Come young master, let me help thee."

Robin:"This is such an adventure. I may never be a knight and see armor, but I will know what it is like to make my bed on God's earth and feel the prick of rain on my face." (John leans over log and puts a blanket on it.)

John-go-in-the-wynd: (Looks at brother Luke while saying this.) "You may never be a knight but each of us has his place in the world. If one cannot serve in one way, there is always another. If we do what we are able a door always opens to something else. (John walks to the front of the stage). I do believe young Robin will sleep soundly in his log house."

Narrator: "Brother Luke, Robin and John-go-in-the-wynd sang heartily as they travelled on their way. They had many experiences including one in which thieves tried to rob them. Robin was able to alert Brother Luke and they escaped with everything intact. Finally after days they arrived at Lindsay. Sir Peter and Lady Constance welcomed Robin immediately. Brother Luke stayed to help look after Robin and John-go-in-the-wynd departed and went to visit his mother who lived not far away. The Welsh began hammering at the town gate. Robin soon realized they were trapped in the castle and would die if something was not done. Robin suddenly sees a door in the wall. Despite his infirmities, he takes it upon himself to escape from Lindsay. Swimming in the dark across the river to find John-go-in-the-wynd. Robin was a hero. John and Robin arrived back at the castle bringing with them an army to conquer the Welsh. Suddenly a hail of arrows dropped the sentries on the bridge and picked off the men manning the wall. Robin was reunited with Sir Peter and hailed as a conqueror and true son of his noble father. The time passed and winter came upon them. But, there was still one more door to come. They began to wonder if the Scottish war might end."

Robin: "It is Christmas eve. I see pages dragging the yule log and branches of holly to decorate the hall. But, wait I see a company of knights and men at arms riding towards the castle. It is true! The Scottish wars are over. My father is alive. I see him and my mother. I must greet them."

Robin's mother: "Robin, my Robin." (Holding his hands while speaking.)

Sir John de Bureford: "He is my son too. You are grown. Your eyes no longer out-race your chin as do a child's. You've now the look of a youth."

Narrator: 'The King and Queen had also arrived with all the soldiers. Robin was commanded to present himself before them. The King and Queen sat enthroned in the great chairs on the dais. Robin wondered what the King would say to him. It is here that we find ourselves."

King: (Rising from his chair.) "Can you kneel my son?"

Robin: "Long enough to say 'Our Father.'" (Robin kneels on the cushion.)

King: "Robin, Son of Sir John de Bureford, it hath been told to us what service you have done for the lord of this castle and me, King of the whole realm of England and France. You are a true son of a noble father. Though but a youth, you have shown courage a man might be proud to call his own." (King spreads out jeweled collar and drops it on Robin's shoulder.)

"This shall be a token of our high regard and with it our grateful thanks. Rise up with you, Robin."(Kings helps Robin to his feet.)

Robin: "I am ever filled with gratitude. I do thank you for this great honor and I beg you to accept my song of Christmas." (Robin picks up the harp and begins to sing.)

Robin: "Come to Bethlehem and see Him whose birth the angels sing. Come adore on bended knee Christ the Lord the new born king. Gloria in excelsis Deo."

Crowd: "Sir Robin. Sir Robin."

Robin: 'Sir Robin, is this what they call me?" (Looking at Sir John.) Sir, mind you not that I must go thus, bent over and with these crutches bent over to help me walk?

Sir John: "The courage you have shown, the craftsmanship proven by the harp, and the spirit in your singing all make so bright a light that I cannot see whether or not your legs are misshapen."

Robin's Mother: "What a comfort it will be to know that the wars will never claim you. And you can come home, for there is no need for you to stay at Lindsay. Nor is their further need for me to be with the Queen. She is now in good health. When the feast of Christmas is over, we shall all go home to London. Brother Luke shall come home with us to be your tutor if he will."

Sir John: "Your mother and I will meet you at midnight office. You rest now." (Robin goes and lies down. Sir John and Robin's mother leave the stage. Brother Luke enters and stands over the sleeping Robin. Robin awakens.)

Robin: "Where am I? What has happened?"

Brother Luke: "Thou'rt here, Sir Robin. Safe with all thy loved ones. Tis the Feast of Christmas, and thou hast found the door in thy wall."

The End

Middle Ages, Reformation and Renaissance
Project

Directions for History-Grammar Integration

We recommend the Shurley Grammar program as being the one which does the best job of teaching students the fundamental structure of the English sentence. Obviously, the sentences in the various sentences groups of Shurley are not all going to have any relationship with the content of their history, but we believe that making up extra practice sentences which have content culled from their history lessons can bring a beneficial "synergy" into the curriculum.

Several sentences derived from the content of the history lessons have been written and parsed as examples. Obviously, the possibilities are limitless.

It would also be worthwhile to have the children make up their own, history-related sentences. This could be done for the whole class to parse, or for their own, individual practice and improved sentences that are integral to the Shurley lessons.

SN V P A ADJ COP C A ADJ COP

1. *SN V* / *P1* Augustine / wrote (of a temporal "City of Man" and an eternal "City of God").

1. Augustine wrote of a temporal "City of Man" and an eternal "City of God".
2. Who wrote of a temporal "City of Man" and an eternal "City of God"? Augustine/SN
3. What is being said about Augustine? Augustine wrote/V
4. Of/P
5. Of what? "City of Man" and "City of God"/COP,COP
6. What kind of "City of Man"? temporal/Adj
7. What kind of "City of God"? eternal/Adj
8. And/C
9. A/A
10. An/A
11. SN V P1 check.
12. (of a temporal "City of Man and an eternal "City of God"), prepositional phrase.
13. Period, statement/D
14. Go back to the verb and divide the complete subject from the complete predicate.

Middle Ages, Reformation and Renaissance

Project, Page 2

A ADJ SN LV ADJ PN P ADJ OP
1. *SN LV* The nomadic Mongols / were fierce warriors (with great skill)
PN P4 *P COP C COP*
(in archery and horsemanship).D

1. The nomadic Mongols were fierce warriors with great skill in archery and horsemanship.
2. Who were great warriors with great skill in archery and horsemanship? Mongols/SN
3. What is being said about Mongols? Mongols were/V
4. Were what? Warriors/verify the noun
5. Does warriors mean the same thing as Mongols? yes
6. Warriors/PN
7. Were/LV
8. What kind of warriors? fierce/Adj
9. With/P
10. With what? skill/OP
11. What kind of skill? great/Adj
12. In/P
13. In what? archery and horsemanship/COP,COP
14. And/C
15. What kind of Mongols? nomadic/Adj
16. The/A
17. SN LV PN P4 check
18. (with great skill), prepositional phrase
19. (in archery and horsemanship), prepositional phrase
20. period, statement/D
21. Go back to the verb; divide the complete subject from the complete predicate.

A SN P OP V-t P DO P A OP
3. *SN V-T* The rise (of Islam) / changed the geography (of the Mediterranean Sea).
DO P2

1. The Rise of Islam changed the geography of the Mediterranean Sea.
2. What changed the geography of the Mediterranean Sea? rise/SN
3. What is being said about the rise? the rise changed/V
4. Changed what? geography/verify the noun
5. Does geography mean the same thing as rise? no
6. Geography/DO
7. Changed/V-t
8. The/A
9. Of/P
10. Of What? Mediterranean Sea/OP
11. The/A

Middle Ages, Reformation and Renaissance
Project, Page 3

12. Of/P
13. Of what? Islam/OP
14. The/A
15. SN V-t DO P2 check
16. (of Islam), prepositional phrase
17. (of the Mediterranean Sea), prepositional phrase
18. Period, statement/D
19. Go back to the verb; divide the complete subject from the complete predicate.

P A OP SN V A
3. *SN V-t* (In the "95 Theses"), Martin Luther / gave the
IO DO P3 *IO PPA DO P OP P ADJ OP*
public his reasons (for disagreeing) (with church practices).D

1. In the "95 Theses", Martin Luther gave the public his reasons for disagreeing with church practices.
2. Who gave the public his reasons for disagreeing with church practices? Martin Luther/SN
3. What is being said about Martin Luther? Martin Luther gave/V
4. Gave What? reasons/verify the noun
5. Does reasons mean the same thing as Martin Luther? no
6. Reasons/DO
7. Gave reasons to whom? public/IO
8. The/A
9. Whose reasons? his/PPA
10. For/P
11. For what? disagreeing/OP
12. With/P
13. With what? practices/OP
14. What kind of practices? church/Adj
15. In/P
16. In what? "95 Theses"/OP
17. The/A
18. SN V-t IO DO P3, check
19. (In the "95 Theses"), prepositional phrase
20. (for disagreeing), prepositional phrase
21. (with church practices), prepositional phrase
22. period, statement/D
23. Go back to the verb; divide the complete subject from the complete predicate.

CHAPTER SUMMARY

EVENT: ______________________ ______________________

______________________ ______________________

Date: ______________________ ______________________

Who: ______________________ ______________________

What: ______________________ *Where:* ______________________

______________________ ______________________

Middle Ages, Reformation and Renaissance

Veritas Press History Song

Listen to a time of castles and kings, a time when God's church went through suffering and change. Back to the Middle Ages, then to the Renaissance, on to the Reformation, we'll all sing this song.

Number One Saint Augustine converted to Christianity in the year 386 AD.
Two, the barbarian invasions and Vikings.
Three, Saint Jerome's translations and writings became the Vulgate in Latin, the Bible, in 405, the language of the people.

The Council of Chalcedon was number four.
Then came five, Saint Benedict and Monasticism.
Number six, Justinian the Great.
Seven, Mohammed and Islam, followed by number
Eight, Charles Martel and his son called Pepin the Short, and his son Charlemagne.

Number nine, Alfred the Great.
Then number 10, Otto, the First and the Holy Roman Empire.
Then number 11, came the East-West Schism.
Number 12, the Feudal System.
Number 13, the Battle of Hastings and William the Conqueror.
Number 14, the cathedrals in Europe.
15, the Crusades in 1095.

Then came number 16, Saint Francis of Assisi.
17, King John of England set his seal on the Magna Charta giving people certain rights in the year of 1215.
Number 18, Saint Thomas Aquinas wrote the *Summa Theologica.*

Number 19, Marco Polo, famous explorer to the Far East.
20 came the Hundred Years' War, the Black Death of Europe, and Joan of Arc.
21, the Great Papal Schism.
22, John Huss and John Wycliffe.

23, the fall of Constantinople to Mohammed the Second. Followed by number
24, the first printing of the Bible. This was done in 1456 by Johann Gutenberg.
25 the Renaissance spread through Europe.

26, Ferdinand and Isabella (Pope Gregory the Ninth) established the Inquisition.
27, Martin Luther began the Reformation in 1517.
Then 28, Ulrich Zwingli and the Anabaptists.
29, the Act of Supremacy by King Henry the Eighth.

30, John Calvin and The Institutes.
31, the Council of Trent.
Number 32, John Knox and the Reformation in Scotland.

This was the time of castles and kings. A time when God's church went through suffering and change. Back to the Middle Ages, then to the Renaissance, on to the Reformation.
Now we've sung our song. Yes, we've sung our song.